GLOBALIZATION AND EU TRADE POLICY AT THE TIME OF CRISES:

GOVERNANCE AND SUSTAINABILITY CHALLENGES

GLOBALIZATION AND EU TRADE POLICY AT THE TIME OF CRISES:

GOVERNANCE AND SUSTAINABILITY CHALLENGES

2023

Edited by
Annette Bongardt
Francisco Torres

ALMEDINA

GLOBALIZATION AND EU TRADE POLICY AT THE TIME OF CRISES: GOVERNANCE AND SUSTAINABILITY CHALLENGES

EDITORS
Annette Bongardt
Francisco Torres

CONTRIBUTORS
Annette Bongardt and Francisco Torres; Vitor Gaspar and David Amaglobeli; Aaditya Mattoo, Nadia Rocha and Michele Ruta; Jeffry Frieden; Helena Guimarães; Francisco Pereira Coutinho; Patrick Leblond and Crina Viju-Miljusevic; Sjorre Couvreur, Ferdi De Ville, Thomas Jacobs and Jan Orbie; Eline Blot; Pompeo Della Posta.

This publication is partly financed by the Portuguese Foundation for Science and Technology and the Portuguese Ministry of Education and Science through national funds — Research Center in Political Science (UIDB/0758/2020), University of Minho / University of Évora.

PUBLISHER
EDIÇÕES ALMEDINA, S.A.
Avenida Emídio Navarro, 81, 3D
3000-151 Coimbra
Tel.: 239 851 904 · Fax: 239 851 901
www.almedina.net · editora@almedina.net

COVER
EDIÇÕES ALMEDINA, S.A.

BOOK DESIGN
EDIÇÕES ALMEDINA, S.A.

PRINTED BY
AAAAAAAAA

April 2023

COPYRIGHT DEPOSIT NUMBER
000000/23

ISBN
978-989-40-1163-7

ALMEDINA | GRUPOALMEDINA

ÍNDICE

LIST OF FIGURES 9
LIST OF TABLES 11
LIST OF BOXES 13

FOREWORD 15
PREFACE 19

INTRODUCTION
THE QUALITATIVE CHANGE IN EU TRADE IN A WEAKENED MULTILATERAL TRADE ORDER
Annette Bongardt and Francisco Torres 21

PART I
ON ECONOMIC AND POLITICAL COORDINATION CHALLENGES FOR GLOBAL GOVERNANCE AND DEEP TRADE AGREEMENTS 25

CHAPTER 1
EU GOVERNANCE AND TRADE DYNAMICS IN THE CONTEXT OF GLOBALIZATION CHALLENGES
Annette Bongardt and Francisco Torres 27

CHAPTER 2
EUROPE IN THE WORLD CIRCA 2030
Vitor Gaspar and David Amaglobeli 41

CHAPTER 3
THE EVOLUTION OF DEEP TRADE AGREEMENTS
Aaditya Mattoo, Nadia Rocha, Michele Ruta 63

CHAPTER 4
GLOBAL TRADE IN THE AGE OF POPULISM
Jeffry Frieden 91

PART II
ON LESSONS FROM THE EU'S BLUEPRINT DEEP TRADE AGREEMENT (CETA) FOR EU TRADE POLICY 111

CHAPTER 5
EU FTAs AND DIVIDED SOVEREIGNTY: TRANSFORMATIVE SHIFTS IN TRADE AUTHORITY
Maria Helena Guimarães 113

CHAPTER 6
THE LEGAL NATURE OF NEW GENERATION FREE TRADE AGREEMENTS: LESSONS FROM THE CETA SAGA
Francisco Pereira Coutinho 133

CHAPTER 7
CETA AS THE EU'S FIRST THIRD-GENERATION TRADE AGREEMENT: DOES IT ACT LIKE ONE?
Patrick Leblond and Crina Viju-Miljusevic 161

PART III
ON PUBLIC AND PRIVATE RESPONSES TO GLOBALIZATION CHALLENGES: EU TRADE POLICY AND GLOBAL VALUE CHAINS 187

CHAPTER 8
THE GOOD GEOPOLITICAL TRADE ACTOR? THE EUROPEAN UNION'S DISCURSIVE JUSTIFICATION OF THE ANTI-COERCION INSTRUMENT
Sjorre Couvreur, Ferdi De Ville, Thomas Jacobs and Jan Orbie 189

CHAPTER 9
GREEN HORIZONS — TOWARDS A MORE SUSTAINABLE TRADE AFTER THE TSD REVIEW
Eline Blot 213

CHAPTER 10
GLOBAL VALUE CHAINS AND THE SLOWING DOWN OF GLOBALISATION
Pompeo Della Posta 237

PART IV
CONCLUSIONS AND OUTLOOK 263

CHAPTER 11
ON GOVERNANCE AND SUSTAINABILITY CHALLENGES FOR EU TRADE POLICY
Annette Bongardt and Francisco Torres 265

NOTES ON CONTRIBUTORS 281

LIST OF FIGURES

CHAPTER 2
EUROPE IN THE WORLD CIRCA 2030
Figure 2.1. World Trade and Global per capita GDP 43
Figure 2.2. Global GDP Weights of Real GDP (in percent of global GDP, 2011 purchasing power parity dollars) 45
Figure 2.3. Major Epidemics, 2000–2022 47
Figure 2.4. Annual Change in SDG Index Scores 49
Figure 2.5. Official Development Assistance (percent of total) 50
Figure 2.6. Official Development Assistance by Provider, 2021 51
Figure 2.7. Global Annual Mean Surface Air Temperature Change 53
Figure 2.8. Frequency of Climate Related Disasters (total for each decade) 53
Figure 2.9. Shares of Countries and Regions in Global CO_2 Emissions, 2030 53
Figure 2.10. Carbon Pricing, Coverage and Average Price 56
Figure 2.11. Fossil Fuel Subsidies, 2020 (in percent of GDP) 56

CHAPTER 3
THE EVOLUTION OF DEEP TRADE AGREEMENTS
Figure 3.1. Number of policy areas covered in PTAs, 1970–2017 67
Figure 3.2. Number of policy areas covered in PTAs, by policy 69
Figure 3.3. A classification of policy areas in DTAs 71
Figure 3.4. Tariffs in PTAs and MFN tariffs 75
Figure 3.5. Number of agreements over time *vs.* average coverage ratio 76
Figure 3.6. Coverage ratios by policy area, over time 77
Figure 3.7. Substantive provisions and a breakdown of non-substantive provisions in PTAs, over time 78
Figure 3.8. Inclusion of substantive commitments in PTAs, by level of development 79

Figure 3.9. Coverage ratio by type of policy and level of development 79
Figure 3.10. Substantive provisions in PTAs by country
Panel a. Average number of provisions 80
Panel b: Maximum number of provisions 81
Figure 3.11. Similarity of agreements 82
Figure 3.12. Boxplot of scores calculated by the RF of variables/provisions in PTAs 86

CHAPTER 7
CETA AS THE EU'S FIRST THIRD-GENERATION TRADE AGREEMENT: DOES IT ACT LIKE ONE?
Figure 7.1. Total Canada-EU Goods Trade, sectors with largest growth (million Euro) 169

CHAPTER 10
GLOBAL VALUE CHAINS AND THE SLOWING DOWN OF GLOBALISATION
Figure 10.1. World Exports of Goods and Services (% of World GDP) 241
Figure 10.2. World Foreign Direct Investment Net Inflows (% of World GDP) 242
Figure 10.3. Annual Rate of Change in the Migrant Stock in 5 years prior to 2020 243
Figure 10.4. Trends in ease of hiring foreign labour, emerging market and developing economies *vs.* advanced economies, 2008–2020 243
Figure 10.5. De Facto Trade Index and De Facto FKO Globalisation Index 244
Figure 10.6. Foreign direct investment and GVC participation 245
Figure 10.7. World distribution of GVCs participation by macro-sector of activity 246
Figure 10.8. The growing role of services in GVCs 247
Figure 10.9. Global Value Chain Participation Rates, World 1995–2020 248
Figure 10.10. Economies with major indirect exports (million $) 249
Figure 10.11. Global Value Chain Production Lengths by Sector, World, 2010, 2019 250
Figure 10.12. Business leaders' opinion on the future of value chains' globalisation 251
Figure 10.13. The Extensive Margin of Trade during the Great Recession 253

LIST OF TABLES

CHAPTER 3
THE EVOLUTION OF DEEP TRADE AGREEMENTS
Table 3.1. Share of policy areas for different PTAs 68
Table 3.2. Number of substantive and other provisions per policy area in all PTAs notified to the WTO 73

CHAPTER 5
EU FTAs AND DIVIDED SOVEREIGNTY: TRANSFORMATIVE SHIFTS IN TRADE AUTHORITY
Table 5.1 Levels of authority in trade policy 127

CHAPTER 7
CETA AS THE EU'S FIRST THIRD-GENERATION TRADE AGREEMENT: DOES IT ACT LIKE ONE?
Table 7.1. Three generations of trade agreements 164

CHAPTER 9
GREEN HORIZONS — TOWARDS A MORE SUSTAINABLE TRADE AFTER THE TSD REVIEW
Table 9.1. The TSD Chapter Action Points and their categorization 216
Table 9.2. Explicit commitments and non-committal phrasings in the TSD review that could foster or challenge sustainable trade 226
Table 9.3. List of upcoming bilateral trade agreements and environmental considerations 230

LIST OF BOXES

CHAPTER 9
GREEN HORIZONS — TOWARDS A MORE SUSTAINABLE TRADE AFTER THE TSD REVIEW
Box 9.1. What is the TSD Chapter and why is it relevant? 214
Box 9.2. Outcomes from the EU-Vietnam DAGs 223

FOREWORD

More than a pleasure, it is a privilege to welcome this book in 4 parts and 11 chapters, first and last by the editors, dear friends since our time in Brussels in the late 1980s. Well aware of their taste for Greece, I will let some atomism shine in since I discover a common allegiance to Canada, featured in most of Part II, where CETA is thoroughly analyzed in legal terms. Let me quote more: "Is the EU Model Viable in a Globalized World?", in Amy Verdun *et al.* (eds.): *Globalization, Development and Integration – a European Perspective*, 2009; "Comprehensive Trade Agreements: Conditioning Globalisation or Eroding the European Model?", 2017; their most recent *Top Cited JCMS Article* "The European Green Deal: More than an Exit Strategy to the Pandemic Crisis, a Building Block of a Sustainable European Economic Model" and of course "the successful publication in December 2022 of a Special Issue of *Perspectivas — Journal of Political Science*".

Part I deals with economic and political coordination and two chapters follow from contributions to *Essays* in my honor, titled *Economic Globalization and Governance* launched in Évora and Lisbon on the occasion of an honorary degree and valedictory lecture, respectively. Chapter 2, by our common friend Vitor Gaspar and David Amaglobeli, encompasses the globe from a European perspective, whereas in Chapter 4, Jeff Frieden, himself no stranger to things Portuguese, swaps "International Cooperation" for "Global Trade". Part II is dedicated to the Canada-EU Trade Agreement, following from Chapter 3 where Additya Mattoo *et al.* survey the international economics and law literature drawing on their recent *Handbook of Deep Trade Agreements*. In Chapter 5, Maria Helena Guimarães combines catchy expressions such as "creeping competences" and "failing forward" to capture the dynamics of negotiations. It reminded me of Alfred de Vigny's *Servitude et grandeur militaires*, written in

1835 shortly after the Portuguese civil war admirably described in the *Essays*. Part III includes original material on the EU as possible "good geopolitical trade actor" given that "the bad offensive geopolitization of trade is linked to China, Russia or the US" implying a double othering strategy in the discursive justification of the Anti-Coercion Instrument, a remarkable assessment on the trade and climate nexus and intriguing evidence on the resilience of Global Value Chains, following a model presented at the 2020 *ECB Forum on Central Banking*. This provides an excuse to remember Paul Krugman's "Trade, Accumulation and Uneven Development", at Yale and NBER Summer Institute, https://econpapers.repec.org/article/eeedeveco/v_3a8_3ay_3a1981_3ai_3a2_3ap_3a149-161.htm. In addition, Paul is the only member of the Lisbon Academy who cycled through Évora in the Summer heat of 2022.

Larger powers' idea of Europe implies domination, whereas small and medium powers attempt to defend their political autonomy in the midst of two millennia of so-called European civil wars. In *The Age of Reason 1700-1789*, Harold Nicolson emphasizes Anglo-American complexities and quotes the 1798 book with the same title where the European allegiance of American settlers is dubbed "obstinate". This forgotten view was refreshed by the quintessentially British (though created by a Canadian) *Monocle* calling for "a bit of lusophilia" in 2012, and it provides a pretext to lament Brexit. Truth be told, I cannot stop loving the oldest ally as host of a Community of Nations speaking the same language, like the one proposed by Brazil just before the fall of the Berlin wall except that the United States forever ignores the Commonwealth. Current parallels in Central and Eastern Europe are dire, but such territorial obstinacy exists around the world, so that G20 is clearly better than an informal "economic G3" with the EU inserted between the US and China.

Rather than pointing to the complementarity between eurozone governance and a single market enhanced by the knowledge society, the failure of Lehman Brothers shelved the Lisbon agenda and the EU recognized that, in order to reach its objectives for 2020, it had to act decisively in the G20 and international forums to produce a full recovery, and help speed up the move toward a greener, more sustainable and more innovative economy as globalization had become more polarized, multilateralism more fragile and the nexus between natural resources, energy and climate change more threatening. Since Francisco was my student at old NOVA *campi* I dare suggest that they consider building on my CIGI Paper nº 132 or on the 2nd Lisbon Conference on Structural Reforms convened by the Ministry of Finance through its think tank, known as Gabinete de Planeamento, Estratégia, Avaliação e Relações Internacionais where I presented three slides on "The EU Dimension: Governance, Complexity and Complementarity". It is indeed the same struggle and I congratulate the editors for carrying it on after all these years.

Jorge Braga de Macedo

PREFACE

This volume on *Globalization and EU Trade Policy at the Time of Crises: Governance and Sustainability Challenges*, edited by Annette Bongardt and Francisco Torres, is a milestone on EU trade policy and globalization studies. It features eleven very rich and diverse chapters and excels at bridging economics, political economy, political science, international relations and international law.

The book follows up on the successful publication in December 2022 of a Special Issue of *Perspectivas — Journal of Political Science* on "New Globalization Challenges and EU Trade Policy". We would like to thank Annette Bongardt and Francisco Torres, *guest editors* of that special issue, for having taken up the most timely challenge to approach such a relevant topic at this time. Doing so they provided a very relevant (and abnegated) academic service to *Perspectivas* and the Research Center in Political Science (CICP), hosted at the University of Minho and the University of Évora, and to the academic community in general. From the editorial board's point of view, the objective of such a special issue was to set in motion a deepening and widening of the Journal's international network, serving both as a landmark for research, contributing to the Journal's Scopus indexation (which is ongoing in the meantime) and contributing to positioning it as a reference in the field of political science. The call for papers of the special issue was an absolute success, as can be easily seen by the list of renowned authors of the different chapters of this volume (and of the special issue).

As academics are well aware, producing a good journal special issue and a good edited volume is not only a very time-consuming but also a challenging affair. The entire process, although very thorough and involving so many authors and reviewers, was extremely efficient and smooth. It also turned out to be a truly agreeable and enriching endeavour. A profound word of gratitude is due for the accomplishment of this project to the editors-authors, authors, reviewers and everybody involved in the production of the Special Issue and of this book.

Finally, and especially so in these times of multiple crises, we hope that the reading and study of this volume contributes to a better understanding of globalization and EU trade policy and the governance and sustainability challenges ahead.

Miguel Rocha de Sousa
(Editor-in-Chief, *Perspectivas*)

Joaquim Filipe Araújo
(Director, CICP-University of Minho)

INTRODUCTION
THE QUALITATIVE CHANGE IN EU TRADE IN A WEAKENED MULTILATERAL TRADE ORDER[1]

Annette Bongardt and Francisco Torres

The EU, a staunch defender of an open trade system and multilateralism, finds itself in a weakened multilateral trade order where world trade is affected by multiple crises. Changing framework conditions present many challenges for the EU. The way the Union responds will define its role as an actor on the global stage in a new chapter of globalization that is being written. It is also bound to have effects domestically.

This book provides an up-to-date take on EU trade, capturing the nature of challenges in a globalized economy facing the Union and their implications for EU trade policy. It brings an interdisciplinary perspective to the study of the topic. It has gathered economists, political scientists, international lawyers and other social scientists both from academia and/or from the International Monetary Fund, the World Bank and the Institute for European Environmental Policy.

In our call for papers at the end of April 2022 for a special issue on 'New Globalization Challenges and EU Trade Policy', published online by *Perspectivas — Journal of Political Science*, Volume 27, 2022, we had encouraged scholars to take in recent developments that promise a break with past practice. Perhaps most acutely, the Covid-19 pandemic and Russia's aggression on Ukraine have exposed vulnerabilities of existing globalization patterns (supply chains, energy dependency, food supply) facing the EU (and not only). The climate crisis highlights the issue of the carbon footprint of international trade. Geopolitics increasingly affect trade relations and indeed the very

[1] The first editor/author, Annette Bongardt, conducted this study at the Research Center in Political Science (UIDB/0758/2020), University of Minho / University of Evora, supported by the Portuguese Foundation for Science and Technology and the Portuguese Ministry of Education and Science through national funds.

functioning of the internal market. This is the case of the EU's and the US's sanctions on Russia and of China's boycott of Lithuanian (content) exports after Lithuania allowed Taiwan to open a representative office under its name. With a view to framing the discussion, a broader discussion of globalization and global governance, which constrain and provide opportunities for an enhanced role of EU trade policy, notably in areas such as the environment, climate change and sustainable development, was also called for.

The book's objective to shed light on how EU trade policy has evolved and to discuss EU trade dynamics in light of new challenges also required taking a closer look at deep free trade agreements and at why EU new generation deep trade agreements imply a qualitative change in EU trade. It furthermore called for discussing the interaction between external trade and EU regulation and the impact on the European (economic, environmental and social) model.

The chapters in this book address EU trade and regulation in the context of the challenges to today's world trading system, spelling out the challenges for global cooperation and those facing the Union as a by-product of its trade dynamics. The latter have been pushing it towards further deepening globalization through an ever-increasing number of deep and comprehensive new generation trade agreements with a growing geographical reach. Also, EU trade policy pays tribute to European values, but it is not clear to what extent the European model — central to the EU's identity — is thereby being upheld, not least in light of the complexity of issues involved that would need to be contemplated in trade talks (Bongardt and Torres, 2017). The experience with the EU-Canada Comprehensive Economic and Trade Agreement (CETA), the EU's showcase new generation trade agreement examined in various articles of this special issue, offers important lessons. It underscored both the complexity of issue areas and the difficulties associated with ratification of mixed agreements. The fact that EU trade policy has been adapted in recent times warrants a closer look at the direction, underlying objectives, and effectiveness in terms of implementation, most notably in regard to sustainability.

A group of renowned authors based in the EU, US, Canada, and China — Vitor Gaspar, David Amaglobeli Aaditya Mattoo, Nadia Rocha, Michele Ruta, Jeffry Frieden, Pompeo Della Posta, Francisco Pereira Coutinho, Eline Blot, Patrick Leblond, Crina Viju-Miljusevic, Helena Guimarães, Sjorre Couvreur, Ferdi De Ville, Thomas Jacobs and Jan Orbie — responded swiftly to our call to jointly address the above-referred issues, providing different perspectives on the topic. In a matter of just a few days we had assembled a rather long but also complete special issue, which could not have taken in one more paper. Moreover, articles/chapters ended up also speaking to each other in substance. Throughout the process we (first as guest editors of the special issue and now as editors of this book) have benefited a lot from the discussion of each submitted article/chapter. We hope and trust that our readers, researchers, students, lecturers, policy makers and the general public, will also find this book valuable for their research and for an enhanced understanding of the topic that we set out to analyse.

We are also very grateful to João Amador (Nova SBE), José Caetano (University of Évora), Valerie D'Erman (University of Victoria), Catherine Moury (Nova FCSH), Miguel Lebre de Freitas (Nova SBE), Miguel Rocha de Sousa (University of Évora), Paul Schure (University of Victoria), Elsa Vaz (University of Évora), Paulo Vila Maior (University Fernando Pessoa, Porto) and Hubert Zimmermann (University of Marburg) for contributing with very useful comments and suggestions.

When preparing the special issue, we learned about projects on the subject running parallel to ours. Those may certainly be of interest to the readers of the special issue and this book. One of them is also to be published in April: Duina, Francesco and Crina Viju-Miljusevic (eds) (2023), *Standardizing the World: EU Trade Policy and the Road to Convergence*, Oxford: Oxford University Press. It happens to have two authors (and a co-editor) in common with our special issue and book. The other, Neuwahl, Nanette and Amy Verdun (eds) (2024), *Canada's EU relations after Brexit*, will be published by Routledge in the beginning of next year. Francesco Duina, Ana Margarida Fernandes and Amy Verdun have also contributed with useful suggestions when we were preparing the special issue and this volume.

We are also most grateful to Miguel Rocha de Sousa, *Perspectivas*'s editor-in-chief, and his colleagues of the editorial team, José Passos Palmeira, Miguel Ângelo Rodrigues and Irene Viparelli, for having invited us in mid-April 2022 to be Guest Editors of a special issue of the journal and for giving us the freedom to choose the subject of study and define the research agenda. We would also like to thank Francisca Abreu, *Perspectivas'* editorial assistant, for guiding the articles to (online) press. We hope that the articles of the special issue, now published as chapters of this book, have confirmed *Perspectivas — Journal of Political Science*, part of the Research Center in Political Science (CICP) of Universidade do Minho and Universidade de Évora, as a journal of reference in its field.

Last but not least, we would like to thank Jorge Braga de Macedo, Treasurer of the Lisbon Academy of Sciences and Professor Emeritus at Nova SBE, who kindly accepted our invitation to write the foreword to this book.

PART I
ON ECONOMIC AND POLITICAL COORDINATION CHALLENGES FOR GLOBAL GOVERNANCE AND DEEP TRADE AGREEMENTS

Summary

Part I includes four chapters that, providing different perspectives on economic and political coordination challenges for global governance and deep trade agreements, frame the discussion in this volume. Those articles cumulatively look at the need for cooperation in global governance in the light of crises, the political difficulties of doing so, seeking to better understand what the observed shift from multilateralism to preferential trade agreements, more specifically the proliferation of deep trade agreements, means, and how EU trade dynamics interact with the European model. **Chapter 1** (Bongardt and Torres) puts forward that EU trade cannot be seen in isolation from the EU (economic, environmental and social) model. This is the result of the very dynamics of EU trade, notably the proliferation of EU new generation deep trade agreements that extend into non-traditional trade areas. Those bilateral rules and beyond-the-border measures feed back into the European model in a way traditional trade agreements have not. **Chapter 2** (Gaspar and Amaglobeli) presents a prospective view on Europe's position in the world by the end of the decade. International trade calls for a stable world economic system, which in present times requires multilateral coordination (pandemic preparedness, progress on the Sustainable Development Goals (SDG), and mitigation of and adaptation to climate change) that goes beyond trade rules and the traditional trade agenda. **Chapter 3** (Mattoo, Rocha and Ruta) zooms in on deep trade agreements and regionalization, setting out what is the nature of deep trade agreements and effects on global trade. As opposed to conventional trade agreements, deep trade agreements aim at economic integration beyond trade and at establishing five types of economic integration rights (goods, services, capital, persons, ideas). **Chapter 4** (Jeffry Frieden) focuses on the politics of trade in regard to the future of international economic cooperation, calling attention for domestic and international political factors. Overcoming opposition to international economic integration within major Western powers, critical to uphold and develop the open trade system, presupposes addressing the domestic reasons for opposition.

CHAPTER 1
EU GOVERNANCE AND TRADE DYNAMICS IN THE CONTEXT OF GLOBALIZATION CHALLENGES[2]

Annette Bongardt and Francisco Torres

Abstract: This chapter argues that European Union (EU) trade dynamics and (old and new) globalization challenges cannot be seen in isolation from their implications for the European (economic, social and environmental) model. The EU, a staunch defender of free trade and multilateralism, faces an increasingly messy international trading system and new realities that affect its external trade (environmental and geopolitical considerations, industrial policy). Its quest to promote external trade may however sit uneasily with European values, to which EU trade policy reviews pay tribute by letter, most recently enshrining the objectives of the European Green Deal. This chapter questions the EU's unfettered defence of the European model in practice through its new generation trade agreements, which are a chief embodiment of its trade policy. Those increasingly stretch into non-traditional areas, which implies that they feed back into the European model in a way that traditional trade agreements have not, via multiple channels, including regulation (standards, also environmental and labour) or investor protection clauses. The issue whether the EU privileges trade over the European model is reflected in the difficulty to find a necessary consensus among member states to ensure the ratification of recent deep trade agreements.

Keywords: European model; EU trade policy; new generation trade agreements; regulation; EU versus member state competences.

[2] We are grateful to our fellow authors in this book as well as to the reviewers for useful comments and discussions. The first author conducted this study at the Research Center in Political Science (UIDB/0758/2020), University of Minho / University of Évora, supported by the Portuguese Foundation for Science and Technology and the Portuguese Ministry of Education and Science through national funds.

1. Introduction

The European Union (EU), a staunch defender of free trade and multilateralism all along, has needed not only to come to grips with an increasingly messy global governance system but also with new realities in the international economic system. Several factors have contributed to a changed setting for EU trade. To start with, the multilateral approach to trade-rule making and even trade dispute arbitration has suffered setbacks. Bilateral and regional trade agreements have proliferated in this setting. To complicate matters further, the globalization of markets as experienced over the past three decades had also brought about manifold phenomena of internationalization beyond traditional goods trade (such as trade-related services, direct and financial investments, intellectual property rights), only partly covered by multilateral rules under the World Trade Organization (WTO) umbrella. On top of that, various shocks have more recently affected the international economic system. Those have highlighted the relevance of geopolitics for trade policy and prompted a reconsideration of globalization patterns, most notably in light of the vulnerability of global value chains.

Global trade takes place under a weakened global governance umbrella. For most of the time in his history, the European integration project could count on a stable and conducive international framework and multilateral institutions that facilitated external trade growth, namely through the General Agreement on Tariffs and Trade (GATT) and its successor, the WTO, and further supported by the Bretton Woods system providing exchange rate stability until the 1970s. The GATT/WTO were the principal vehicle and forum for opening up world trade and dealing with trade disputes. The multilateral approach had been rather successful in doing away with conventional trade barriers in successive negotiation rounds but started to encounter increasing difficulties in concluding multilateral agreements and to set new rules collectively.[3] It may hence not be surprising that multilateral trade rules should not have evolved in step with the global economic integration of markets and its accompanying phenomena. In recent times, even the WTO's smooth functioning regarding multilateral trade rules (trade dispute arbitration) has

[3] In the 1990s, the Uruguay round was already drawn out. In the following decade, the Doha round failed. In the WTO, an international organization with currently 164 members, agreements require unanimity of its membership, which in this millennium has come to include notably also Russia and China.

been cast in doubt.[4] Countries are thus more exposed to power relations in international trade.

Against this background of a weakened multilateral trade governance *cum* increasingly integrated world markets since the 1990s, the world has seen a remarkable proliferation of bilateral and regional agreements in general and of deep trade agreements in particular. As Fernandes *et al.* (2021a) observe, bilateral and regional trade agreements have surged from about 50 in 1990 to about 300 in this millennium, with regional agreements taking over the trade agenda.

At a first glance, preferential trade agreements may seem to constitute a second-best solution to multilateral agreements for furthering free trade. However, the picture is much more complex.

Mattoo *et al.* (2022) show that deep trade agreements go much beyond the tariff cutting that is the object of conventional free trade agreements, in terms of breadth (scope) of issue areas but also depth (complexity). Moreover, by involving regulatory and other non-tariff measures they get into what were formerly exclusively domestic policy domains (Lamy, 2020). Fernandes *et al.* (2021a) clarify that WTO multilateral rules are still at the basis of regional agreements, but that in their absence deep trade agreements establish new trade rules; their details hence matter. As important determinants of international trade patterns, global value chain integration and welfare, deep trade agreements therefore shape economic development.

The deepening of preferential trade agreements beyond traditional trade policy, encompassing areas like competition, investment, and intellectual property right protection has driven globalization (Laget *et al.*, 2019). Specifically, the authors find that those deep trade agreements promote and facilitate global value chains in intermediate (rather than final) goods and services and that it is provisions that are outside the WTO's current mandate (such as investment and competition policy) that drive the effect on value added trade and on North-South trade in parts and components. Conversely, regarding South-South trade in parts and components it is provisions under the current WTO mandate (such as tariff reduction and customs facilitation) that are observed to drive the effect of deep preferential trade agreements.

[4] Referring here to the WTO appellate body, out of function due to unfilled vacancies (https://www.wto.org/english/tratop_e/dispu_e/appellate_body_e.htm). US President Biden continued his predecessor's policy of not nominating judges. For an appreciation of the background, see Bacchus (2022).

More recently, various crises have opened the perspective of a break with or induced changes to past globalization practice. Most acutely, there are the worldwide repercussions of the Covid-19 pandemic that erupted in 2020 and Russia's full-scale invasion of Ukraine in 2022. Those have exposed vulnerabilities of existing globalization patterns (resilience of supply chains, energy dependency, food supply). And, more long-term (hence more easily put on the backburner), there is the lingering issue of the carbon footprint of international trade (environmental sustainability). What is at stake is how to preserve the economic benefits from global economic integration, when the focus shifted to the viability of globalization patterns and the inclusion of strategic considerations linked to geopolitics and industrial policy. Plus, for the international economic system, addressing climate change is a (if not the) chief challenge, requiring the internalization of environmental costs via carbon pricing also in international trade (Gaspar and Amaglobeli, 2022).

2. Main challenges for EU trade policy

Regardless of remaining a (increasingly lonely) defender of multilateralism and free trade on the global stage, the EU, too, initially reluctantly, embarked on an increasing number of bilateral and regional international trade agreements. By summer 2021, the EU had summed some 130 trade agreements — in place (77), pending (24) or in the process of being adopted or ratified (24) or being negotiated (5). As a result, up to 40 per cent of EU external trade is governed by bilateral and regional agreements (Blot and Kettunen, 2021).

However, to the extent that preferential trade agreements have moved away from conventional tariff-cutting, becoming broader and deeper over time, their welfare effects are no longer clear-cut. As Fernandes *et al.* (2021b: 2) put it, the economists' traditional approach to evaluate (preferential) trade agreements, based on the creation of market access, is inadequate to capture the complexity of policy areas that are covered by deep trade agreements. Economists (and not only) need to take a more differentiated view and account for the fact that specific policy areas and provisions in trade agreements have consequences, not all of them beneficial. A similar point has been emphasized by Rodrik's work, notably that economists have also failed to contribute to a full picture on trade, tending to emphasize gains from trade and not to discuss more complex consequences such as the distribution of benefits and the impact of regulation (Rodrik, 2018).

In parallel to the growth of deep trade agreements, EU trade policy underwent several modifications over the years in support of EU objectives. The Global Europe Strategy (European Commission, 2006) affirmed that EU trade agreements were to complement the EU's growth and jobs strategy (the Lisbon Agenda) through an external dimension. In 2015, EU trade policy was put also at the service of European values and principles such as high social and environmental standards (European Commission, 2015). Still, according to Felbermayr (2016) the EU's more active policy of negotiating bilateral trade agreements became guided by economic objectives rather than by political affinities and objectives. In 2021, the European Commission (2021) presented its new trade policy strategy dedicated to the European Green Deal (EGD), which aims at reinforcing the EU's capacity to act as a global champion of open, rules--based trade that is sustainable and fair. It includes efforts to reform the WTO, strengthen the EU's regulatory impact and implement and enforce trade agreements, ensuring a level playing field for EU economic actors. In mid-2022, the Commission (2022) presented a communication on its new approach to trade agreements as to promote green and just growth, in which it puts forward how the implementation and enforcement of Trade and Sustainable Development (TSD) chapters of the EU's trade agreements are to be strengthened. TSD chapters had already become to be systematically included in recent, modern EU free trade agreements, aiming at putting to good use the leverage of trade and investment issues with respect to EU objectives (European Commission, 2018). The new approach is to include the use of trade sanctions if core TSD provisions are breached and is applicable to future negotiations and ongoing ones as appropriate.[5] Existing trade agreements are thus not covered by the upgrading effort.

Unlike what had happened in the case of conventional trade agreements, EU deep trade agreements became politically fraught. The EU used to be able to negotiate and/or conclude (traditional) trade agreements without arousing much public interest or opposition, despite protests against globalization. That changed with the EU-US Trans-Atlantic Trade and Investment Partnership (TTIP) and the EU-Canada Comprehensive Economic and Trade Agreement (CETA).[6] The fact that they were much contested (with investment

[5] The Commission's Communication (2022) replaces the Commission's (2018) non-paper on TSD chapters in EU free trade agreements.

[6] With respect to the plurilateral level, the same can be said for the Trade in Services Agreement (TiSA). The backlash against globalization became directed against the Union, perceived as prioritizing economics over making sure that economic goals were compatible with social and environmental concerns.

protection clauses and regulation among the key concerns), crystallized popular concern with the effects of globalization on society and the environment (see Rodrik, 2016). The difficulty to find the necessary consensus among member states to ensure the ratification of recent deep trade agreements is another factor to be reckoned with, indicating divergent preferences.

Leblond and Viju-Miljusevic (2019) explain that the EU has taken two strands of actions in response to the perceived politicisation of trade. On the one hand, it tried to make trade agreements and negotiations more transparent (for example, the Commission publishes explanatory documents, textual proposals and third-party correspondence and makes results of meetings with stakeholders and policy officials public). On the other hand, it has aimed at making agreements more progressive in order to make free trade more legitimate and politically acceptable in the eyes of European citizens and in light of their concerns, meaning that it seeks to find an adequate balance between barrier-free trade and the right to regulate (environmental protection, labour standards). Those progressive elements include defending and exporting EU regulations and norms, increased transparency and implementing a new framework for screening foreign direct investment.

The approach that the EU takes to global trade is set to define its credibility as a global actor and its soft power. More importantly still, it will impact the (political) sustainability of the European integration project, which has come to incorporate the European Green Deal as one of the pillars of its economic model (Bongardt and Torres, 2022a). After all, there is an economic case for the internalization of environmental costs (economic efficiency reasoning).[7] Longer-term environmental concerns have for long and consistently been among European citizens' priorities. They should not be alienated in trade in the name of a short run need to deliver results, whatever results. It is hence important to consider whether EU deep trade agreements incorporate and live up to EU objectives as enshrined in the European Green Deal. In a comparative analysis of the treatment of the environment across the most recent EU trade agreements (final or proposed), Blot and Kettunen (2021) conclude that as yet none is fully compliant with the European Green

[7] Also the ECB considers to introduce a climate-neutral monetary policy (ECB, 2022). Moreover, as stressed in the timely encyclical letter on the environment by Pope Francis (2015), there is also a moral obligation (especially by a supranational body that at the time represented over 500 million European citizens) that trade and growth policies be directed at achieving social and environmental sustainability and quality of life.

Deal's objectives, although some moved in the right direction.[8] Still, Blot (2022) concludes that the new approach on TSD chapters is going in the right direction by setting a path for embedding sustainability in free trade agreements, introducing new measures and mechanisms to ensure that trade delivers sustainable outcomes.

The EU will also have to address the implications of recent geopolitical events and resulting impacts (notably Russia's attack on Ukraine) on globalization patterns. Foreign policy and geopolitics increasingly affect trade relations and indeed the very functioning of the internal market (the example of the EU's and the US's sanctions on Russia; China's boycott of Lithuanian (content) exports after Lithuania allowed Taiwan to open a representative office under its name). It has to come to terms, also in its trade policy, with a reality in which blocks. including allies, put their interests first (including the USA, the latest case being the Inflation Reduction Act (IRA) in late 2022). For the EU it becomes difficult to defend the purity of free trade in response to geopolitics and third country's industrial policy. As Couvreur *et al.* (2022) observe, while the practice had not been that pure before, the discourse is being adjusted to a more pragmatic and active stance.

As Lagarde (2022) put it, shifting value systems, and shifting alliances are redoing the global map of economic relations, in three ways: prompting shifts from dependence to diversification, from efficiency to security, and from globalisation to regionalisation. These shifts occur at a time when domestic political pressures already appear to be pushing the major powers apart (Frieden, 2022). Yet, multilateral cooperation in the areas of climate change, international corporate taxation and sustainable development is a necessary public good for the international economic system to function (Gaspar and Amaglobeli, 2021).

In sum, the challenge facing the EU is hence no less than to find an equilibrium in which external trade serves also European objectives and values.[9] The issue is whether the Union actively works towards a rules and value based international order, which delivers on EU preferences for quality growth and fairness and which prioritizes the overdue link between environmental

[8] See also Blot, Oger and Harrison (2022).

[9] This is what Rodrik (2011: xix) calls the ultimate globalization paradox, namely an incompatibility between globalisation and democratisation: "A thin layer of international rules that leaves substantial room for manoeuvre by national governments is a *better* globalization. It can address globalization's ills while preserving its substantial economic benefits. We need smart globalization, not maximum globalization".

sustainability and trade. The EU's self-declared leadership role in combating climate change provides a test case for its resolve. After all, economic growth cannot be sustained over time if the limits of the planet are not accounted for nor is trade sustainable (economically and politically) if negative externalities are not priced in or taken care of.

3. A qualitative change in EU trade, with repercussions on the European model

At the time when the European Commission embarked on negotiating a new generation of international trade agreements tariff barriers were already relatively low among WTO members. The fact that those — unlike conventional free trade agreements — aimed at abolishing also non-tariff barriers to trade might hence have seemed merely a logical next step in trade. Yet, moving into doing away with non-tariff barriers and therefore into other, domestic policy domains meant a qualitative change from trade into economic integration. In the fully integrated EU, it affects the European model, which aims to make compatible economic growth with high social and environmental standards and could consolidate or weaken it.

That said, EU trade dynamics have been pushing the Union towards further deepening globalization through an ever-increasing number of deep and comprehensive new generation trade agreements with a growing geographical reach. Of course, for the EU promoting external trade is attractive also as an exit from crises, even more so since trade is mostly an EU competence. While EU trade policy pays tribute to European values and objectives, it is not clear to what extent the European model — central to the EU's identity — is thereby being upheld, not least in light of the complexity of issues involved that would need to be contemplated in trade talks (Bongardt and Torres, 2017). The experience with CETA, the EU's showcase new generation trade agreement, has underscored both the complexity of issue areas and the difficulties associated with ratification of mixed agreements (Bongardt and Torres, 2018; Forum, 2018; Coutinho, 2022; Leblond and Viju-Miljusevic, 2022).

Fears voiced by member states or civil society that deep and comprehensive free trade agreements might not correspond to the preferences or values of society cannot be dismissed out of hand.[10] For instance, this could be the case if

[10] See De Ville and Siles-Brügge (2017) on the case of the TTIP.

there was a race to the bottom of standards through regulatory competition and/or regulation being hollowed out by regulatory cooperation and being beyond democratic reach, or when investor state arbitration came to limit the policy space for future more stringent consumer and environmental protection.

More generally, any discussion on the EU's approach to global trade needs to take into account that external trade and regulation interact and impact the European model. As we have argued elsewhere, it is noteworthy that the EU's new generation of deep trade agreements magnifies the issue of regulation, which is already complex in internal EU trade, in an international trade context (Bongardt and Torres, 2017 and 2020b). In regard to economic integration in the single market, preference convergence determines the possibility of harmonization. Mutual recognition is the default option in the case of divergent preferences. Crucially, its acceptability hinges on sufficient trust among member states that rules will be similar in their effect as well as functioning supervision and enforcement capacity. Systems competition and regulatory arbitrage have at times proven problematic even within the Union since the EU has become more heterogeneous over time. They are bound to be a larger issue with respect to third countries, be it Canada, the US, or others. As Duina (2019) puts it, the complex regulatory issues ultimately were seen as putting at stake European values and beliefs, put differently, the European way of life as opposed to the American way of life.

On the upside, international trade agreements offer the EU an opportunity to condition globalisation in line with societal preferences. Deep trade agreements in particular could be an easier and speedier way to disseminate EU values and principles on the global stage. Yet, there is little evidence that the EU has aimed to be a global rule maker in the past. Young (2015) finds that the EU has not used regulatory coordination to try to export its rules and standards and that it has generally settled for granting equivalence. Unsurprisingly then, critiques persist and centre on fears that those trade agreements could undermine environmental and labour standards and give multinational firms the power to challenge national laws and limit the EU's and member states' regulatory space. That said, at the time of writing, the jury is still out as far as the EU's recent, and more active trade policy is concerned.

The issue remains that a trade focus may easily lead the EU to overlook the complex and potentially broad consequences for society of the new generation economic and trade agreements. Just recall that the EU only belatedly integrated the environment and the Paris Climate Agreement in recent trade deals (with Japan and South Korea), that it abandoned the climate issue to achieve a trade truce with the US, and that in (the EU-Mercosur agreement), the potential environmental impact (of agricultural trade on the deforestation of the Amazon rainforest) might still derail the ratification of the mixed agreement. It remains to be seen to what extent the TSD chapters align trade with EU principles. As Blot (2022) points out, there is significant progress but some concerns remain with respect to monitoring efficacy, the evolving nature of trade and environmental issues, and the applicability of the enforcement mechanisms.

Still, EU ambitions to condition globalization could also become frustrated at the outset if the bloc were not able to ratify negotiated and signed deep trade agreements. The EU has successfully negotiated many deep trade agreements but ratification has proven more complicated (even CETA, the EU's blueprint for deep trade agreements, is still only provisionally applied, awaiting ratification by all member states[11]). In its Singapore decision, the Court of Justice of the European Union had clarified the competence distribution between the EU and the member states. Trade agreements that involve member state competences qualify as mixed agreements and require ratification by all member states and even some regions. The Commission proposal to split trade agreements into two separate ones, in line with competence distribution, is meant to speed up ratification with respect to those issue areas falling under the EU's exclusive competence on trade.

However, while doing so could bolster the EU's credibility as a global player, by itself it does nothing to address the source of unease at the member state level with the erosion of competences, which is ultimately rooted in divergent preferences. And, of course, it presupposes that trade partners agree with this split. On the other hand, national and regional veto power might work as checks and balances, obliging the Commission to widen its trade focus to the defence of (a modernized and sustainable) European model. CETA provides an interesting case study.[12]

[11] To date, 10 out of 27 EU member states have not yet ratified CETA (https://carleton.ca/tradenetwork/research-publications/ceta-ratification-tracker/)

[12] In the case of CETA, contestation by civil society and the refusal by the Belgian region of Wallonia to sign the original agreement resulted in some amendments before CETA could be signed by at the EU-Canada summit. Wallonia obtained a number of assurances, among others on investor-state dispute settlement, ISDS (which was initially not to be replaced by the investment court system, ICS), regulatory cooperation (requiring common agreement by member states), safeguards with respect to genetically modified organisms, a guarantee of the precautionary principle (see Magnette, 2016).

Assuring the voice of the European model (preferences) in trade-focussed negotiations is a challenge that the EU needs to take up in its new trade dynamics for the sake of its own (environmental, economic and political) sustainability.

REFERENCES

Bacchus, James (2022), "Echoing Trump, Biden embraces international trade lawlessness", blog, Cato Institute, 12 December (https://www.cato.org/blog/echoing-trump-biden-embraces-international-trade-lawlessness).

Blot, Eline (2022), "Green horizons — Towards more sustainable trade after the TSD Review", Special Issue on New Globalization Challenges and EU Trade Policy, *Perspectivas - Journal of Political Science*, Vol 27.

Blot, Eline and Marianne Kettunen (2021), *Environmental credentials of EU trade policy — A comparative analysis of EU free trade agreements*, Brussels and London: Institute for European Environmental Policy.

Blot, Eline, Antoine Oger and James Harrison (2022), *Enhancing sustainability in EU Free Trade Agreements: The case for a holistic approach*, policy report, Brussels: Institute for European Environmental Policy.

Bongardt, Annette and Francisco Torres (2017), "Comprehensive Trade Agreements: Conditioning Globalization or Eroding the European Model?", *Intereconomics*, 52, 3, 165-170.

Bongardt, Annette and Francisco Torres (2018), "What should be the EU's approach to global trade?", *Review of European Economic Policy*, Vol. 53, 5, 245-49.

Bongardt, Annette and Francisco Torres (2022a), "The European Green Deal: More than an Exit Strategy to the Pandemic Crisis, a Building Block of a Sustainable European Economic Model", *JCMS: Journal of Common Market Studies*, Vol. 60(1), 170-185. https://doi.org/10.1111/jcms.13264

Bongardt, Annette and Francisco Torres (2022b), *Lessons on the Political Economy of European Integration*, Lisbon: Universidade Católica Editora.

Coutinho, Francisco Pereira (2022), "On the Legal Nature of New Generation Trade Agreements: Lessons from the CETA Saga", Special Issue on New Globalization Challenges and EU Trade Policy, *Perspectivas - Journal of Political Science*, Vol 27.

Couvreur, Sjorre, Ferdi De Ville, Thomas Jacobs and Jan Orbie (2022), "The good geopolitical trade actor? The European Union's discursive justification of the Anti-Coercion Instrument", Special Issue on New Globalization Challenges and EU Trade Policy, *Perspectivas - Journal of Political Science*, Vol 27.

De Ville, Ferdi and Gabriel Siles-Brügge (2017), "Why TTIP is a game-changer and its critics have a point", *Journal of European Public Policy*, Vol. 24: 10, pp. 1491-1505.

Duina, Francesco (2019), "Why the excitement? Values, identities, and the politicization of EU trade policy with North America", *Journal of European Public Policy*, Vol.26, issue 12, 1866-82. https://doi.org/10.1080/13501763.2019.1678056

European Central Bank (2022), "ECB takes further steps to incorporate climate change into its monetary policy operations", Press release, 4 July.

European Commission (2006), *Global Europe. Competing in the world*, Brussels: European Commission, External Trade.

European Commission (2015), *Trade for all. Towards a more responsible trade and investment policy*, Brussels: European Commission.

European Commission (2018), Feedback and way forward on improving the implementation and enforcement of Trade and Sustainable Development Chapters in EU Free Trade Agreements, non-paper of the Commission services, 26 February.

European Commission (2021), Trade Policy Review — An Open, Sustainable and Assertive Trade Policy, Communication from the Commission to the European Parliament, the Council, the European Economic and Social Committee and the Committee of the Regions, COM(2021) 66 final.

European Commission (2022), *Commission unveils new approach to trade agreements to promote green and just growth*, press release, Brussels, 22 June, available at: https://ec.europa.eu/commission/presscorner/detail/en/ip_22_3921.

Felbermayr, Gabriel (2016), "The EU and the US: TTIP", *in* Badinger, Harald and Volker Nitsch (eds), *Routledge Handbook of the Economics of European Integration*, Routledge, 220-237.

Fernandes, Ana, Nadia Rocha and Michele Ruta (2021a), The Economics of Deep Trade Agreements: a new e-book, VoxEU.org: https://voxeu.org/article/economics-deep-trade-agreements-new-ebook

Fernandes, Ana, Nadia Rocha and Michele Ruta (eds) (2021b), *The Economics of Deep Trade Agreements*, e-book, London: CEPR press. https://voxeu.org/content/economics-deep-trade-agreements-new-ebook

Forum (2018), 'The European Response to a Challenging World Trade Regime', *Intereconomics*, 53, 5, 245-265.

Frieden, Jeffry (2022), "Global Trade in the Age of Populism", Special Issue on New Globalization Challenges and EU Trade Policy, *Perspectivas - Journal of Political Science*, Vol 27.

Gaspar, Vitor and David Amaglobeli (2021), "Tax, Climate Change, and Sustainable Development: Global Problems, Global Solutions?", in Mata, M. E., M. Rocha de Sousa and L. Brites Pereira (eds.), *Economic Globalization and Governance - Essays in honor of Jorge Braga de Macedo*, Springer, 211-226.

Gaspar, Vitor and David Amaglobeli (2022), "Europe in the World circa 2030", Special Issue on New Globalization Challenges and EU Trade Policy, *Perspectivas - Journal of Political Science*, Vol 27.

Lagarde, Christine (2022), "A new global map: European resilience in a changing world", speech at Peterson Institute for International Economics, Washington, D.C., 22 April.

Laget, Edith, Alberto Osnago, Nadia Rocha and Michele Ruta (2019), "Deep Trade Agreements and Global Value Chains", Working Paper, EUI RSCAS 2019/86 (https://cadmus.eui.eu/handle/1814/64725)

Lamy, Pascal (2020), "Foreword", in A. Mattoo, Nadia Rocha and Michele Ruta (eds), *Handbook of Deep Trade Agreements*, World Bank.

Leblond, Patrick and Crina Viju-Miljusevic (2019), "EU trade policy in the twenty-first century: change, continuity and challenges", Journal of European Public Policy, 26:12, 1836-1846, doi: 10.1080/13501763.2019.1678059

Leblond, Patrick and Crina Viju-Miljusevic (2022), "CETA as the first EU third-generation trade agreement: does it act like one?", Special Issue on New Globalization Challenges and EU Trade Policy, *Perspectivas - Journal of Political Science*, Vol 27.

Magnette, Paul (2016), "Wallonia blocked a harmful EU trade deal — but we are not isolationists", *The Guardian*, 14 November.

Mattoo, Aaditya, Nadia Rocha and Michele Ruta (2022), "The Evolution of Deep Trade Agreements", Special Issue on New Globalization Challenges and EU Trade Policy, *Perspectivas - Journal of Political Science*, Vol 27.

Pope Francis (2015), *Laudato Si'. On Care for our Common Home*, Encyclical Letter, Vatican City: Libreria Editrice Vaticana.

Rodrik, Dani (2011), *The Globalization Paradox: Democracy and the Future of the World Economy*. New York and London: W.W. Norton.

Rodrik, Dani (2016), "Have economists been honest enough about trade", World Economic Forum, 17 November; also as "Straight talk on trade", Project Syndicate, 15 November.

Rodrik, Dani (2018), "What Do Trade Agreements Really Do?", Feb., NBER Working Paper No. 24344 https://www.nber.org/papers/w24344.

Young, Alasdair R. (2015), "Liberalizing trade, not exporting rules: The limits to regulatory coordination in the EU's new generation preferential trade agreements", *Journal of European Public Policy* 22 (9), 1253-1275.

CHAPTER 2
EUROPE IN THE WORLD CIRCA 2030[13]

Vitor Gaspar and David Amaglobeli

Abstract: This chapter examines how several underlying evolutionary dynamics will shape the global economy, from a European perspective. The chapter also discusses some areas of multilateral cooperation focusing on climate change, the pandemic preparedness, and sustainable development. At a time of heightened geopolitical tensions, international cooperation is key to avoid fragmentation and aggravating instability in the global economy.

Keywords: Europe; Global cooperation; Climate change; Sustainable Development; Pandemic preparedness.

1. Introduction

As the world economy is experiencing shock after shock, multilateral cooperation is urgently needed to tackle numerous problems requiring collective action on a global scale. Pandemic management and prevention, climate change, poverty, food and energy security, debt and development in low-income countries are a few examples. More cooperation between all countries, especially the largest, is crucial to avoid the spectre of fragmentation. Such international cooperation is even more warranted because there is not a single natural "hegemon" — following Charles Kindleberger — who can stabilize

[13] The views expressed in this chapter are those of the authors and do not necessarily represent the views of the IMF, its Executive Board, or IMF management. The authors would like to thank Maureen Burke, Paolo Mauro, James Roaf, Abdel Senhadji, Genet Zinabou, and an anonymous referee, for their helpful comments and suggestions. Virat Singh provided outstanding research assistance.

the international economic system (especially) in times of stress or crises. When in 1929 "the British could not and the United States would not" act as a lender and consumer of last resort, the world economy ended in a deep and protracted depression (Kindleberger 2013).

Confronting these formidable challenges together is in the best interest of all countries. Future pandemics may be unavoidable, but the risks and costs can be reduced through joint efforts by countries and organizations. The WHO provides a platform for cooperation between governments to prevent and manage future pandemics among other health objectives. Given that epidemics can impose significant economic and financial costs on affected countries closer collaboration between the WHO, on one hand, and multilateral financial institutions, such as the IMF and the World Bank, on the other hand, is crucial. Cooperation between countries to support development objectives in developing countries is crucial for a more stable and socially cohesive world. With about 60 percent of the world population projected to live in today's low and lower-middle income countries by 2050 (compared with 52 percent today), developed countries and international organizations should provide support to these countries in achieving the Sustainable Development Goals (SDGs). Finally, no country can combat climate change on its own. Global cooperation is required. Such cooperation needs to create incentives for countries at various development stages to exceed their climate objectives, which is necessary to limit the rise in temperature well below 2°C (as agreed in Paris, in 2015).

Unfortunately, the temptation to free ride and risks to such cooperation have become stronger. If history is any guide, the global economy prospered when the international community agreed on the rules for cooperation and set up a system of multilateral institutions to aid the implementation of those rules. Recognizing the benefits of international cooperation is crucial. Unfortunately, developments in the last few years, such as Covid-19 and Russia's invasion of Ukraine, have created risks of polarization and division, which need to be overcome. The European Union (EU), as one of the major economic powers in the world, can play a crucial role in promoting the common agenda and effectively facilitating international cooperation. In this paper we briefly review the experience of international cooperation and its benefits and focus on three key areas in which global cooperation is needed going forward: pandemic preparedness, SDGs and combating climate change.[14]

[14] Combating climate change is one of SDGs (SDG 13) but we single it out given the existential threat presented by climate change to the world.

2. Benefits of and Risks to Global Cooperation

The establishment of the Bretton Woods institutions in 1944 marked the beginning of a new era of multilateral cooperation. The key objective of the new institutions — the International Monetary Fund and the World Bank — was to rebuild the shattered global economy after the disastrous effects of the Second World War by promoting international economic cooperation and development among the participating nations. Later, in 1947, the agreement was reached to create the General Agreement for Tariffs and Trade (GATT), the predecessor of the World Trade Organization (WTO). The creation of the new post-war economic order was truly an international effort—involving countries from all parts of the world including the Western countries such as the United States and the United Kingdom, and other global players like China, India, and the Soviet Union. Stability and structure provided by the new global order has helped many countries to grow their economies as economic interconnectedness increased. The share of international trade in percent of the global GDP rose 2.5 times in the period between 1970 and 2021 (Figure 2.1).

Figure 2.1. World Trade and Global per capita GDP

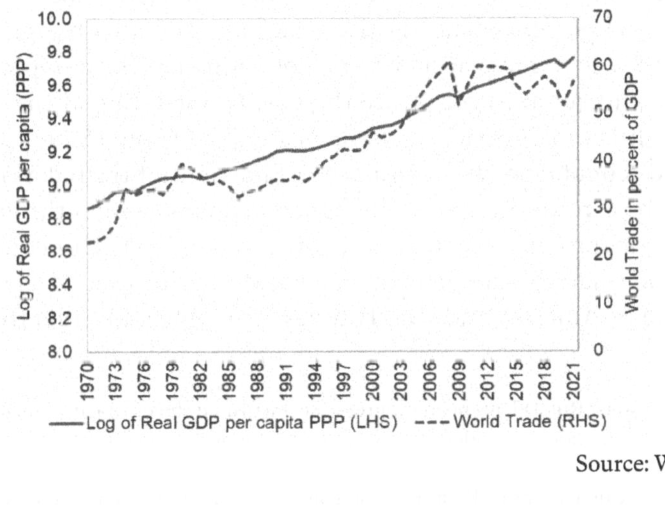

Source: World Bank.

Real average world per capita as well as GDP per capita of the European Union also increased by about 2.5 times. Concurrently, the share of the world population living in extreme poverty declined. Following the successful launch of new institutions of global economic governance other crucial international organizations, such as the World Health Organization (WHO) and the Food and Agriculture Organization (FAO) were created.

Russia's invasion of Ukraine is threatening to upend the system of global economic cooperation and fragment the world into us-versus-them blocs. The war and the policies adopted by a number of developed country governments and firms against the aggressor have resulted in colossal human losses, triggered the largest population displacement since the Second World War and disrupted global trade and financial flows.[15] Russia is a major exporter of oil and gas products, grains, fertilizer, and other key commodities and has a much larger footprint in the global economy than other countries that had been under sanctions in previous historical episodes, such as Iran, South Africa, or Venezuela. Therefore, the impact on the rest of the world is much more profound. The fighting has also disrupted trade routes in the Black Sea limiting Ukraine's ability to export grains, sunflower oils, and other goods from its seaports. Isolation of Russia from the international financial system (especially the exclusion of several Russian banks from the SWIFT system in March 2022) and from trade have prompted some redirection of Russian trade and financial flows. For example, bilateral trade between Russia, on the one hand, and China and India, on the other hand, has been growing during 2022.[16] The trade between Russia and China and India is increasingly denominated in local currencies.

The global power balance is also changing as China has emerged as a major global economic player. The rise of China has been impressive since the 1980s. During most of twentieth century, including at the time when the key multilateral institutions were created, the United States was a dominant world economic power (Figure 2.2). Shortly after the recovery from the WWII, Europe restored some of its former economic might through its own regional cooperation. As Jean Monnet observed in 1954 "Our countries have become too small for the present day world, for the scale of modern technology and of America and Russia today, or China and India tomorrow."[17]

[15] Sanctions against Russia have been progressively instituted since 2014 after its illegal annexation of Crimea. Sanctions expanded massively in 2022 following the Russia's military aggression against Ukraine.

[16] According to calculations by Reuters (based on Chinese customs data) year on year growth in Chinese exports to Russia stood at nearly 27 percent in August 2022 while Chinese imports from Russia were at 59 percent.

[17] The statement was made on November 9, 1954 and is reproduced in his Memoirs: the Architect and Master Builder of the European Economic Community, New York, Doubleday, 1978.

Even so, in purchasing power parity (PPP) dollar terms, the weight of the EU (after accounting for the expansion of its membership and for Brexit) in the global economy has been consistently declining since the 1960s because of the rapid growth of the Chinese and Indian economies. China, in particular, has more than tripled its PPP GDP weight in the global economy and now exceeds that of the United States. Meanwhile, Russia (Soviet Union before its independence), a country with the largest land mass in the world, has been losing its weight in the global economy in PPP terms and is projected to continue its decline partly as a result of its declining population[18].

Figure 2.2. Global GDP Weights of Real GDP (in percent of global GDP, 2011 purchasing power parity dollars)

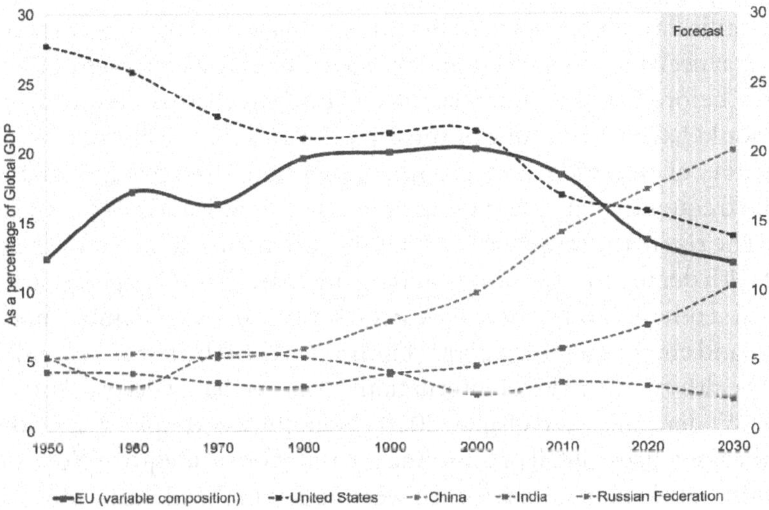

Sources: Maddison Database Project 2019; IMF WEO; and the authors calculations. Note: Each datapoint corresponds to a 10-year average for each country/group in the global economy. The variable used is real GDP in 2011 US dollars. Projections are based on extrapolations of the Maddison data assuming real GDP growth rates from the IMF World Economic Outlook (WEO) database (April 2022 vintage). Beyond 2027 (the terminal year of the IMF WEO projections extrapolation is done using the growth projection for 2027.

[18] The population of Russia started declining in the 1990s. The turning-point is well before the corresponding point for Japan (normally referred as the paradigm of early demographic transition). See United Nations, Department of Economic and Social Affairs, Population Division, Population Projections.

3. Strengthening Pandemic Preparedness

If there is one main lesson to draw from Covid-19 it is that strengthening international cooperation for pandemic preparedness is crucial. The effects of the Covid-19 pandemic have been catastrophic. The officially reported figures put the global death toll at nearly 7 million. Credible estimates by independent researchers are much higher, at 17.2 million as of May 31, 2022 (Sachs and others, 2022).[19] The difference between the reported and estimated numbers of results from the fact that more than 100 countries do not collect reliable statistics on expected or actual deaths, or do not release them in a timely manner (Adam 2022). In addition to the staggering human toll, the pandemic has resulted in massive economic losses estimated to be close to $13.8 trillion through 2024 relative to pre-pandemic forecasts (Gopinath 2022). These estimates could have been significantly higher if not for the extraordinary work of scientists to develop vaccines at neck-breaking speed, and the swift policy responses across the world.

Even before Covid-19 outbreak it was evident that pandemic preparedness should have become one of the top priorities for the global community. The history of emerging or re-emerging infectious disease pandemics shows that the frequency of pandemics has increased significantly (Ross and others 2016). The rise in the frequency of emerging infectious diseases is largely associated with demographic changes and the increased world population density (Jones and others 2008). There have been several major epidemics (both established and emerging) since 2000 (Figure 2.3).[20] In the last 15 years alone six public health emergencies of international concern have been declared by the WHO (Wilder-Smith and Osman 2020). Nonetheless, despite major advances in medical sciences global preparedness has not been adequate. For example, the Ebola outbreak in 2014 exposed weaknesses in the identification of community outbreaks, limited capacity of local health systems, poor communication between response teams and the population, and the slow and poorly coordinated international response (Sands and others 2016).

[19] The Economist excess deaths model available at https://ourworldindata.org/grapher/excess-deaths-cumulative-economist-single-entity?country=~OWID_WRL, puts the total deaths estimate at 21 million.

[20] Established infectious diseases are those that have been prevalent for a sufficient period of time to allow for a relatively stable and predictable level of morbidity and mortality. Emerging diseases include newly emerging diseases—i.e., diseases that are recognized in the human host for the first time—and re-emerging diseases—diseases that historically have infected humans but continue to reappear either in new locations or in resistant forms or reappear after apparent control or elimination or under unusual circumstances (Fauci and Morens 2012).

The international community should recognize that investing in pandemic preparedness helps address a systemic risk to the global economy. All nations need to mobilize additional financing to invest in strengthening their capacity to fight the next pandemic. It is crucial that as countries upgrade their systems, they let themselves be guided by International Health Regulations, which provide an overarching legal framework for handling public health events and emergencies. Such investments in health systems can reduce the probability of future pandemics occurring and the costs (both human and economic) associated with the fight against them. Moreover, these investments can also help tackle other long-standing infectious diseases, such as HIV/AIDS and Malaria. Eradication of smallpox in the 1970s — an endemic disease of 20th century — was an outstanding practical achievement and was possible owing to international cooperation in public health and investments in vaccination programs and information and knowledge sharing (Cooper and others 1989). The total annual financing needs for investing in the strengthening pandemic prevention and preparedness is estimated at US$ 31.1 billion, which implies additional financing needs of US$ 10.5 billion after considering current and expected domestic and international financing (G20 2022a). Many emerging and developing economies will not be able to mobilize substantial additional financing needed. Therefore, the cooperation among all key stakeholders, such as national governments, multilateral and specialized institutions, and the private sector will be needed to scale up financing for pandemic preparedness. In addition, a new dedicated multilateral financing mechanism has been proposed to signal the importance of pandemic preparedness, sustain global attention in inter-pandemic years and mobilize and deliver additional resources (G20 2022b).

Figure 2.3. Major Epidemics, 2000–2022

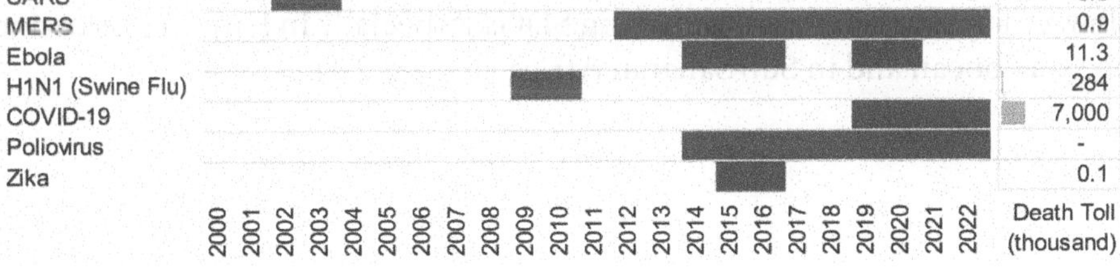

Source: various sources.

4. Achieving Sustainable Development Goals

Even prior to the pandemic many low-income developing countries faced colossal challenges to reach the SDGs by 2030. Delivering on SDGs in the areas of primary physical infrastructure (roads, electricity, and water and sanitation) and in the social sector (health and education) was estimated at 15 percent of GDP in low-income developing countries and 4 percent of GDP in emerging market economies prior to the pandemic (Gaspar and others 2019). Most emerging market economies could finance the additional spending to achieve the SDGs by raising tax revenues through major, sustained efforts to strengthen tax capacity. In low-income developing countries, however, the magnitude of required additional spending implies than an ambitious but realistic increase in tax revenues could potentially finance only one-third of the total additional spending. Improving efficiency through better economic management together with enhanced transparency and governance could also allow governments to achieve more with less. Estimates suggest that about one-half of the spending on public investment in developing countries is wasted (Schwartz and others, 2020). Strengthening the institutional framework through better governance and a more robust regulatory environment would help catalyse additional private investment. For countries in Sub-Saharan Africa, for example, increasing spending efficiency could yield 2½ percent of GDP in savings (Desruelle, Razafimahefa, and Sancak 2019) while the private sector, both domestic and international, could bring an additional 3 percent of GDP over the next decade (Eyraud and others 2021). Even with these efforts, a sizable financing gap would remain, which in many countries could potentially be financed through support from international partners by stepping up efforts to increase Official Development Assistance (ODA) to meet the target of 0.7 percent of aggregate DAC GNI.

The pandemic first and then the war in Ukraine were major setbacks for the achievement of the SDGs by 2030. The pandemic has markedly slowed down the progress toward achieving SDGs, especially in Latin America and the Caribbean and in Sub Saharan Africa (Figure 2.4).

Figure 2.4. Annual Change in SDG Index Scores*

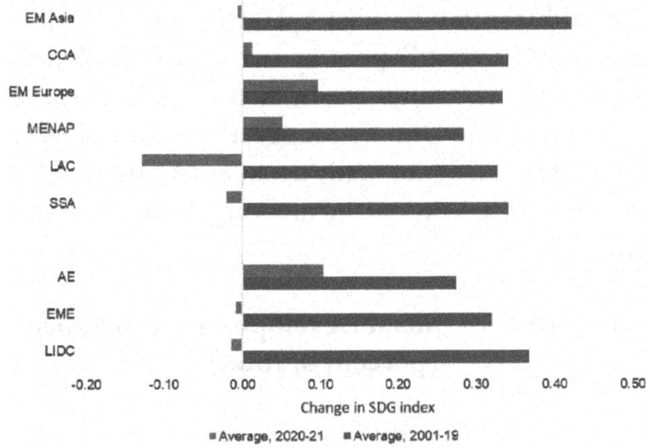

Sources: Sustainable Development Report; and authors' calculations.

Note: AEs — Advanced Economies; EME — Emerging Market Economies;
LIDC — Low-Income Development Countries; CCA — Caucasus and Central Asia;
MENAP — Middle East, North Africa, and Pakistan;
LAC — Latin America and Caribbean; SSA — Sub Saharan Africa.

* The SDG Index is an assessment of each country's overall performance on all SDGs. The score ranges between 0 (the worst possible outcome) and 100 (the target).

The pandemic has also substantially raised the financing needs to reach the SDGs. In the five key development areas — education, health, roads, electricity, and water and sanitation — the financing needs for four case study countries increased by about 2½ percentage points of GDP (Benedek and others 2021). The pandemic also affected other SDGs. For example, the number of people living in extreme poverty is estimated to have increased by 124 million to 779 million in 2020, implying a global poverty rate of 10 percent, which is 1.9 percentage points higher than forecasted for 2020 before the onset of the pandemic (World Bank 2022). The war in Ukraine has brought about further challenges to ambitions of reaching various SDGs. In addition to devastating effects to Ukraine itself, the war is having a profound impact on global food security, making the achievement of the SDG2 on ending hunger by 2030 significantly more challenging.[21] Moreover, higher food prices are

[21] The SDG2 is on ending hunger, achieving food security and improving nutrition and promoting sustainable agriculture.

hurting the poor the most as food normally represents a higher share in the consumption basket of lower-income households. The eventual poverty impact could be substantial. For example, the 2010–2011 food price spike raised the number of the world's poor by an estimated 8.3 million (Ha, Kose and Ohnsorge 2019). The confluence of factors, such as the pandemic, climate change, and the war in Ukraine, suggest that the risk of famine today is much higher than it has been for many decades (Alfani and O Grada, 2022). These multiple crises have jeopardized meeting the agenda for SDGs by 2030 (United Nations, 2022).

Figure 2.5. Official Development Assistance (percent of total)

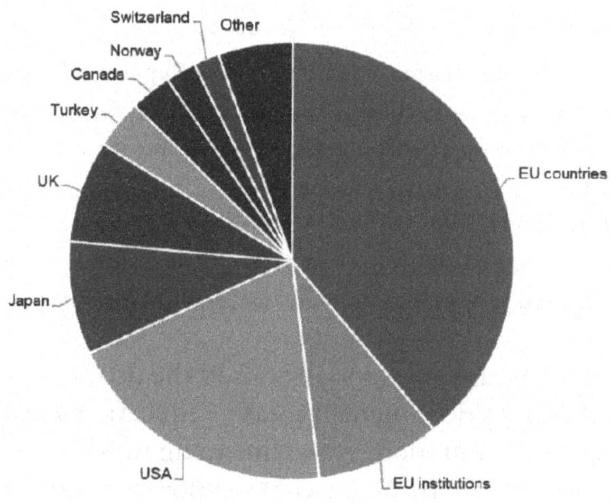

Sources: OECD, and authors' calculations.

The current predicament requires a more intense global partnership to salvage the SDGs against the backdrop of recent shocks. The consequences from Russia's invasion of Ukraine necessitate that the international community stand together to provide crucial support to those most affected by the war. More than 14 million displaced individuals within and outside Ukraine, mostly across Europe, need urgent aid to support their livelihoods. Meanwhile, it is equally important that the assistance provided to the victims of the war does not crowd out support from the members of the international community to low-income countries in their efforts to meet the SDGs. The EU member states in particular, which account for nearly half of total official development assistance, should stay the course and step up their efforts in supporting countries whose development agendas have been set back by the two major shocks (Figure 2.5). Demonstrating the EU's steadfast support for low-income countries would also help ensure that these countries continue to view the EU, and the global community more generally, as constructive partners in their quest for economic development. Among the largest providers of official development assistance only a handful meet the 0.7 percent of GNI target set by the UN resolution adopted in 1970 (Figure 2.6). Meeting the 0.7 percent of gross national income target would provide about US$230 billion in additional funding to contribute to closing development gaps (Gaspar and others 2019).

Figure 2.6. Official Development Assistance by Provider, 2021

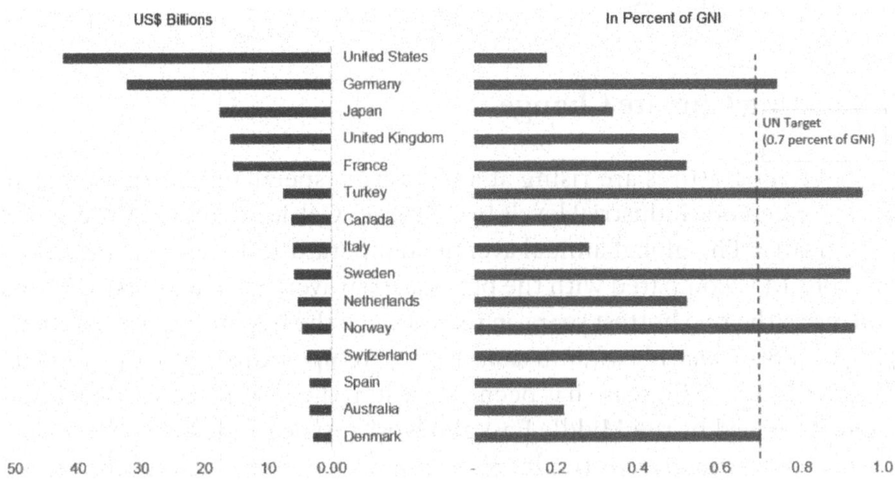

Source: OECD.

Note: includes those countries that are part of the Development Assistance Committee of the Organization for Economic Co-operation and Development and those that are not.

Promoting economic growth is the most effective way to rapidly achieve SDGs. Growth expands the pool of available resources for investing in SDGs creating a virtuous circle of growth and development. To accelerate growth rates, countries need to rigorously implement structural reforms that strengthen macroeconomic fundamentals, the quality of key institutions and the regulatory environment for the private sector. For a typical emerging market and developing economy, major simultaneous reforms in domestic and external finance, international trade, labour and product market regulations, and governance could raise annual economic growth by about 1 percentage point over five to ten years, doubling the current speed of income-per-capita convergence to advanced economy levels over the next decade (IMF 2019a). Doubling projected GDP per capita in 2030 would reduce additional spending needs by some 4½ percentage points (Gaspar and others 2019). As a successful example, Vietnam managed to achieve a remarkable progress thanks to structural reforms implemented starting from the late 1980s. Being initially poorer than most of todays' low-income developing countries, Vietnam managed to lift its per-capita GDP 10-fold, and as a result reduce the poverty rate (living at below $1.90 per day) from more than 60 percent in the 1980s to below 5 percent of the population now and to become a country that ranks in the top quarter of SDG performance across emerging market economies for the majority of indicators (Baum 2020).

5. Tackling Climate Change

Global temperatures are rising at an alarming speed and, if unaddressed, could exceed pre-industrial levels by 3 degrees Celsius or more by the end of the century. The global annual average temperature has already increased by about 1.1°C compared with the preindustrial average. The years 2020 and 2016 were the two hottest years on record since the beginning of recordkeeping in 1880.[22] Decade after decade average temperatures kept creeping up (Figure 2.7). The increase has been greatest in the Europe and Central Asia region followed by the Middle East and North Africa and North America.

The consequences of the increase in temperatures include the rise in extreme weather events, such as heatwaves, droughts, and flooding. The frequency of such extreme weather events has accelerated over the last three decades across many geographic areas (Figure 2.8). In addition to their large human toll, extreme weather events bring about significant socio-economic disruption. Moreover, extreme weather events tend to affect the poor more than the rich. The poor are also most exposed to the more gradual, slow, and more pervasive environmental disasters caused by climate change (Stern 2019). Empirical evidence suggests that an increase in climate vulnerability is positively associated with rising income inequality, after controlling for economic

[22] Source: NASA's Goddard Institute for Space Studies (GISS).

and demographic factors (Cevik and Jalles 2019). Therefore, climate change could undermine poverty eradication efforts as it disproportionately impacts the poorest regions and worsens income inequality within countries (World Bank 2020). Climate change may also prompt international migration.

Figure 2.7. Global Annual Mean Surface Air Temperature Change

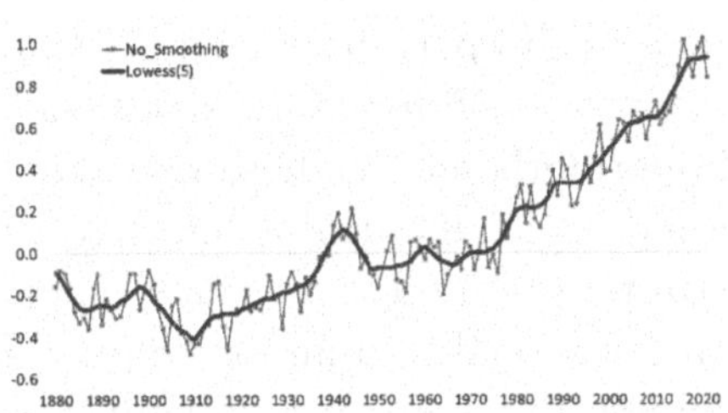

Source: NASA.

Note: Land-ocean temperature change with respect to the base period of 1951–1980.

Figure 2.8. Frequency of Climate Related Disasters (total for each decade)

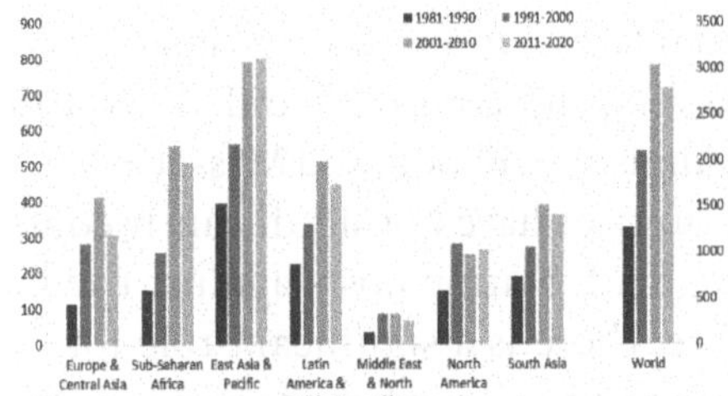

Source: The Emergency Events Database (EM-DAT), Centre for Research on the Epidemiology of Disasters (CRED) / Université catholique de Louvain (UCLouvain), Brussels, Belgium — www.emdat.be.

Note: Includes droughts, extreme temperatures, floods, landslides, and storms.

Figure 2.9. Shares of Countries and Regions in Global CO_2 Emissions, 2030

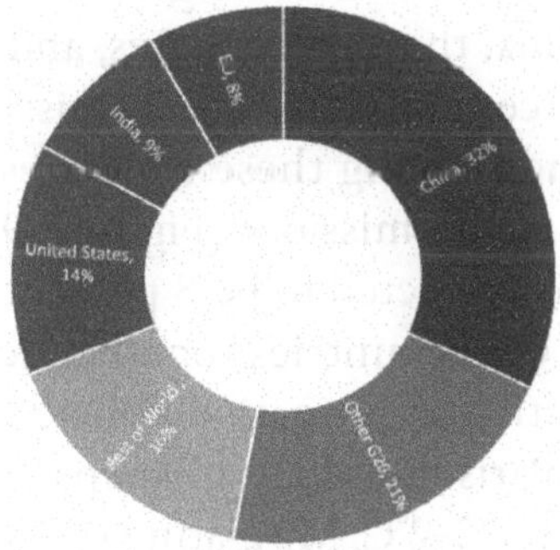

Source: Parry, Black and Roaf 2021.

Given that temperature rises impact the entire globe, all countries need to invest in resilience to adapt to climate change. It is clear that even with the best mitigation efforts climate change will continue. Therefore, national adaptation plans should be developed and implemented using a three-pillar approach that focuses on (a) structural resilience by building climate-resistant infrastructure; (b) financial resilience that ensures countries have fiscal buffers to cope with disasters; and (c) post-disaster resilience requires that requires contingency planning (IMF 2019b). The costs of adaptation, especially building structural resilience, are high for low-income developing countries. Annual adaptation costs could exceed 1 percent of GDP for some developing countries and above 10 percent of GDP for some island states (Aligishiev, Bellon, and Massetti 2022). Importantly, most of these low-income countries have not significantly contributed to global warming but they face high adaptation costs against the backdrop of limited fiscal space. Therefore, there is a significant role for the international community to provide support to climate change vulnerable countries anchored in nationally developed disaster-resilience strategies. Advanced economies should deliver on their promise to provide additional $100 billion to developing economies in climate finance. The IMF's new policy instrument — the Resilience and Sustainability Trust (RST) — will provide crucial financing to eligible low-income countries to enhance their economic resilience and sustainability with a special emphasis on climate change (IMF 2022).

If adaptation policies are needed for all countries climate mitigation by large emitters matters most to avoid catastrophic effects on the planet. Recognizing that low-income countries have historically contributed less to global greenhouse gases (GHG) emissions, the international community adopted the principle of "common but differentiated responsibility and respective capabilities" to fight climate change. The top three emitting countries in the world — China, the United States, and India—are projected to account for about 55 percent of global CO2 emissions in 2030, suggesting that a pragmatic approach among these countries could have a profound effect on the overall volume of emissions (Figure 2.9). The EU's contribution to the global emissions is projected to be 8 percent (one-quarter of China's contribution), while all G20 countries together account for up to 85 percent. The ultimate objective of mitigation policies, which was endorsed by 196 signatory parties in Paris in 2015, is to keep the increase in global temperature by 2100 within 1.5°C–2°C. Mitigating the climate and the attendant decline in extreme weather events will have a very positive long-term economic impact, especially considering health and productivity gains from reduced local pollution. However, the progress to date in achieving emissions reductions has been limited.

Carbon pricing is the most effective policy instruments to curb climate change. Each country would have to take measures to set carbon prices at appropriate levels to ensure the required carbon emissions reductions. To avoid a collective action problem an international carbon price floor (ICPF) has been proposed as a pragmatic solution (Parry, Black and Roaf 2021). The ICPF would be negotiated among key large emitters and focuses on the minimum price for carbon. For equity considerations, including for application of the principle of "common but differentiated responsibility and respective capabilities", the carbon price floors would be differentiated depending on countries income level. For illustration, a price floor of $75 per ton of carbon could be adopted for advanced economies, $50 for emerging market economies and $25 for low-income developing countries. The ICPF with a tiered price system, appropriately designed and simultaneously adopted by countries, would likely be sufficient to achieve the target of keeping the global temperature increase within 2°C, would have only a small impact on global economic growth and would help ensure a fairer redistribution of burden of reducing emissions across countries (Chateau, Jaumotte, and Schwerhoff 2022).

Strong global action to raise carbon pricing is urgently needed as current levels of carbon prices remain woefully low. Although several countries, including EU members, have been aggressively raising carbon pricing, either through carbon taxes or emissions trading systems (ETS), this has not been sufficient to meaningfully raise the global average price. About four-fifths of global GHG emissions remain unpriced and the global average carbon price in 2021 was only $3 per ton (Figure 2.10). The slow progress has triggered discussions in countries with high carbon prices to place charges on the carbon content of imports from low carbon price countries. However, this is a highly ineffective instrument for emissions reduction compared to the ICPF because carbon embodied in trade flows is typically less than 10 percent of countries' total emissions.

In contrast to mitigation objectives, many governments are underpricing fossil fuels, which leads to overconsumption and subsequently to faster global warming. Fossil fuel subsidies, measured as underpricing compared to the full supply and environmental costs of the fuels, stood at nearly 7 percent of GDP in 2020 (Parry, Black, and Vernon 2021). Such subsidies are particularly high in the Middle East and North Africa region and the lowest in North America (Figure 2.11). The size of these subsidies has very likely increased in 2021 and 2022 with the substantial rise in global energy prices. In addition to their contribution to global warming, fossil fuel subsidies lead to worsening in local air quality problems, with knock-on social and healthcare effects. Fossil fuel subsidies are also costly, poorly targeted, and crowd out other productive government spending. Reforming fossil fuel subsidies can be politically difficult but if designed appropriately such reforms can become acceptable. Subsidy reform needs to rely on a comprehensive reform plan consisting of a far-reaching communications strategy, appropriately phased energy price increases, sequenced differently across energy products, targeted mitigation measures for vulnerable households, improvements in the efficiency of state-owned enterprises, and depoliticization of energy pricing (Clements and others 2013).

Figure 2.10. Carbon Pricing, Coverage and Average Price

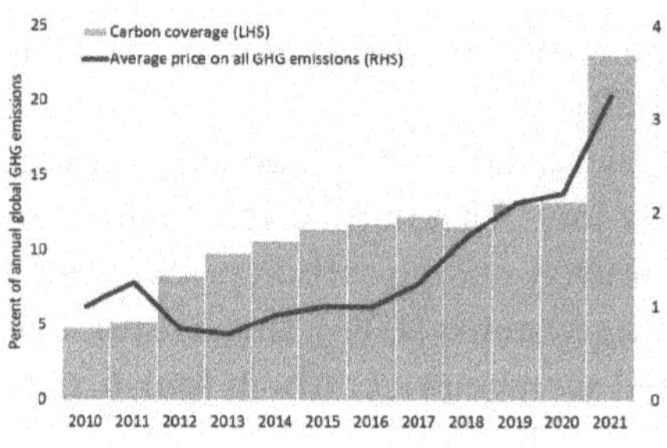

Source: World Bank.

Note: Carbon coverage shows the share of global carbon emissions subjected to a carbon price.

Figure 2.11. Fossil Fuel Subsidies, 2020 (in percent of GDP)

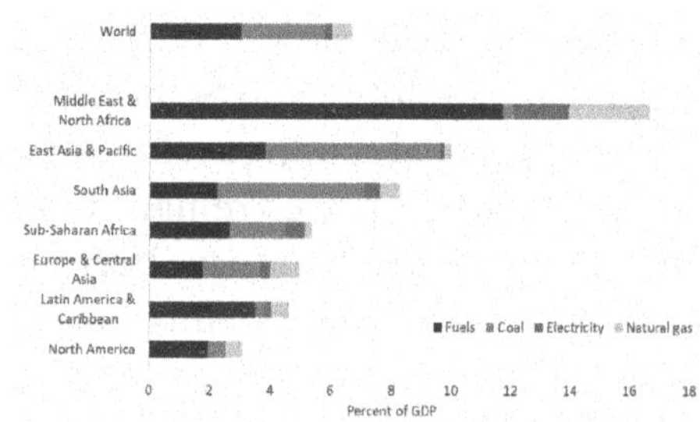

Sources: Parry, Black and Vernon (2021); and authors calculations.

Note: Subsidies include explicit (subsidies due to supply costs being greater than the retail prices) and implicit subsidies (subsidies due to the efficient price being greater than the retail price, exclusive of any explicit subsidy).

Russia's invasion of Ukraine has put energy security at the forefront of the policy agenda for many countries creating risks for the green transition. In response to rising energy prices many countries have announced emergency measures to cushion the effects of higher prices on vulnerable households and firms. In most cases the key objective of announced policies was to limit the pass-through of the increase in international prices to domestic consumers (Amaglobeli and others 2022). Some governments also took measures to boost local fossil fuel productions to ensure affordable access to energy. These measures are aimed at further boosting coal production to reduce reliance on imported coal (for example, China), or to sustain household consumption of coal briquettes through price subsidies (for example, Mongolia). It is crucial that the current energy price shock does not derail the world from meeting the target to limit global warming to below 2°C and is managed in a way that is consistent with the climate ambition. Diversification of energy supplies can help accelerate the transition to green economies and strengthen energy security. Speedily increasing investments in the production of renewables and reducing dependence on fossil fuels are urgent priorities to ensure both energy security and climate change mitigation. However, in the short run, as economies grapple with supply shortages, alternative supply sources of non-renewable energy, including, for example, enhancing markets for liquefied natural gas, and temporarily expanding production of shale oil and gas may be unavoidable.

6. Conclusion

In this paper we argue that even in today's highly interdependent but polarized world international cooperation is crucial and feasible. Effective cooperation should focus on areas where collective action is urgently needed. Cooperation in public health to eradicate smallpox in 1970s serves as an inspiring example when key global players, the United States and the Soviet Union, then rivals in the Cold War, joined forces to introduce a program under the auspices of the WHO. In today's world, strengthening pandemic preparedness, supporting low-income countries in achieving SDGs and tackling climate change are priority problems. Russia's war in Europe, the disastrous effects of the Covid-19 pandemic, derailed efforts to achieve SDGs and the increased frequency of extreme weather events should prompt countries, and especially all major players, to embrace collaborative action for the ultimate benefit of the entire world.

The EU can act as a centre of gravity for multilateral cooperation. It has a special role to play given its unique position on the global arena. In particular,

- The EU is a large and successful global player. Despite its declining weight in the global economy the EU still accounts for about 15 percent of the world GDP in PPP terms. Moreover, the EU has been successful in building an inclusive economy with its member states enjoying one of the highest levels of social protection globally.
- The EU is an example of multilateral cooperation, based on collective institutions and community law. The EU is a union of nations, peoples and citizens that has reached a deep level of international integration. The single market and the euro are its most emblematic achievements.
- The EU has established itself as a reliable partner on global arena. The EU has been forceful in taking actions in all crucial transnational areas. Over the last several decades the EU has made strong progress in reducing its greenhouse gas emissions. For many years the EU has been providing financial and technical support to low-income countries to implement necessary policies in support of SDGs. The EU has been an important actor in helping countries strengthen pandemic preparedness and has contributed considerably, for example, to increasing Covid-19 vaccine access globally.

Global cooperation is a vital priority for the EU. Its exercise of soft power requires global peaceful coexistence to deliver security and prosperity to European citizens. The EU can play a constructive role in finding practical ways forward. One good example is climate change. By 2030, the EU emissions are projected to be below those of China, the US and India. Differences in numbers are stark: 8 percent projected for the EU against 55 percent for the sum of these three countries. China alone is projected to represent almost one-third of total emissions. Nevertheless, the EU is most advanced in the use of carbon pricing. In this area, the EU could help push a comprehensive agenda that would include financing, innovation, technology transfer, and development. In such agenda, adaptation would have to be considered together with mitigation. By playing such a role, the EU would be pushing for security and prosperity for all citizens of the world.

REFERENCES

Adam, D. (2022), "The pandemic's true death toll: millions more than official counts", Nature, 18 january, available at: https://www.nature.com/articles/d41586-022-00104-8

Alfani, G., and C. O Grada (2022), *Famine, war, and climate change: From the Middle Ages to the Russia-Ukraine War*, available at https://cepr.org/voxeu/columns/faminewar-and-climate-change-middle-ages-russia-ukraine-war (Accessed: 06 march 2023).

Aligishiev, Z., M. Bellon, and E. Massetti (2022), *Macro-Fiscal Implications of Adaptatin to Climate Change*, IMF Staff Climate Note 2022/002, Washington, DC: International Monetary Fund.

Amaglobeli, D., E. Hanedar, G. Hong, and C. Thevenot (2022), *Fiscal Policy for Mitigating the Social Impact of High Energy and Food Prices*, IMF Notes No 2022/001, Washington, DC: International Monetary Fund.

Baum, A. (2020), *Vietnam's Development Success Story and the Unfinished SDG Agenda*, IMF working paper 2020/031, Washington, DC: International Monetary Fund.

Benedek, D., E. Gemayel, A. Senhadji, and A. Tieman (2021), *A Post-Pandemic Assessment of the Sustainable Development Goals*, IMF Staff Discussion Note 2021/003, Washington, DC: International Monetary Fund.

Cevik, S., and J. Jalles (2022), *For Whom the Bell Tolls: Climate Change and Income*, Washington, DC: International Monetary Fund.

Chateau, J., F. Jaumotte, and G. Schwerhof (2022), "Economic and Environmental Benefits from International Cooperation on Climate Policies", IMF Departmental Paper DP/2022/007, Washington, DC: International Monetary Fund.

Clements B., D. Coady, S. Fabrizio, S. Gupta, T. Alleyne and C. Sdralevich (eds.) (2013), *Energy Subsidy Reform: Lessons and Implications*, Washington, DC: International Monetary Fund.

Cooper, R., B. Eichengreen, G. Holtham, R. Putnam, and C. Henning (eds.) (1989), *Can Nations Agree? Issues in International Economic Cooperation*, Washington, DC: Brookings Institution Press.

Desruelle, d., I. Razafimahefa, and C. Sancak (2019), "Sustainable development, sustainable debt: Finding the right balance", IMF conference paper, Washington, DC: International Monetary Fund.

Eyraud, L., H. Devine, A. Peralta-Alva, H. Selim, P. Sharma, and L. Wocken (2021), "Private Finance for Development: Wishful Thinking Out of The Box?", IMF Departmental Paper, DP/21/11, Washington, DC: International Monetary Fund.

Fauci, A., and D. Morens (2012), "The Perpetual Challenge of Infectious Diseases", New England Journal of Medicine, 366: pp. 454-461, available at: https://www.nejm.org/doi/full/10.1056/NEJMra1108296.

Gaspar, V., D. Amaglobeli, M. Garcia Escribano, D. Prady, and M. Soto (2019), "Fiscal Policy and Development: Human, Social, and Physical Investments for the SDGs", IMF Staff Discussion Notes No. 2019/003, Washington, DC: International Monetary Fund.

Gopinath, G. (2022), "A Disrupted Global Recovery", blog, IMF, January 25, 2022, available at: https:// blogs.imf.org/2022/01/25/a-disrupted-global-recovery/.

Ha, J., A. Kose, and F. Ohnsorge (2019), "Inflation in Emerging and Developing Economies: Evolution, Drivers and Policies", World Bank, available at: https://open knowledge.worldbank.org/handle/10986/30657.

International Monetary Fund (2019), "Reigniting Growth In Low-Income And Emerging Market Economies: What Role Can Structural Reforms Play?" in IMF, *World Economic Outlook*, Washington, DC: International Monetary Fund, pp. 98-119.

International Monetary Fund (2019), "Building Resilience in Developing Countries Vulnerable to Large Natural Disasters", IMF Policy Paper, Washington, DC: International Monetary Fund.

International Monetary Fund (2020), "Mitigating Climate Change—Growth and Distribution-Friendly Strategies", in *World Economic Outlook*, Washington, DC: International Monetary Fund, pp. 85-113.

International Monetary Fund (2020), "Proposal to Establish A Resilience and Sustainability Trust", IMF Policy Paper, Washington, DC: International Monetary Fund.

Jones, K., Patel, N., Levy, M. *et al.* (2008), "Global trends in emerging infectious diseases" *Nature* 451, pp. 990–993, available at: https://doi.org/10.1038/nature06536.

Kindleberger, C., (author), B. DeLong (foreword) and B. Eichengreen (foreword) (2013), "The World in Depression, 1929–1939", Oakland: University of California Press.

Mott, G., C. Razo and R. Hamwey (2021), *Carbon emissions anywhere threaten development everywhere*, available at: https://unctad.org/news/carbon-emissions-anywhere-threaten-development-everywhere.

Parry, I., S. Black, and J. Roaf (2021), "Proposal for an International Carbon Price Floor among Large Emitters" IMF Staff Climate Notes 2021/001, Washington, DC: International Monetary Fund.

Parry, I., S. Black, and N. Vernon (2021), "Still Not Getting Energy Prices Right: A Global and Country Update of Fossil Fuel Subsidies", Working Paper No. 2021/236, Washington, DC: International Monetary Fund.

Ross, A., S. Crowe, M. Tyndall (2016), "Planning for the Next Global Pandemic", International *Journal of Infectious Diseases*, Volume 38, September 2015, pp. 89-94.

Sachs, J., S. Abdool Karim, L. Aknin, J. Allen, K. Brosbol, F. Colombo, G. Cuevas Barron, M. Fernanda Espinosa, V. Gaspar, A. Gaviria, A. Haines, P. J Hotez, P. Koundouri, F. Larrain Bascunan *et al.* (2022), "The Lancet Commission on lessons for the future from the Covid-19 pandemic", *The Lancet*, Volume 400, issue 10359, pp. 1224-1280, available at: https://www.thelancet.com/journals/lancet/article/PIIS0140-6736(22)01585-9/fulltext

Sands, P., C. Mundaca-Shah and V. Dzau (2016), "The Neglected Dimension of Global Security — A Framework for Countering Infectious-Disease Crises", *The New England Journal of Medicine*, 374, pp. 1281-1287.

Schwartz, G., M. Fouad, T. Hansen, and G. Verdier (eds) (2020), "Well Spent: How Strong Infrastructure Governance Can End Waste in Public Investment", Washington, DC: International Monetary Fund.

Stern, N. (2019), "Poverty and Climate Change", in Atkinson, Anthony, *Measuring Poverty around the World*, New Jersey: Princeton University Press.

United Nations (2022), "The Sustainable Development Goals Report", New York: United Nations.

Wilder-Smith, A. and S. Osman (2020), "Public health emergencies of international concern: a historic overview", *J Travel Med.* 27(8): taaa227, available at: https://www.ncbi.nlm.nih.gov/pmc/articles/PMC7798963/.

World Bank (2020), "Poverty and Shared Prosperity 2020: Reversals of Fortune." Washington, DC: World Bank, doi: 10.1596/978-1-4648-1602-4.

World Bank, 2022, *Poverty and Shared Prosperity Report: Toward Inclusive Recovery*, Washington, DC: World Bank.

World Health Organization & the World Bank (2022), "Analysis of Pandemic Preparedness and Response (PPR) architecture, financing needs, gaps and mechanisms", Paper prepared by the WHO and World Bank for the G20 Joint Finance & Health Task Force, Geneva: World Health Organization.

World Health Organization & the World Bank (2022), "Financing Modalities for Pandemic Prevention, Preparedness and Response (PPR)", paper prepared by the World Bank and the World Health Organization for the G20 Joint Finance & Health Task Force, Geneva: World Health Organization.

CHAPTER 3
THE EVOLUTION OF DEEP TRADE AGREEMENTS[23]

Aaditya Mattoo, Nadia Rocha, Michele Ruta

Abstract: This paper takes a first look at new data on the content of Preferential Trade Agreements (PTAs). The data contain detailed information on the eighteen policy areas most frequently covered in PTAs, focusing on the stated objectives, substantive commitments, and other aspects such as transparency, procedures and enforcement. A number of new stylized facts emerge: (i) PTAs have reduced trade-weighted average tariff rates to less than 5 percent for more than two-thirds of countries; (ii) the number of commitments in PTAs has increased over time, particularly since the 2000s and in areas aiming at facilitating flows of services, goods and capital; (iii) deepening commitments have been accompanied by an increase in regulatory requirements, namely on enforcement; (iv) developing countries tend to have fewer commitments in PTAs, with larger gaps in areas such as labour and environment; (v) PTAs are more similar within blocs, but similarity can be significant even across blocs. The paper also discusses the challenges of quantification of PTA "depth" and its effects and proposes a research agenda for future work on trade agreements.

Keywords: Preferential Trade Agreements; Deep Integration.

[23] This paper is based on the Introduction of the Handbook of Deep Trade Agreements (Mattoo, Rocha and Ruta, 2020). We would like to thank Francisco Torres and Annette Bongardt (the Editors), Petros Mavroidis, Tom Prusa, an anonymous referee and seminar participants at Columbia Law School, USITC, and the World Bank for helpful comments and suggestions. We are highly indebted to Alvaro Espitia for providing background research for this paper. Kazusa Yoshimura and Edith Laget worked on the quantification exercise using machine learning techniques in Section 4.

1. Introduction

This paper takes a first look at new data on the content of all Preferential Trade Agreements (PTAs) that have been notified to the World Trade Organization (WTO) and highlights the emergence of Deep Trade Agreement (DTA).[24] The detailed description of the data and the methodology used to collect them are discussed in the Handbook of Deep Trade Agreements (Mattoo, Rocha and Ruta, 2020).

DTAs are reciprocal agreements between countries that cover not just trade but additional policy areas, such as international flows of investment and labor, and the protection of intellectual property rights and the environment, amongst others. While these legal arrangements are still referred to as trade agreements, their goal is integration beyond trade or *deep* integration. DTAs aim at establishing five "economic integration" rights: free (or freer) movement of goods, services, capital, people and ideas. DTAs also include enforcement provisions that limit the discretion of importing governments in these areas, as well as provisions that regulate the behaviour of exporters.

Preferential trade agreements have always been a feature of the world trading system but have become more prominent in recent years. The number of PTAs has increased from 50 in the early 1990s to roughly 300 in 2019. All WTO members are currently party to one, and often several, PTAs. While WTO rules still form the basis of most trade agreements, PTAs have in some sense run away with the trade agenda. Traditional trade policy areas, such as tariff reduction or services liberalization, are now more frequently negotiated in regional contexts rather than at the WTO, with PTAs often going beyond what countries have committed to at the WTO. The result is that PTAs have expanded their scope. While the average PTA in the 1950s covered 8 policy areas, in recent years they have averaged 17. In other words, there is some

[24] In the international economics and law literature, PTA is an umbrella term encompassing several types of reciprocal agreements between trading partners: Regional Trade Agreements (RTAs), Free Trade Agreements (FTAs), and Customs Unions (CUs). This definition differs from that of the World Trade Organization (WTO), which defines PTAs as agreements that grant *unilateral* (i.e., non-reciprocal) trade preferences such as the Generalized System of Preferences schemes, under which developed countries grant preferential tariffs to imports from developing countries. This study, following the definition from international economics and law, uses the term PTA to refer to all types of trade agreements, both within and across regions, and uses DTA to refer to PTAs that contain provisions aimed at deepening economic integration between trading partners.

preliminary evidence that PTAs are becoming DTAs, both on the *intensive* margin (specific commitments within a policy area) and the *extensive* margin (number of policy areas covered). In this paper, we do not draw a sharp distinction between DTAs and other PTAs. Rather, the aim is to demonstrate the progressive deepening of PTAs.

Deep trade agreements matter for economic development. The rules embedded in DTAs, along with the multilateral trade rules and other elements of international economic law such as International Investment Agreements, influence how countries (and, hence, the people and firms that live and operate within them) transact, invest, work, and, ultimately, develop. Trade and investment regimes determine the extent of economic integration, competition rules affect economic efficiency, intellectual property rights matter for innovation, environmental and labor rules contribute to social and environmental outcomes. It is, therefore, vital that rules and commitments in DTAs are informed by evidence and shaped more by development priorities than by international power dynamics or domestic politics. An impediment to this goal is that data and analysis on trade agreements have not captured the new dimensions of integration, which makes it difficult to identify the content and consequences of DTAs.

The new data collected by the World Bank (Mattoo, Rocha and Ruta, 2020) take a first step towards filling this important gap in our understanding of international economic law and policy. It presents detailed information on the content of the eighteen policy areas most frequently covered in PTAs, focusing on the stated objectives, substantive commitments, and other aspects such as transparency, procedures and enforcement. In terms of the coverage of policy areas and the granularity of information within each area, this is the most comprehensive effort up to date.

The primary goal of this paper is to take a first look at the new data. This allows to establish a set of new stylized facts on the deepening of trade agreements: (i) PTAs have reduced trade-weighted average tariff rates to less than 5 percent for more than two-thirds of countries; (ii) the number of commitments in PTAs has increased over time, particularly since the 2000s and in areas aiming at facilitating flows of services, goods and capital; (iii) deepening commitments have been accompanied by an increase in regulatory requirements, namely on enforcement; (iv) developing countries tend to have fewer commitments in PTAs, with larger gaps in areas such as labor and environment; (v) PTAs are more similar within blocs, but similarity can be significant even across blocs.

The new data build on previous research by the World Bank and others. A first database on the content of deep trade agreements was published in 2017 with the goal of documenting how the policy areas covered by PTAs had increased over time (Hofmann *et al.*, 2019). This dataset allowed researchers to construct a first series of indicators which capture the scope of trade agreements; i.e., what policy areas they cover. We refer to this as the *extensive margin* of PTA depth. Based on this first dataset, several research papers then looked, respectively, at the impact of deep trade agreements on trade, global value chains, foreign direct investment, and the effect of breaking up such agreements.[25]

The new data that we briefly review in this paper offer insights into a different dimension of PTAs depth. They capture the detailed commitments to establish and preserve the rights to economic integration, and the procedures, institutions and enforcement mechanisms that countries set up to make deep integration work. The focus is therefore not on the extensive margin of integration (number of policy areas that are covered by the agreement), but on its *intensive margin* (the specific commitments within a policy area).

While there are a number of individual studies that have documented the deepening of PTAs in specific areas, two major data collection projects — Dür *et al.* (2014) and Acharya (2016) — also aimed at documenting the specific commitments for a group of policy areas covered in PTAs. Both efforts have important merits. Dür *et al.* (2014) covered a large set of PTAs, including those that have been notified to the WTO but are no longer in force. Acharya (2016) provided a series of databases on the content of PTAs that go beyond specific policy areas and cover emerging issues such as e-commerce or the rules on dispute settlement in PTAs. Relative to these data collection projects, the new dataset is more comprehensive, both in terms of the number of policy areas covered and in terms of the information on detailed disciplines in each area.

The paper is organized as follows. Section 2 describes the scope and methodology underlying the research agenda on deep trade agreements. Section 3 highlights a novel set of stylized facts that can be inferred from a first look at the new data, while Section 4 offers some insights into future applications and areas for analysis. Concluding remarks follow.

[25] Mattoo *et al.*, 2017, Mulabdic *et al.*, 2017, Laget *et al.*, 2018, Laget *et al.*, 2019.

2. Scope and methodology

The number of policy areas covered by PTAs has increased in the last two decades. Up until the late 1990s, when the number of PTAs started increasing, the majority of new agreements covered fewer than 10 policy areas. Since the 2000s, most new PTAs have covered between 10 and 20 policy areas, with some having even more than 20 (Figure 3.1). In a study of 28 trade agreements signed by the US and the EU, Horn *et al.* (2010) identify up to 52 policy areas that have been covered by at least one of the agreements. The inclusion of new policy areas in PTAs is not random. As shown in Mattoo *et al.* (2017), trade agreements covering few policy areas generally focus on traditional trade policy, such as tariff liberalization or customs (Table 3.1). Agreements with broader coverage (between 10 and 20 policy areas) tend to include trade-related regulatory issues, such as subsidies or technical barriers to trade. Finally, agreements with more than 20 provisions often include policy areas that are not directly related to trade, such as labor, environment and movement of people.

Figure 3.1. Number of policy areas covered in PTAs, 1970–2017

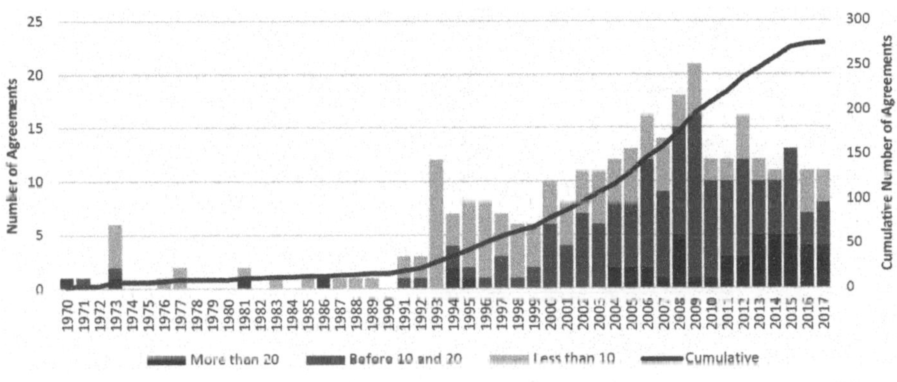

Source: Authors' calculations based on Hofmann *et al.*, 2019.

Table 3.1. Share of policy areas for different PTAs

No. Provisions	Less than 10	Between 10 and 20	More than 20
Tariffs on manufacturing goods	97%	100%	100%
Tariffs on agricultural goods	96%	100%	100%
Export taxes	73%	81%	95%
Customs	67%	95%	100%
Competition policy	58%	73%	88%
State aid	39%	69%	88%
Anti-dumping	35%	88%	98%
Countervailing measures	22%	77%	98%
Statistics	20%	0%	23%
TRIPS	18%	75%	98%
STE	18%	69%	68%
TBT	17%	73%	95%
Movement of capital	15%	68%	93%
GATS	14%	67%	98%
SPS	12%	72%	98%
Public procurement	12%	59%	80%
IPR	6%	56%	75%
Environmental laws	3%	14%	83%
Labor market regulations	3%	13%	75%
Investment	2%	58%	75%
TRIMS	2%	42%	73%
Visa and asylum	2%	37%	57%
Industrial cooperation	2%	5%	33%
Social matters	2%	5%	30%
Agriculture	1%	10%	45%
Energy	1%	8%	40%
Data protection	1%	5%	20%
Anticorruption	1%	5%	18%
SME	1%	4%	25%
Regional cooperation	1%	3%	15%
Taxation	1%	2%	30%
Approximation of legislation	1%	2%	25%
Political dialogue	1%	1%	8%
Research and technology	0%	6%	38%
Public administration	0%	6%	5%
Consumer protection	0%	5%	38%
Mining	0%	5%	13%
Education and training	0%	4%	33%
Information society	0%	4%	15%
Innovation policies	0%	4%	5%
Illegal immigration	0%	3%	23%
Illicit drugs	0%	3%	3%
Economic policy dialogue	0%	2%	43%
Cultural cooperation	0%	2%	38%
Financial assistance	0%	2%	25%
Audiovisual	0%	2%	18%
Terrorism	0%	2%	8%
Money laundering	0%	2%	3%
Health	0%	1%	38%
Human rights	0%	1%	3%
Nuclear safety	0%	0%	15%
Civil protection	0%	0%	5%

Source: Mattoo *et al.*, 2017.

The policy areas under analysis are those that appear most frequently in trade agreements. They include (a) a set of 18 policy areas that are covered in 20 percent or more of trade agreements notified to the WTO (Figure 3.2): (b) tariffs on industrial and agricultural goods, which are covered by all trade agreements; (c) customs and export taxes, which are regulated in more than 80 percent of PTAs; (d) services and movements of capital, which are regulated in roughly half of the PTAs; and (e) environmental and labor issues, which are covered by around 20 percent of all trade agreements. The focus on individual areas helps us to identify specific policies that are the object of negotiation but may obscure cross-cutting issues — such as electronic commerce — that may be disciplined under multiple policy areas.

Figure 3.2. Number of policy areas covered in PTAs, by policy

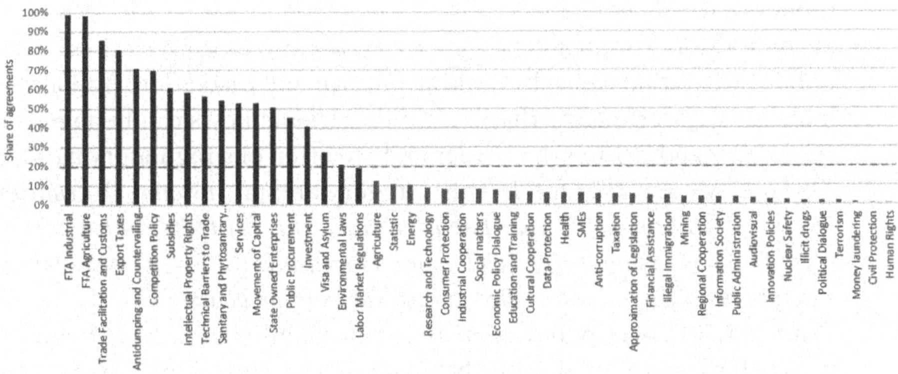

Source: Authors' calculations based on Hofmann *et al.*, 2019.

The classification of policy areas used in Figure 3.2 deviates slightly from the one of Horn *et al.*(2010).[26] Specifically, we decided to include rules of origin, a policy area that was absent from the Horn *et al.*(2010) classification, and to treat as a single policy area: (a) *trade remedies*, which include anti-dumping and countervailing measures; (b) *investment*, which includes the areas covered under the WTO's Trade Related Investment Measures, or TRIMs; and (c) *intellectual property rights* (IPR), which include the areas covered under the WTO's Trade Related Intellectual Property Rights, or TRIPs.

Trade agreements are generally assessed in terms of the market access they create. Given the complexity of policy areas that are covered by DTAs, the metric of market access—while still important—appears inadequate. In this paper, we propose to define deep trade agreements as international arrangements that aim to regulate three (partially overlapping) sets of policy areas (Figure 3.3).

[26] The Horn *et al.* 2010 classification was used to collect data on the extensive margin of PTA depth.

- First, the core policy areas included in DTAs aim to establish five economic integration rights: *free (or freer) movement of goods, services, capital, people* and *ideas.*[27] The policy areas that directly impact these flows include: (a) *tariffs and export taxes,* which affect the movement of goods; (b) *services,* which regulate services trade flows; (c) *investment and movement of capital,* which affect the movement of capital; (d) *visa and asylum,* which regulate the movement of people; and (e) *intellectual property rights,* which influence the flows of ideas.
- Second, DTAs also include policy areas that aim to support these economic integration rights by limiting government discretion. Actions by importing governments that limit international flows can be taken at the border and behind the border and are often of a regulatory nature. The policy areas that fall in this category are: (a) *customs*; (b) *rules of origin*; (c) *trade remedies*; (d) *public procurement*; (e) *technical barriers to trade* (TBT); (f) *sanitary and phytosanitary measures* (SPS); (g) *state-owned enterprises* (SOEs); (h) *subsidies;* and (i) *competition policy.*[28]
- Third, DTAs cover policy areas that aim to enhance social or consumer welfare by regulating the behavior of exporters. Policy areas such as environment and labor impose obligations on exporters to further consumer or social interests in importing countries. Rules in areas such as competition, SOEs, and subsidies can have a dual aspect: in addition to regulating action that undermines economic integration rights, they can aim to address distortionary actions that lower economic efficiency thus hurting consumer or social welfare.

[27] We use the words "aim to establish" rather than "establish" for two main reasons. First, DTAs may cover only a subset of integration rights. Second, provisions may not be justiciable. A contribution of the new data is to identify the extent to which integration rights are established in PTAs.

[28] Some of these provisions apply only to cross-border trade in goods (e.g., customs, TBT and SPS). Others can also apply to cross-border trade in services (e.g., public procurement and competition policy). In some cases, services-related provisions are included separately in a services agreement.

Figure 3.3. A classification of policy areas in DTAs

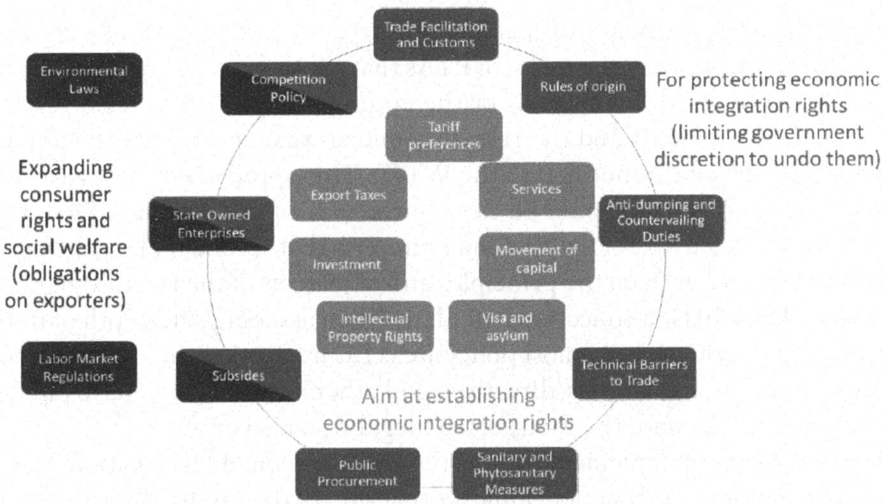

In Mattoo *et al.* (2020), the experts followed a uniform approach to coding for all policy areas.[29] The coding templates encompass several common headings such as objectives and definitions, institutional framework, enforcement mechanism, plus a series of discipline-specific questions. Under each heading, questions on specific provisions in the agreement are formulated so that they can be answered with Yes/No. For some policy areas, additional information is provided at the provision level, including (a) the relationship between the coverage of the disciplines on and the corresponding regulation in the WTO; (b) the level of enforceability of each provision;[30] (c) whether the specific commitment can be applied discriminatorily or whether it is de facto non-discriminatory. Finally, when applicable, for example in

[29] One exception is preferential tariffs. Differently from the other policy areas, tariff commitments apply at the product level. The information for this area is therefore collected at the country-pair-product level. For rules of origin a sub-sample of agreements in Latin America and East Asia, the dataset on regime-wide provisions is accompanied by a mapping of the rules of origin that apply at the product level.

[30] The legal enforceability of the PTA provisions is coded according to the language used in the text of the agreements. It is assumed that commitments expressed with a clear, specific and imperative legal language, can more successfully be invoked by a complainant in a dispute settlement proceeding, and therefore are more likely to be legally enforceable. In contrast, unclearly formulated legal language might be related with policy areas that are covered but that might not be legally enforceable.

services and government procurement, the coders included information at the sectoral level on exclusion of certain sectors from an agreement, or the applicability of an agreement to a specific industry.

The analysis covers the realm of PTAs that are in force and notified to the WTO as of end-2017. The basis of the coding analysis is the legal text of the trade agreements and the relevant annexes that accompany the agreement (and have been notified to the WTO). This approach comes with two main limitations that should be clear to the user of the database. First, the focus on the legal text of the agreement implies that secondary law (the body of law that derives from the principles and objectives of the treaties) has not been coded. This is a concern particularly when assessing the depth of integration of the EU, since in most policy areas EU institutions have used secondary law such as regulations, directives, and other legal instruments to pursue integration.[31] Second, the focus on the legal text also excludes from consideration issues of implementation of the trade agreement into national laws and regulations or subsequent annexes that the parties might agree on which are not reported to the WTO. These are important areas for future research.

Despite the similarity in the coding approach, policy areas differ widely from each other. First, some policy areas are inherently more complex than others and their description requires a larger number of questions to reflect the more detailed provisions. IPR has the highest number of provisions (120), while labor has the lowest (18). Second, some policy areas focus primarily on substantive provisions: specific commitments on integration, such as market access commitments, and specific obligations such as harmonization of standards. Others tend to have a larger number of procedural provisions, such as transparency provisions and procedural requirements.

Table 3.2 provides an overview, showing the heterogeneity across policy areas in these different dimensions and identifying the set of "substantive" provisions as those that require specific integration/liberalization commitments and obligations.

[31] Note that the figures and tables in this paper refer to the EU as a single entity (i.e. the European Union agreement and enlargements are excluded) and report data for EU PTAs with third countries where this concern does not apply.

Table 3.2. Number of substantive and other provisions per policy area in all PTAs notified to the WTO

Category \ Discipline	Export Taxes	Services	Investment	Movement of Capital	Intellectual Property Rights	Visa and Asylum	Trade Facilitation and Customs	Anti-dumping and Countervailing Duties	Technical Barriers to Trade	Sanitary and Phytosanitary Measures	Public Procurement	Subsidies	State Owned Enterprises	Competition Policy	Environmental Laws	Rules of Origin	Labor Market Regulations	Total provisions
Objectives				1		1		8	1	2		2	2	2	2		2	**23**
Scope and definitions	1	16	11	7		2		17	2	4	2	1	10	8	10			**91**
Transparency	4	9	3		13	3	8	6	3	10	7	4	5	1				**76**
Substantive commitments	17	19	13		59	3	6	2	19	20	4	3	8	11	27	20	12	**243**
Liberalization/ Integration	*14*	*8*	*11*		*19*		*4*	*1*	*3*	*4*	*3*					*13*		***80***
Conditions/Obligations	*3*	*11*	*2*		*40*	*3*	*2*	*1*	*16*	*16*	*1*	*3*	*8*	*11*	*27*	*7*	*12*	***163***
Procedural requirements	17	8			12	3	28	10		3	28		2	2		17		**130**
Enforcement mechanism		1	3	8	22	1		2	4		5	7	5		4	1		**63**
Sectoral coverage	2	1	2		5						33	9	8					**60**
Specific coverage		2	1	13		9					8	2	8	1				**44**
Exceptions	5	6	2	35	4	4						3	1	3				**63**
Safeguards		1	10	31		1												**43**
Special and differentiated treatment											7	2	2					**11**
Institutional framework		1	1		2	2	2	6	2	11				2	1		2	**32**
Cooperation			2		3	1	8		3	3	1	1	1	5	4		1	**33**
Miscellaneous			9							6	5	2	2				1	**25**
Total provisions	**46**	**64**	**57**	**95**	**120**	**30**	**52**	**51**	**34**	**59**	**100**	**36**	**54**	**35**	**48**	**38**	**18**	**937**

Source: Authors' calculations based on Mattoo *et al.*, 2020.

We also make an effort to identify the set of provisions within each policy area that are essential to achieve the objectives of the agreement. The provisions we refer to as "essential" comprise the set of substantive provisions plus the disciplines among procedures, transparency, enforcement or objectives, which are viewed as indispensable and complementary to achieving the substantive commitments. Non-essential provisions are referred to as "corollary." A caveat is that this exercise is based on judgment on the relative importance of different provisions and is thus subjective. However, this approach has the advantage of limiting the dimensionality of the data in an informed way.[32]

3. Stylized facts

A number of new stylized facts emerge from a preliminary analysis of the data. Given the differences among policy areas and among provisions within each policy area, this approach presents many quantification challenges, which are discussed below. In this section, we rely on simple counts of the provisions and on coverage ratios[33] to investigate the evolution of the content of deep trade agreements. The underlying assumption in this approach is that deeper trade agreements imply a larger number of provisions.

As shown in Espitia *et al.* (2019), liberalization in PTAs has reduced trade-weighted average tariff rates to less than 5 percent for more than two-thirds of countries (Figure 3.4). While there are still pockets of high protection in some countries, most notably lower-income economies, PTAs have been broadly successful in committing national governments to maintaining low tariffs. Trade-weighted applied tariffs are, on average, 2.3 percentage points lower than average most-favoured nation (MFN) rates, with gaps of greater than 6 percentage points for countries like Tunisia, Morocco, Bosnia and Herzegovina, Namibia and Lao PDR. So, while from an efficiency perspective, preferential tariff liberalization is inferior to non-preferential liberalization, the commitments countries have taken in the network of preferential trade agreements may provide a safety net at a time when trade tensions are escalating and some countries are disregarding their multilateral commitments.

[32] A statistical approach on how to assess the importance of specific provisions included in the different policy areas in explaining trade outcomes is presented in section 4.

[33] The coverage ratio is defined as the share of provisions for a policy area contained in a given agreement relative to the maximum number of provisions in that policy area or agreement.

Figure 3.4. Tariffs in PTAs and MFN tariffs

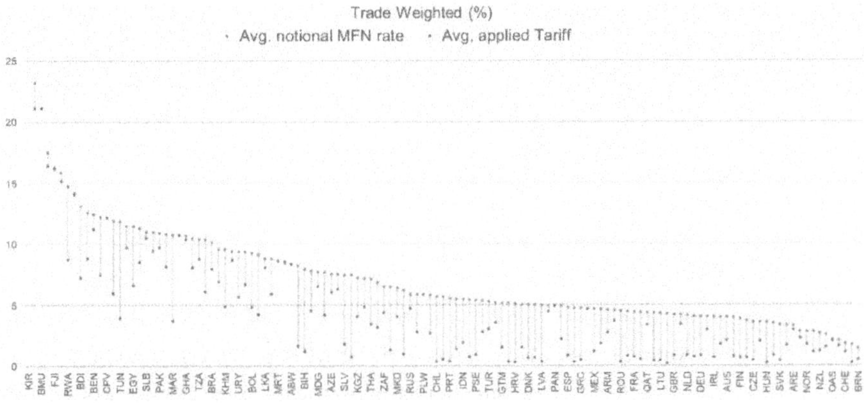

Source: Espitia *et al.*, 2019.

The number of commitments that governments have taken in trade agreements, particularly since the early 2000s, has increased over time.

Figure 3.5 shows how the coverage ratio has changed over time for the 17 policy areas analysed (all but tariffs) in aggregate. With only few exceptions, the majority of new PTAs signed after 2000 have a coverage ratio higher than 25 percent. This stands in sharp contrast to the trade agreements signed in the 1980s and 1990s, when coverage ratios were below 15 percent and, in many cases, even below 5 percent. The reduction in tariffs accomplished through preferential trade liberalization, together with the increased depth of agreements over time, suggests that countries that are willing to cut tariffs reciprocally may also be willing to accept deeper mutual commitments in other areas.

Figure 3.5. Number of agreements over time *vs.* average coverage ratio

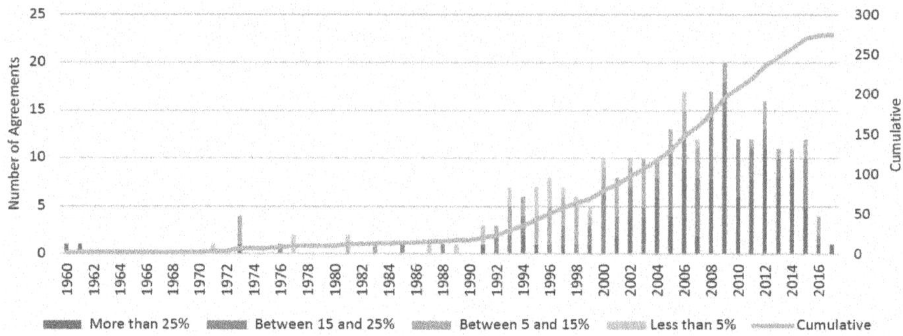

Note: Coverage ratio refers to the share of provisions contained in a given agreement relative to the maximum number of provisions. European Union agreement and enlargements excluded.
Source: Authors' calculations based on Mattoo *et al.*, 2020.

While the overall number of provisions is suggestive, it can hide important elements of the evolution of deep trade agreements. First, as discussed above, some provisions imply substantive commitments while others concern broad objectives, definitions or procedural matters. Second, deep trade agreements do not only concern themselves with market access in goods, but also aim to establish freedom of mobility for services, capital, ideas and people, as well as regulating policy areas that have an impact on consumer and/or social welfare, such as labor and the environment. To gain a better understanding of how the commitments in PTAs have changed over time, we look at the evolution of coverage ratios by policy area.

Figure 3.6 shows that the coverage of *essential* disciplines in PTAs has increased over time across all policy areas. This is most clearly the case for the policy areas aimed at facilitating the flows of goods (customs and trade facilitation), capital (investment and movement of capital) and services. IPR and movement of people (visa and asylum) also saw a steady by less remarkable increase in essential commitments over time. Along with economic integration rights, PTAs increasingly include essential commitments in policy areas that support these rights or impose obligations on exporters. The ones that appear to stand out are subsidies, competition and SOEs, areas that are either excluded from the WTO or for which reform of multilateral rules is considered difficult. Interestingly, while essential commitments in labor have largely increased in recent years, this happened to a lesser extent for provisions on the environment.

Figure 3.6. Coverage ratios by policy area, over time

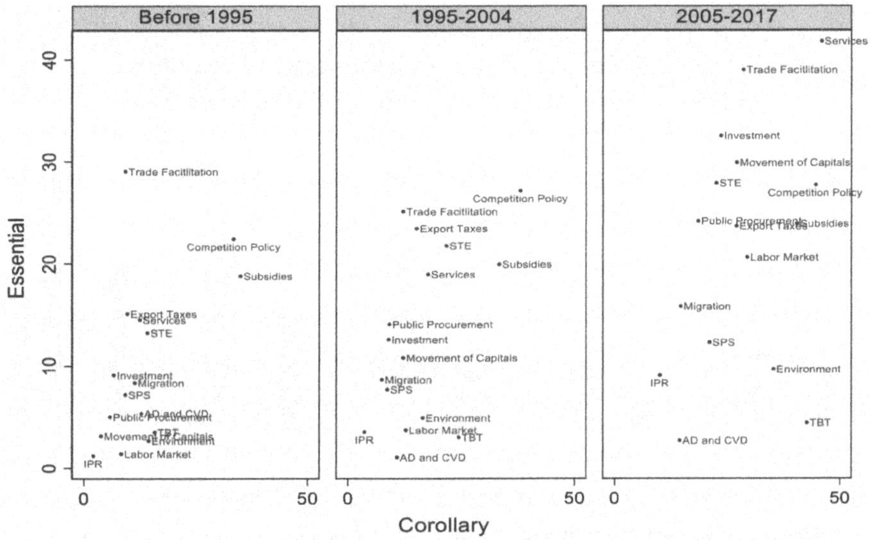

Note: Coverage ratio by policy area refers to the share of provisions for a policy area contained in a given agreement relative to the maximum number of provisions in that policy area. Years refer to entry into force date. European Union agreement and enlargements excluded.
Source: Authors' calculations based on Mattoo *et al.*, 2020.

The presumption is that the increase in the essential disciplines in deep PTAs has been driven by countries taking on more substantive commitments over time. Indeed,

Figure 3.7 shows that this is the case, but it also uncovers interesting insights about the evolution of non-substantive commitments. We focus on the three (numerically) most relevant non-substantive provisions: procedural rules, transparency and enforcement provisions. The deepening of substantive commitments has been accompanied by an increase in the number of corollary provisions, suggesting that achieving deeper commitments may require more procedural rules for implementation, transparency, and enforcement. A second insight is that, while these disciplines are all necessary to render substantive commitments in trade agreements effective, they have evolved differently in recent years. Starting in the early 2000s, the relevance of enforcement provisions in DTAs has increased disproportionally relative to procedural and transparency provisions. The growing enforcement capacity of DTAs may help explain the success of these institutional arrangements as tools for deep integration.

Figure 3.7. Substantive provisions and a breakdown of non-substantive provisions in PTAs, over time

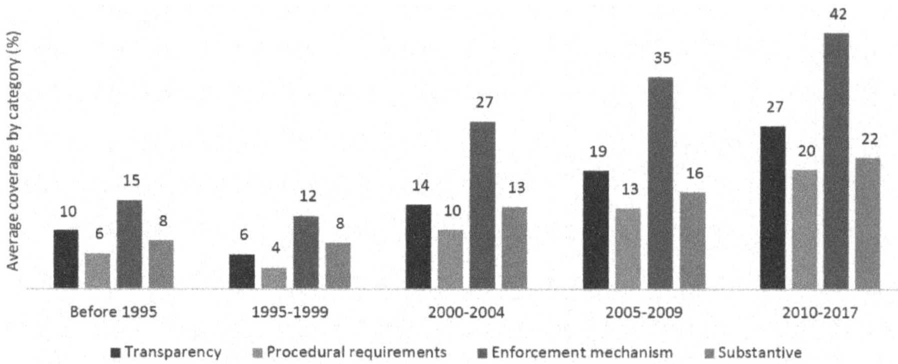

Note: Coverage ratio refers to the share of provisions for a policy area contained in a given agreement relative to the maximum number of provisions in that policy area. Years refer to entry into force date. European Union agreement and enlargements excluded.

When we break down the trade agreements by level of development of the signatories, we observe two facts. First, the deepest PTAs are those involving developed economies, followed by PTAs between developed and developing economies. PTAs between developing countries are the shallowest. Indeed, there is a sizeable gap between average coverage ratios for the latter group of PTAs relative to the first two (Figure 3.8). This could reflect a focus of negotiations on tariffs and traditional trade barriers, which are still high for several low-income economies. Second, in terms of composition, PTAs between developed countries and those between developed and developing economies include similar shares of provisions establishing economic integration rights, supporting these rights and aiming to regulate exporters (Figure 3.9). PTAs between developing countries are shallower across the board, with a stronger gap in areas such as environment and labor that aim at improving social welfare.

Figure 3.8. Inclusion of substantive commitments in PTAs, by level of development

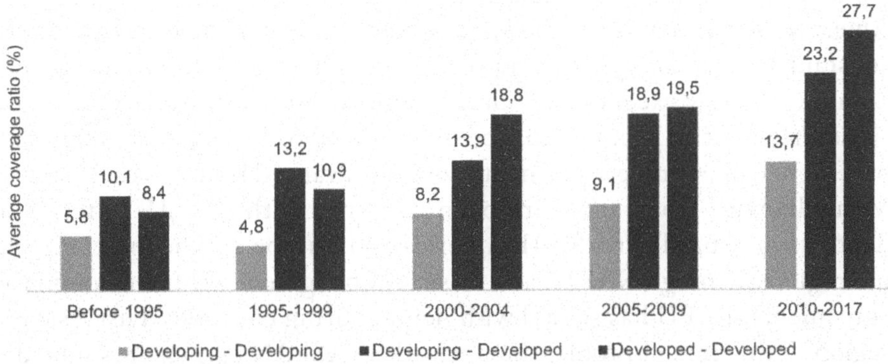

Note: Coverage ratio refers to the share of provisions for a policy area contained in a given agreement relative to the maximum number of provisions in that policy area. Years refer to entry into force date. European Union agreement and enlargements excluded.

Figure 3.9. Coverage ratio by type of policy and level of development

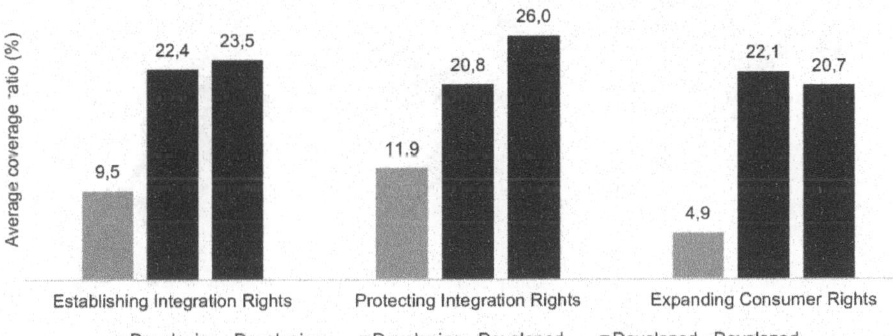

Note: Coverage ratio refers to the share of provisions for a policy area contained in a given agreement relative to the maximum number of provisions in that policy area. Years refer to entry into force date. European Union agreement and enlargements excluded.

We next analyse the depth of trade agreements by country. Here, we focus on the substantive commitments. As several countries have multiple agreements with different levels of depth, we present the average number of substantive commitments per country in panel a of Figure 3.10 and the maximum number in panel b of Figure 3.10. The main takeaway is that developing countries in Sub-Saharan Africa, Middle East and North Africa, South America, South Asia and, to a lesser extent, East Asia tend to have fewer substantive commitments in trade agreements relative to advanced economies. The few exceptions include countries in South America that are signatories of the Pacific Alliance and other developing economies that have signed deep trade agreements with an advanced trade partner, such as Mongolia with Japan and Caribbean countries with the EU. In terms of depth as measured here, North America and Europe are the most integrated regions, through NAFTA and its successor agreement, and through the agreements the EU has signed with neighbouring countries. East Asia is a region with a mixed profile: the network of ASEAN agreements includes most countries but tends to have fewer substantive commitments relative to North America and Europe, except for some countries such as Vietnam, which have signed onto the Comprehensive Agreement for the Trans-Pacific Partnership (with a coverage ratio of 61 percent).

Figure 3.10. Substantive provisions in PTAs by country
Panel a. Average number of provisions

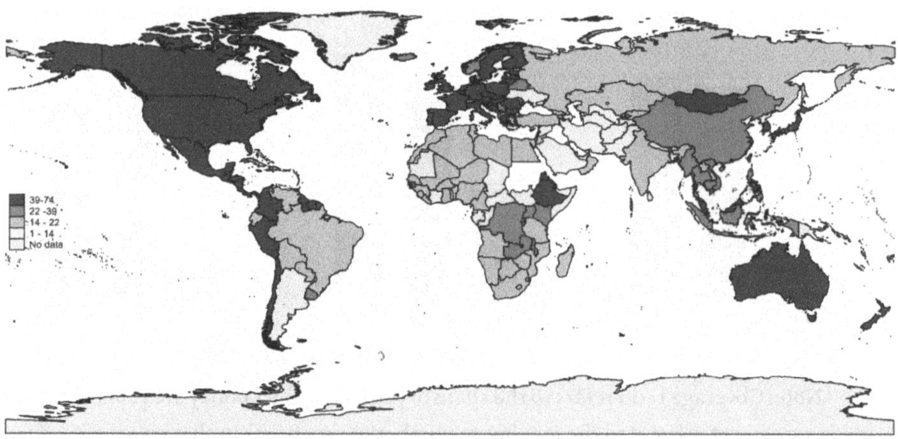

Panel b: Maximum number of provisions

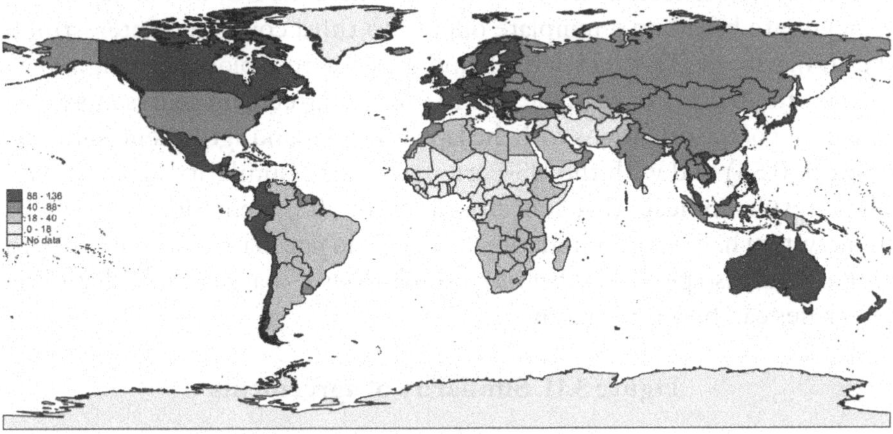

With the increasing depth and complexity of trade agreements, both similarities and dissimilarities between PTAs could potentially increase. Older agreements that covered only preferential tariff liberalization and other aspects of market access tended to be very similar. As PTAs now cover more ground, there can be provisions that are included in two agreements, making them more similar, or there can be provisions that are covered by one PTA but not by another, making them more dissimilar. To capture this information, we construct a similarity index for DTAs, calculated as the ratio between the number of provisions for which two agreements have a "yes" (a measure of similarity) and the total number of provisions covered by the agreements, independently of whether they have the same answer or not. The closer the similarity index is to one (or zero), the more (or less) similar are the two DTAs; i.e., include the same type(s) of provisions.

Figure 3.11 plots the degree of similarity for the PTAs signed by the three major trading blocs: the European Union, United States, and Japan. Each colour represents a DTA signed by a third country with the US (dark blue), EU (light blue) or Japan (red). The size of the bubbles represents the depth of the agreements, measured as the number of provisions covered. Each agreement is connected to the one which is most similar within a trading bloc. The figure also links the three trading blocs, by connecting the pair of agreements that are the most similar between two blocs.

As expected, within each bloc, DTAs are highly similar: up to 0.89 for the US (US-Peru; US-Colombia), up to 0.80 for the EU (EU-Republic of Moldova;

EU-Ukraine), and up to 0.75 for Japan (Japan-Indonesia; Japan-Mongolia). This fact often reflects a "template effect," where the EU, US and Japan tend to negotiate based on a template offered to third countries. Interestingly, the similarity of DTAs is relatively high even across blocs, although lower than within blocs. For example, the EU-Korea agreement shares more than 50 percent of the provisions with the Japan-Switzerland agreement (similarity index of 0.54) and with the US-Peru agreement (similarity index of 0.51). These results indicate that concerns about the fragmentation of the global trade system have some foundation (*i.e.*, they do not share almost half of provisions), but also point to substantial similarities — based on which multilateral rules can be agreed upon.

Figure 3.11. Similarity of agreements

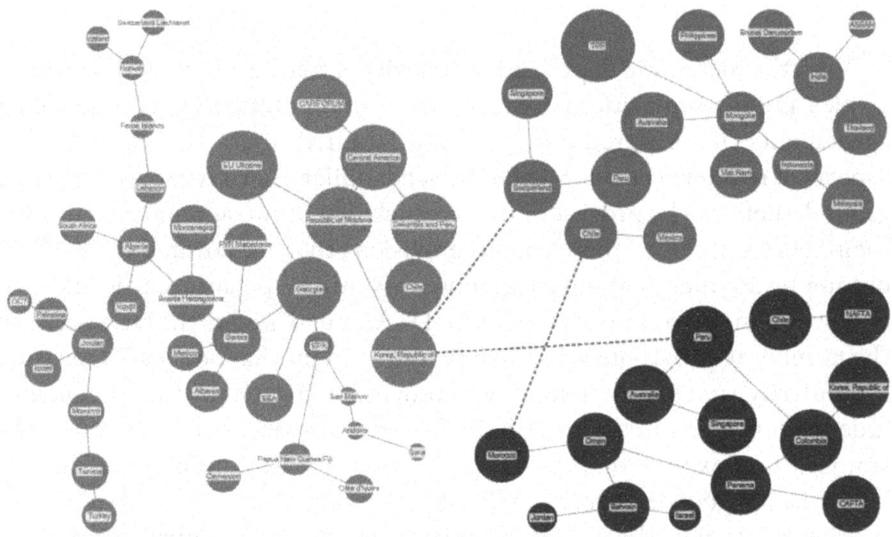

Note: The size of the bubbles represents the depth of a trade agreement, as captured by the number of provisions included in the agreement. Each edge connects an agreement with one that is most similar. Light blue bubbles represent EU agreements with non-EU countries, dark blue represent US agreements, and red represent Japan agreements.

4. The challenge of quantifying the effects of DTAs

Quantification of the effects of DTAs poses a serious challenge. DTAs cover heterogeneous areas: tariffs, contingent protection, export taxes, customs procedures, technical barriers in goods; a wide range of restrictions across modes in services; investment measures, subsidies, procurement, state enterprises, competition policy affecting both trade and investment in goods and services, visas and asylum, and a range of regulatory requirements affecting labour mobility; and a variety of policies affecting the protection of intellectual policy rights and the environment. How can the diversity of policies be quantified and aggregated within separate areas? How can we aggregate across the different areas? We briefly discuss here two approaches to quantification—directly constructed indices and indirectly estimated measures — and some analytical issues going forward.

4.1 Directly constructed indices

The count variables and coverage ratios presented in the previous section are the simplest directly constructed indices of depth. They provide an immediate view of how commitments in PTAs have changed over time, across countries and for subsets of provisions. Still, aggregate indicators based on some form of counting disregard the fact that DTAs cover multiple policy areas and sectors and that the "value" of each provision is unlikely to be the same even within the same policy area.

In some cases, it may be possible to construct a hierarchy of measures. For example, in the areas of services and government procurement, provisions could be divided into three tiers. Tier 1 would comprise provisions ensuring market access and national treatment at entry. Tier 2 would comprise provisions on post-entry operation; *e.g.*, preferences or offsets. Tier 3 would comprise procedural rules limiting discretion in licenses and awards. The construction of an index could then be lexicographic, in that we would consider first only differences between countries or sectors in Tier 1 and move to subsequent tiers only to break ties. Such an approach is ideally suited to the construction of an ordinal rather than cardinal (i.e., qualitative rather than quantitative) measure.

4.2 Indirectly estimated measures

These measures are obtained by estimating the impact of the provisions on a variable of interest. For example, we could infer the value of individual provisions by estimating their impact on bilateral trade, controlling for other influences. In principle, each binary element in the relevant DTA areas could be included in a country-product import regression as a right-hand variable while controlling for applied policies, including tariffs and non-tariff measures. Similar methods have been used to estimate the Overall Trade Restrictiveness Index.[34] However, even for trade in goods we have limited degrees of freedom, and in other areas (such as services), we do not have sufficiently fine outcome data. In these areas, it may be necessary to take a hybrid approach, based on first constructing more aggregated indices.

Another approach is to quantify the effects of DTAs and build indicators of depth is to use new statistical methods. As a first example, we employ machine learning techniques to detect the influential variables/provisions in DTAs for trade.[35] Machine learning is a generic term referring to a wide variety of algorithms which detect a certain pattern from a large dataset, often referred to as "Big Data", and make predictions based on that pattern. In this case, we use a method called Random Forest (RF) to calculate the importance of each variable/provision for international trade flows.[36] Specifically, we run as a first step a structural gravity model with the standard set of fixed effects and then use the residuals as the left-hand variable in the RF.

Figure 3.12 shows the boxplot of scores calculated by the RF of variables/provisions in PTAs belonging to the 17 (non-tariff) policy areas analysed in this paper.[37] The areas are coloured according to their categorization into the three main groups illustrated in Figure 3.3; red indicates policies that

[34] Kee, Nicita and Olarreaga, 2009.

[35] This exercise has been carried out in collaboration with Kazusa Yoshimura and Edith Laget. Parallel work by Breinlich *et al.* (2020) also uses machine learning techniques to precisely quantify the impact of individual provisions in trade agreements on trade flows.

[36] RF is a frequently used machine learning algorithm that predicts a Y variable by combining the results from hundreds of regression/classification trees. It has the merit of not imposing a linear relationship between the Y and X variables, which is an advantage when analyzing the impact of a highly heterogenous set of variables, such as the provisions in PTAs.

[37] A score should not be interpreted as a coefficient in a regression analysis. It measures how much the accuracy of the prediction for Y gets worse if the particular X variable is randomly permuted.

establish economic integration rights, blue is assigned to those supporting these rights, and green to those that promote welfare. Each box shows the range of the first (25 percent) and third (75 percent) quartiles, and the black line in the box shows the median of the scores. The vertical lines extending from the box indicate the variability outside the above quartiles, and the dots outside of the line are regarded as outliers. Boxplots are ordered according to the magnitude of the median.

Focusing on the entire set of PTAs, we find that provisions such as investment, subsidies, and services, and to a lesser extent, rules of origin and movement of capital have a median score above the overall score average, suggesting that these policy areas are good predictors of bilateral trade, after controlling for the usual gravity determinants of trade flows. Provisions in policy areas such as SPS, environmental laws, and visa and asylum are located at the other extreme of the distribution of median scores, suggesting a more limited role in predicting bilateral trade flows. The size of the boxes and the vertical lines also indicate that there are policy areas such as movement of capital and IPR for which the contribution to trade is more or less uniform across provisions. For other policy areas such as competition policy and SOEs, there is more heterogeneity within provisions in terms of their contribution to trade.

Figure 3.12. Boxplot of scores calculated by the RF of variables/provisions in PTAs

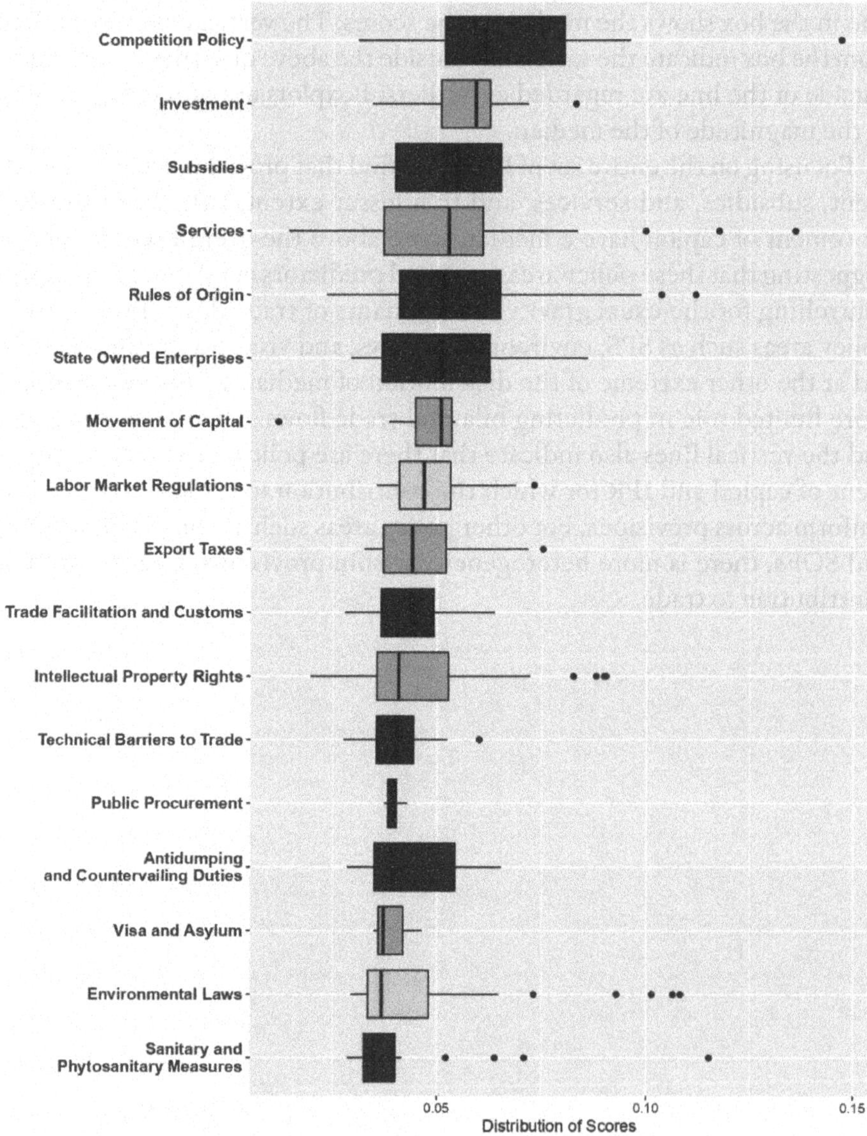

4.3 Quantification challenges: some analytical issues going forward

Looking ahead, there is a need for stronger analytical underpinnings for any quantification exercise. Ideally, the "value" of a commitment must be evaluated in light of the objective that the provision or the deep trade agreement is trying to achieve. In other words, depth indicators could use different weights depending on whether the outcome variable is market access, welfare or another metric. For trade policy, market access may seem to be the most obvious metric, but for intellectual property rights, welfare may be the more relevant. In still other areas, such as competition policy, both might be relevant: the market access measure would include only provisions restricting barriers to foreign entry and operation while the welfare measure would include provisions requiring action against anti-competitive behavior affecting consumers.

One indicator cannot provide a measure of both the trade distortions a country imposes on its trading partners (market access) and the trade distortions a country imposes on itself (welfare). For a market access-based measure in the goods context, the relevant question could be: what is the uniform tariff that if imposed on home imports instead of the existing structure of protection would leave aggregate imports at their current level? And for a welfare-based measure: what is the uniform tariff that if applied to imports instead of the current structure of protection would leave home welfare at its current level? The relationship between the two measures is likely to vary across policy areas: positive correlation for tariffs; perhaps negative for environmental standards; and ambiguous for intellectual property rights.

A further issue relates to whether we should be interested in what legal commitments do to the level of a policy or to its variance. Provisions such as the elimination of tariffs, or of a national treatment rule in services or government procurement, fix the level of protection at zero. Provisions which legally bind policy (*e.g.*, the permissible levels of fees, subsidies or preferences) truncate the distribution of possible policy outcomes by reducing the variance and hence the expected level of protection. Provisions which reduce discretion, such as rules on customs valuation, licensing or procurement procedures, narrow the distribution of possible policy outcomes.

Finally, we also need to consider whether we should assess agreements per se or agreements relative to applied policies. If we have the relevant data, the mean and variance shift would ideally be assessed relative to the prevailing policy (and not just the law or policy on paper but how it is implemented).

For example, a legal binding tariff at 10 percent might have a different value depending on whether the existing tariff was 5, 10 or 20 percent. The creation of new databases on applied policies in goods and services trade may facilitate such analysis.

5. Conclusions

The *World Development Report 2009* made the case that "thicker" borders between countries hurt economic growth, especially in developing countries. Policies that directly or indirectly restrain the international mobility of goods, services, capital, people and ideas limit, among other things, the scale of the market, which is vital for development.[38] Deep trade agreements aim at establishing the rights of economic integration, protecting these rights from importing governments' actions that could undo them, and regulating actions of exporters that can have negative welfare effects. These agreements have developed over time into a key institutional mechanism for countries to overcome the constraints to economic development created by the thick borders that fragment markets.

Of course, deep integration is not an end in itself. First, countries at different levels of development may have different institutional needs, and trade agreements still need to strike the right balance between rules in PTAs and the needed discretion at the national level to pursue desirable social objectives. Second, while many deep provisions may be de facto non-discriminatory and apply to members and non-members alike, there is still a tension between the proliferation of regional approaches and multilateral rules enshrined in the WTO. Therefore, from the perspective of both economic development and global governance, the efficient set of rules in DTAs is an empirical question.

The wealth of information on the content of the policy areas commonly included in PTAs could provide new impetus to the analysis on the determinants and impact of deep trade agreements. Such analysis would also provide the necessary tools to further understand the opportunities and challenges that countries face in terms of negotiation and implementation of deep trade agreements.

[38] World Bank, 2009.

We suggest three areas of work going forward. A first step is to improve the measurement of the depth of trade agreements and quantification of its effects. Beyond simple count variables and coverage ratios, more work will be needed to develop new analytic methods to overcome the challenges discussed in the previous section. As shown, machine learning techniques may provide a useful innovative approach. Second, the detailed information at the level of individual policy areas could inform a series of studies to assess how specific provisions impact trade and other relevant economic variables. As trade policy experts well understand, the devil is often in the details. Finally, the new data and analysis could provide essential information to policymakers on priorities for the negotiation and implementation of trade agreements: finding what potential partners include in their trade deals, identifying best practices in DTAs and areas where practices diverge or overlap across different players, and assessing gaps between international commitments and domestic legislation.

REFERENCES

Acharya, R. (ed.) (2016), *Regional Trade Agreements and the Multilateral Trading System*, Cambridge, UK: Cambridge University Press.

Baldwin, R. (2010), "21st century regionalism: filling the gap between 21st century trade and 20th century trade rules", Geneva Graduate Institute, *Working Paper* No. 2010-31., Geneva: World Trade Organization.

Breinlich, H., V. Corradi, N. Rocha, M. Ruta, J. Santos Silva, T. Zylkin (2020), *Machine learning in international trade research: Evaluating the impact of trade agreements*, available at: https://openknowledge.worldbank.org/handle/10986/35451.

Dur, A., L. Baccini and M. Elsig (2014), "The design of international trade agreements: introducing a new dataset", *The Review of International Organizations* 9(3), pp. 353-375.

Espitia, A., A. Mattoo, M. Mimouni, X. Pichot and N. Rocha (2019), "Preferential tariffs" in A. Mattoo, N. Rocha and M. Ruta (eds.), *Handbook of Deep Trade Agreements*. Washington, DC: World Bank.

Freund, C. and Ornelas, E. (2010), Regional trade agreements, *Annual Review of Economics* 2, pp. 139-166.

Hofmann, C., A. Osnago and M. Ruta (2019), The Content of Preferential Trade Agreements. *World Trade Review*, 18(3), pp. 365-398.

Horn, H., P.C. Mavroidis and A. Sapir (2010), Beyond the WTO? An anatomy of EU and US preferential trade agreements, *World Economy* 33, pp. 1565-1588.

Kee, Hiau Looi, Alessandro Nicita and Marcelo Olarreaga (2009), Estimating trade restrictiveness indices, *Economic Journal* 119: 534, pp. 172-199.

Laget, Edith; Roch, Nadia; Varela, Gonzalo (2021), Deep Trade Agreement and Foreign Direct Investments, Policy Research Working Paper;No. 9829. World Bank, Washington, DC.: World Bank, available at: https://openknowledge.worldbank.org/handle/10986/36480 License: CC BY 3.0 IGO.

Laget, Edith; Roch, Nadia; Varela, Gonzalo (2021), Deep Trade Agreement and Foreign Direct Investments. Policy Research Working Paper No. 9829. Washington, DC: World Bank, available at: https://openknowledge.worldbank.org/handle/10986/36480 License: CC BY 3.0 IGO.

Limao, N. (2016), "Preferential trade agreements", in K. Bagwell and R. Staiger (eds.), *Handbook of Commercial Policy* Vol. 1, Amsterdam: North Holland, pp. 279-367.

Mattoo, A., A. Mulabdic and M. Ruta (2017), "Trade creation and trade diversion in deep agreements", Policy Research Working Paper 8206, World Bank, paper funded by the World Bank's Strategic Research Program, Washington, DC: World Bank.

Mattoo, A., N. Rocha and M. Ruta (eds.) (2020), *Handbook of Deep Trade Agreements*, Washington DC: World Bank.

Mulabdic, A., A. Osnago and M. Ruta (2017), "Deep integration and UK-EU trade relations", Policy Research Working Paper 7947, Washington, DC: World Bank

Viner, J. (1950), *The Customs Union Issue,* New York: Carnegie Endowment for International Peace.

World Bank (2009), *World Development Report 2009: Reshaping Economic Geography*. Washington, DC: World Bank.

World Bank (2019), *World Development Report 2020: Trading for Development in the Age of Global Value Chains*, Washington, DC: World Bank.

World Trade Organization (2011), *World Trade Report 2011: The WTO and Preferential Trade Agreements: From Co-Existence to Coherence*, Geneva: World Trade Organization.

CHAPTER 4
GLOBAL TRADE IN THE AGE OF POPULISM[39]

Jeffry Frieden

Abstract: The growth rate of world trade appears to be slowing. Some of this slowdown is undoubtedly due to the combined impact of the global COVID pandemic, the Russian invasion of Ukraine, and tensions between the United States and China. However, broader, more general, factors are also at work. Trade depends upon cooperation among the principal economic centres, and both economic and political trends have called this cooperation into question. Within the advanced industrial countries an upsurge in "populist" sentiment with an economically nationalistic tenor often expresses explicit hostility to "globalist" approaches to economic cooperation. These domestic political pressures in particular call into question the future of international economic cooperation.

Keywords: Keyword: Populism, trade, trade policy, economic integration, geopolitics

1. Introduction

The coming decade promises to be rife with challenges to international economic openness. A global pandemic, international geopolitical upheavals, and increasing tensions among the major powers have all brought home the fact that the international economy is subject to a wide range of non-economic shocks. Perhaps most important of all, a drumbeat of domestic political scepticism about economic integration — and even opposition to it — has continued and even strengthened. There are now widespread and legitimate

[39] Written for a special issue of the journal *Perspectivas – Journal of Political Science* on "New Globalization Challenges and EU Trade Policy," edited by Annette Bongardt and Francisco Torres.

concerns that the open world economic order that has characterized much of the globe since the 1950s may be headed toward closure.

It is worth remembering, in light of contemporary pessimism, that it was not so long ago that globalization appeared to be the inevitable future of the international economy. From the vantage point of, say, the year 2000, it seemed a foregone conclusion that global economic integration would bring with it substantive and institutionalized cooperation among the world's major economies. The lessons of European integration argued for ever greater collaboration, and ever more cohesive forms of global governance. Logic supported it: global markets, global problems, and global externalities all demanded global solutions. Policymakers seemed increasingly committed to an unprecedented level of inter-state economic integration and policy coordination. An expansive class of globalists — prosperous, cosmopolitan, educated, self-confident — had coalesced. Economic and political integration in Europe, now joined in a single market heading toward the free movement of goods, capital, and people, and mostly sharing a common currency, seemed to foreshadow the future of the world. Europe's dramatic experiment in integration seemed well on its way to prove that global governance was feasible — even necessary.

The Global Financial Crisis of 2007–2009 seemed only to demonstrate the need for international cooperation to deal with the problems that might arise in this new globalizing reality. To the satisfaction of global financial markets — and to the surprise of some observers — the monetary and financial authorities of the major economic powers worked closely together to engineer coordinated policies to address the frightening prospect of a crisis that might well have been longer and deeper than the Great Depression of the 1930s. This hardly amounted to the existence of a global lender of last resort and a global financial regulatory agency to provide the global public goods of monetary and financial stability. Nonetheless, the cooperative measures among policymakers came close enough to fill this bill that there was speculation that the next step would in fact be to create such a global institution — or to transform the International Monetary Fund (IMF) into one. Difficult as the crisis was, the early returns suggested guarded optimism about the possibility of global governance provided by far-seeing policymakers.

Perhaps even more striking was the fact that the Global Financial Crisis did not appear to lead directly to a major increase in protectionist measures. To be sure, there were the usual complaints from distressed industries. But the Global Trade Alert's accounting shows that the number of discriminatory trade interventions implemented in 2009 was 278, roughly in line with previous years. And the number of protectionist measures stayed stable for nearly a decade.

In retrospect, this optimism appears excessive. Perhaps it was born of a decades-long era of extremely low interest rates and macroeconomic stability. Perhaps it was simply the result of assuming that the future would be like the (immediate) past. Certainly it underestimated the longer-term impact of the crisis on socio-economic and political developments (of which more below). For today the prospects for international trade, and international integration more generally, now seem much less promising. Indeed, in 2018 Global Trade Alert's count of discriminatory trade measures shot up to 944, and in 2021 it identified 2,470 such interventions — nearly ten times the level barely a decade before.[40] Meanwhile, foreign direct investment flows are barely at the level of 15 years ago. The growth rate of world trade — and more broadly of world economic integration — has slowed. Indeed, for the first time since World War Two the "trade openness index" — the sum of world exports and imports as a share of world output — has declined significantly.[41] A global pandemic and great-power geopolitics have highlighted sensitivities to disruptions in trade, while domestic political controversy has made the future of world trade highly uncertain.

2. Biology, geopolitics, and climate assert themselves

The first major shock to the relative rosiness of expectations about world trade came with the global pandemic that began in December 2019 and which is still playing itself out. In the face of shortages of personal protective equipment and medicine, government after government restricted trade and travel, even sequestering health-care supplies where feasible. Beyond the health-care sector, disease and lockdowns disrupted supply channels throughout the world economy. The experience led many governments to conclude that their economies had become too reliant upon foreign supplies of essential — or simply important — materials. This was compounded in some cases by the sense that the producers of these materials were either politically or economically unreliable or undesirable. The result has been a flurry of measures to ensure the domestic production of a host of goods — and not only in the health-care sector — to avoid the supply shocks experienced in 2020 and 2021. The purpose is to reduce dependence upon trade.

[40] https://www.globaltradealert.org/

[41] https://www.piie.com/research/piie-charts/globalization-retreat-first-time-second-world-war

Much of the concern about supply in the OECD centred on the fact that China was a principal — often *the* principal — producer of the goods in question. Concern along these lines grew as tensions between China, some of its neighbours, and the United States grew. China embarked on an ambitious expansion of its economic and geopolitical influence, with substantial forays into development finance and a commitment to a massive investment in Eurasian and African infrastructure, including the Belt and Road Initiative. It also began challenging some of its neighbours with territorial claims in the South China Sea. The rise of China led many across the political spectrum in the United States to regard China as a major national security threat. In this context, measures to restrict American trade with China gained support for both protective and national-security reasons.

Geopolitical realities reasserted themselves with even greater vengeance in February 2022, when Russia invaded Ukraine. The invasion, and subsequent sanctions, massively disrupted world trade in food, fuel, and other commodities. Apart from the distress it caused, the disruption underlined to many governments their sensitivity to external events. As with the pandemic, the Russian invasion and its impact further encouraged many governments to attempt to bring some economic activities home and reduce reliance upon imports.

Climate policy, too, started to call international economic openness into question. As requirements that traded-goods industries reduce greenhouse emissions grow, whether by way of regulation or carbon pricing, these industries face competitive pressure from imports originating in countries with less stringent requirements. This has led to demands from affected industries for countervailing measures — typically in the form of "border adjustment mechanisms (BAMs)," tariffs to raise the price of such imports by the cost of the domestic climate-policy measures. Apart from appearing fair to domestic firms, these mechanisms have the appealing feature of giving other governments incentives to enact more stringent climate policies, creating incentives for a "race to the top." Yet these BAMs are restraints on trade, and developing countries may — not without reason — complain that they impose unfair burdens on countries that cannot easily afford the expensive climate policies the OECD is enacting. Nonetheless, most OECD government are moving rapidly in this direction. In addition, some OECD governments have adopted or are considering climate-related policies, such as subsidies, that discriminate in favour of domestic producers and thus against imports.

The global COVID pandemic, the Russian invasion of Ukraine, the rise of China, and the evolution of climate policy have all contributed to uncertainty about the future of world trade and investment. However, broader, more general, domestic and international political factors are also at work, and it is on them that I concentrate here.[42] Trade depends upon cooperation among the principal economic centres, and both economic and political trends have called this cooperation into question.

Indeed, perhaps the most striking development in the politics of trade over the past 15 years is the onset of a wave of anti-globalist, and anti-European, sentiment throughout the developed world — and into many developing countries. Within the advanced industrial countries an upsurge in "populist" sentiment with an economically nationalistic tenor often expresses explicit hostility to "globalist" approaches to economic cooperation. While China and Russia may challenge "Western" economic interests and norms, the fact that long-standing principles of international economic cooperation are now challenged *within* the major Western powers is truly unprecedented, and truly significant. How can international economic cooperation be sustained when domestic political pressures appear to be pushing the major powers apart, rather than together?

In fact, stirrings of discontent with the reigning economic order surfaced almost as soon as countries began to emerge from the depths of the Global Financial Crisis. In the United States, nationalist right-wing reaction took the form of the Tea Party movement, which helped the Republican Party sweep the midterm election of 2010. Europe's governments collapsed into bitter disputes over how best to address accumulated debts, and the region fell into a second recession as leftist movements and parties opposed to austerity shot to prominence in the debtor nations.

Even after the purely economic impact of the crisis began to fade, its political effects matured and grew. In both the developed and much of the developing world movements arose and proliferated that varied on many dimensions but were similar on several. They rejected most existing political institutions, parties, and politicians. They couched their rejection in absolutist terms, pitting "the people" against a spent and corrupt elite. They were hostile to globalism and the stateless cosmopolitanism of the new global ruling class. These "populist" movements of Right and Left grew almost everywhere — and were able to win elections in some cases, most prominently in the United States.

[42] Some earlier thoughts on the process are in Frieden 2021.

What explains this rejection of global economic and political integration? Will it put a stop to efforts to create and extend global governance? What might slow or stop the march of populism?

3. The rise of populist nationalism

The 2016 presidential election in the United States was a watershed in American political history. For the first time in over 80 years, candidates for the presidential nomination of both political parties ran on platforms of explicit hostility to international trade, international finance, and international investment. The rhetoric of Bernie Sanders and Donald Trump was, indeed, strikingly similar. Donald Trump said:

> Our politicians have aggressively pursued a policy of globalization, moving our jobs, our wealth and our factories to Mexico and overseas. Globalization has made the financial elite very, very wealthy.... But it has left millions of our workers with nothing but poverty and heartache.

For his part, Bernie Sanders argued:

> [T]rade is....a significant reason why Americans are working longer hours for low wages and why we are seeing our jobs go to China and other low-wage countries....[W]e should have a trade policy which represents the working families of this country, that rebuilds our manufacturing base, not that just represents the CEOs of large multinational corporations.

By the same token, Trump claimed that "NAFTA was the worst trade deal in history....And China's entrance into the World Trade Organization has enabled the greatest job theft in the history of our country."

Sanders was only slightly less bombastic:

> NAFTA, CAFTA, PNTR with China...have been a disaster for the American worker....Working people understand that after NAFTA, CAFTA, PNTR with China we have lost millions of decent paying jobs.

Of course, one of those candidates won the nomination of his party and went on to win the presidency. And this brought to the most powerful office in the world, again for the first time in 80 years, a policymaker who was avowedly hostile to international trade, finance, investment, and immigration, as well as to what he called "globalism," and to multilateralism.

In office, the Trump administration was true to its word. The administration embarked on a trade war with China, and an almost as vehement trade conflict with allies in North America and Europe. It forced renegotiation of the NAFTA and US-Korea trade agreements, and pulled the United States out of any remaining potential trade agreements. Although the succeeding Biden administration was more cooperative in its rhetoric, its trade policies have not varied much from those pursued by the Trump administration.

The root causes of this striking turn in American politics, and in American foreign economic policy, go back at least forty years. The country's income distribution has deteriorated almost continually — with a pause in the 1990s — since the early 1970s. Almost from the start, many Americans connected this trend with the position of the United States in the international economy. In the 1970s and 1980s, there were those who blamed the stagnation and decline in the wages of unskilled workers on a dramatic increase in imports from developing countries. It is worth noting that this had little to do with China and referred primarily to what were then called the Newly Industrializing Countries (NICs): South Korea, Taiwan, Hong Kong, Singapore, Mexico, and Brazil. As late at 1990, China ranked fourth among developing-country exporters to the United States, after South Korea, Taiwan, and Mexico. The connection was based on good Heckscher-Ohlin logic: greater trade with countries rich in unskilled labor would put downward pressure on unskilled wages in the United States.

This logic led to the original "trade and wages" debate, about the relative importance of trade and skill-biased technological change respectively to the deterioration of the return to unskilled labor in the United States. It is useful to recall that this debate raged in the late 1980s and early 1990s, long before China was a major force (Freeman 1995). The consensus was that technological change was far more important than trade, although more recent re-evaluations tend to find a greater impact of trade than had previously been expected (Krugman, 2008; Krugman *et al.*, 2013).

In the 1990s and early 2000s, as unskilled wages largely stabilized — at a lower level — much of the attention shifted to the increasing separation between the middle class and the top registers of the income distribution. Whether the target was the top 1 percent or the top 10 percent, activists and others pointed to the emergence of "headquarters cities" and "superstar firms" collecting in prosperous urban agglomerations, pushing out the middle class and leaving them behind. Again, many made a connection to globalization, and regarded the problem as result of an alliance among internationalist firms and banks, globalist governments, and international organizations that privileged markets over social goals. This perspective, largely from the Left, was especially prominent in the late 1990s, culminating in the so-called Battle for Seattle in 1999, on the occasion of a WTO Ministerial Conference.

The American middle class had reason to complain: over the 1980s and into the early 1990s, median household income was largely stagnant in real terms. Rapid economic growth in the 1990s served to paper over some of the discontent. But into the 2000s, real median household income again stagnated. Some of this middle-class stagnation was masked by the 2001–2007 boom in housing and asset prices, which helped increase middle-class wealth. But even during those go-go years, the gains from economic growth were not distributed evenly. During the expansion, two-thirds of the country's income growth went to the top one percent of the population. These American families, each earning more than $400,000 a year, saw their incomes rise by more than 60 percent between 2002 and 2007, while the income of the rest of the country's households rose by 6 percent. And even that meagre growth was taken back by the Great Financial Crisis (GFC) that began late in 2007.

The GFC exacerbated trends that had been in train for decades. We see it easily in Europe, where the crisis in the Eurozone was so severe that it took almost ten years for GDP per capita to recover to its pre-crisis levels. Moreover, the unequal distribution of the burden of adjustment is clear in the European context, where the heavily indebted countries suffered Depression-like economic collapses. In Spain and Greece, GDP per capita fell by 10 and 25 percent respectively, while unemployment peaked at over 25 percent — and over 15 percent in Portugal and Ireland.

The crisis in the United States was almost as severe, and almost as unequally distributed. It took six years for American GDP per capita to recover, nine years for median household income. As in Europe, the aggregate numbers mask substantial regional variation. Median household income in prosperous states like Massachusetts and New York rose by 10 or 15 percent in the ten years after the crisis, while troubled states like Michigan, Wisconsin, and Florida remained below pre-crisis levels. The regional contrast was also clear in differential rates of unemployment. The unemployment rate in

Michigan peaked at 15 percent, while it never reached 9 percent in New York and Massachusetts.

The disparities in the impact of the American crisis among social groups were even greater. At the height of the GFC the national unemployment rate was 10 percent. Among the poorest third of American households, however, unemployment was 18 percent; if the underemployed (including discouraged and involuntary part-time workers) are included, the rate rises to 35 percent. Meanwhile, in the richest third of American households, unemployment peaked at 4 percent; including the underemployed, at 9 percent. Perhaps most striking has been the collapse of middle-class wealth: median household wealth in 2016 was 34 percent below where it had been in 2007 — this while the household wealth of the top 20 percent of the population grew by 33 percent. Indeed, by 2016, the richest 20 percent of American households owned 77 percent of the country's wealth — more than three times that owned by the entire middle class (the middle 60 percent of households). Even more striking, the richest one percent of American households owned substantially more than the middle class combined. The most striking imbalances in the American crisis and recovery were — as in the expansion that preceded it — among groups in the population. Not only had the rich gotten richer during the boom, but they also continued to get richer during the crisis and the recovery.

In both Europe and the United States, the crisis and its aftermath highlighted the failures of existing elites to address their societies' problems. In Europe, the member states of the Eurozone were unable to arrive at a reasonable resolution of the Eurozone debt crisis. The catastrophic mess that enveloped the Eurozone was entirely avoidable, and yet the region's political leaders could not avoid it. In the United States, politicians and pundits emphasized the general recovery of the economy — and of the stock market — and focused on the booming prosperity of the big cities. They ignored the fact that vast swaths of the population, including much of the middle class, were worse off than they had been before the crisis.

Existing political institutions, parties, and leaders had failed on two dimensions. There was a failure of compensation: an unwillingness or inability to safeguard the interests of those harmed by international and domestic economic events, while catering to and celebrating the beneficiaries. There was a failure of representation: an unwillingness or inability to accurately reflect and address the needs of large portions of the population. For decades since World War Two, in Europe and North America, a centrist consensus had reigned. The centre-left and the centre-right, for all their differences, agreed on the broad contours of domestic and international economic policies. As large portions of these economies fell farther behind, those left out of the consensus had nowhere to turn — until they did.

The domestic political reaction to these failures came even as the crisis was fading. Over the course of 2009, the Tea Party movement swept the United States and the Republican Party, culminating in major successes in primary and general elections in 2010. The movement lay the groundwork for Donald Trump's populist campaign of 2016 and played a major role in remaking the Republican Party in its, and Trump's, images. On the Democratic side, Senator Bernie Sanders led the "progressive" wing in attacking Democratic Party moderates. In Europe, populists of the left quickly rose in Greece and Spain, soon taking power in the former and becoming a major political force in the latter. Within a few years, almost every western European country had a powerful populist movement, whether of the Right or of the Left. Indeed, in 1998 populist parties drew support from less than 10% of European citizens and only two governments included populist politicians.[43] In 2019, populist parties received 24% of votes in national parliamentary elections across Europe and served in eleven different governments; they were part of the pro-government bloc, but not in government, in four others (Heinö, 2019).

Although there were substantial differences among the various populist movements, some things tied them together. They all, to one extent or another, rejected existing political institutions, parties, and leaders. And they all harboured a basic hostility toward economic and political integration. In the United States the target was globalization, "globalism," and multilateralism in general. Donald Trump told the United Nations General Assembly in no uncertain terms: "America is governed by Americans. We reject the ideology of globalism.... [R]esponsible nations must defend against threats to sovereignty...from global governance.... We will never surrender America's sovereignty to an unelected, unaccountable, global bureaucracy."[44]

[43] https://www.theguardian.com/world/ng-interactive/2018/nov/20/how-populism-emerged-as-electoral-force-in-europe

[44] https://news.un.org/en/story/2018/09/1020472

In Europe, the European Union was the principal target. As Marine Le Pen put it:

> The European Union has become a prison of peoples. Each of the 28 countries that constitute it has slowly lost its democratic prerogatives to commissions and councils with no popular mandate....I will be Madame Frexit if the European Union doesn't give us back our monetary, legislative, territorial, and budget sovereignty.[45]

There is not always a direct connection between this sort of populism — especially of the Right — and opposition to globalization. In Europe it often takes the form of opposition to European integration, or of aspects of integration that they see as impinging upon national sovereignty. The target of the hostility might be EU-imposed austerity, in the debtor nations, or EU policies toward regulation or immigration, in other countries. Some in the Trump administration, like some British supporters of Brexit, might have argued that their economic nationalism is in pursuit of the ultimate goal of a more open economy. Nonetheless, virtually all these movements share an aversion to "globalism," and to the kind of international collaboration and integration that has been the norm since the 1940s.

4. Nationalist populism and international cooperation

Populists of the modern variety have made abundantly clear that they are uninterested in — and often hostile to — the previous elites' quest for global cooperation. The Trump Administration eschewed multilateralism in favour of bilateral, or unilateral, action on trade. It was hostile to the World Trade Organization (WTO), ignoring it in most of its actions and actively impeding the work of the Dispute Settlement System. Such central European populists as Hungarian prime minister Viktor Orban boast about building "a new state built on illiberal and national foundations." They reject EU oversight of their domestic policies, and EU attempts to allocate refugees and asylum-seekers among member states. They may welcome the openness of European markets

[45] https://www.nytimes.com/2016/06/28/opinion/marine-le-pen-after-brexit-the-peoples-spring-is-inevitable.html; and https://www.bloomberg.com/news/articles/2015-06-23/call-me-mrs-frexit-le-pen-sees-france-euro-exit-next?leadSource=uverify%20wall

to their goods and people, but they resist the attempts of other EU member states to harmonize and coordinate policies and principles.

This is not to take a position on the correctness or less of the populists' positions. In most instances, there is a logic to their arguments. There is a great diversity of socio-economic realities and political views among the member states of the European Union and attempts to create common policies may well be unrealistic in many arenas. Supporters of the populist nationalists in Europe often argue that integration has gone too far, too fast, and that the EU needs to correct its course and set its integrationist sights lower. This view is also held by some decidedly non-populist observers (such as Mody 2018).

The American populist variant shares with its European counterparts a bitter disdain for elite internationalism, which it blames for inflicting hardship on "the people" and for steering the country away from its traditions. Donald Trump's 2016 presidential campaign, and his rhetoric in office afterwards, emphasized his dedication to the middle class, and to the country's industrial base. Trump on campaign, and Trump in office, were explicitly hostile to globalization. The Trump Administration moved sharply away from the country's post-war commitment to multilateralism. The Administration's trade policy, in particular, has been a notable departure from that of past administrations. It undertook undertaken a series of unilateral measures and bilateral negotiations, most of which are clearly inconsistent with reigning WTO principles. Trade is only one foreign-policy arena in which America's nationalist populists have largely jettisoned previous patterns of multilateral engagement.

The Biden administrations' rhetoric has been more favourable to international cooperation and multilateral institutions. This reemphasis on traditional alliance partners and traditional institutions was reinforced by the geopolitical realities brought home by the Russian invasion of Ukraine and heightened concern about China's ambitions in Asia. But in practice, the Biden administration has continued many of the Trump-era trade policies. The main streams of both the Democratic and Republican parties seem to have drifted away from their traditional pro-globalization views; how far they have drifted, and how far they might continue to drift, remains to be seen.

While the specific policies pursued by populists in power are important — especially in the case of the United States — their policy principles are less important than the underlying political realities they reflect. For if it were simply a matter of one political party of two, or among many in the European cases, one might expect an eventual reversion to the strategies of the past. However, there is substantial evidence that the populists — in or out of office — are a political reflection of powerful socio-economic trends that affect most industrial societies. The power of these trends was shown, as noted, by the movement of the Democrats in a decidedly more protectionist direction — something evident as early as the 2016 presidential campaign, when Hillary Clinton felt constrained to disavow the Trans-Pacific Partnership she had helped design. Similar pressures have led many European centre--right (and even centre-left) parties to move closer to the positions of their populist challengers.

The new economic nationalists in western Europe and the United States find their principal bases of support in regions of their respective countries that are economically distressed — and, in particular, in regions that have experienced deindustrialization. While, as previously noted, there are many reasons for the loss of manufacturing jobs in rich countries, foreign competition and the relocation of production offshore are prominent causes and causes that — unlike automation — suggest potential policy responses.

The problems of formerly industrial regions in decline are complex and of long standing, and they are not amenable to quick fixes. Their recovery will require some combination of adjustment policies to soften the blows from technological change and globalization, and structural policies whose impact is likely to be felt only over decades. These regions need substantial improvements in education, in workforce development, and in the economic and social infrastructure. They also need good jobs for their residents, although we have little clear guidance as to the measures best suited to ensure a steady supply of such good jobs.

There are substantial, long-term, structural sources of the discontent that has rippled — or torn — through advanced industrial societies over the past decade. It was probably not preordained that the discontent would be captured and channelled by nationalist populists, largely of the Right but also of the Left. However, that is how the politics developed, and they are unlikely to recede any time soon.

The underlying politics of the present day — and of the present-day backlash against globalization and integration — must be the foundation for any sensible projection of the prospects for international economic cooperation. Current trends would not seem promising even for a maintenance of current levels of cooperation, let alone for their deepening into some meaningful forms of global governance.

5. Past and present of international cooperation

The battle for international economic cooperation will be won or lost on the field of domestic politics. This much seems clear from current trends, and how they have affected international economic relations in the past few years. A look at the history of the successes and failures of global economic integration — and there is a long history to draw upon — is equally instructive.

The central problem of an integrated international economy is to manage the delicate relationship between the demands of international economic collaboration, on the one hand, and the demands of domestic social and political realities, on the other. The first era of globalization, in the nineteenth and early twentieth centuries, solved this problem by excluding most domestic groups from meaningful participation in political and social life. This proved untenable in the interwar years and led to catastrophe. During the first decades of the post-World War Two order, which we may call the Bretton Woods period, the balancing act was managed with a series of important compromises. As the world transitioned to the "high globalization" of the 1990s and after, that balancing act became increasingly difficult — and its difficulties are central to the problems of today. A short sketch of this trajectory is illustrative.

For decades before 1914, the international economy was roughly as integrated as it is today. That first era of globalization was remarkably successful by the standards of the time. The world economy grew more in the 75 years before 1914 than it had in the previous 750, and there was substantial convergence among countries of the core and lands of recent settlement. Macroeconomic conditions were relatively stable, despite periodic crises and 'panics.' None of this is to ignore the uglier sides of the period — colonialism, authoritarian governments, agrarian crises and grinding urban poverty were all parts of the 19th and early 20th century world order. Nonetheless, compared to what had come before — and what came immediately after — this was a flourishing global economy.

And yet that globalized economy came to a grinding halt in 1914. After WWI was over, the world's political and economic leaders attempted to restore the classical order that had prevailed for so long — and failed. It was not for lack of trying, as conferences, meetings, treaties and international organizations proliferated as never before. But nothing worked; the global economy fragmented and eventually, after the 1929 downturn hit, broke up into trade and currency wars, and eventually shooting wars (Eichengreen 1992 is the classic account).

There are some interesting parallels between the interwar period and the present day. Apart from the superficial similarities between some of the current populist movements and interwar ones — such as the re-use of the America First label by the Trump Administration — there are deeper connections. One is that the regional political base of the Trump Administration, and in particular of its more protectionist trade policies, is to be found in the regions of the country that were the principal sources of isolationist sentiment in the 1920s and 1930s, especially the industrial belt in the Midwest along with states in the Great Plains and the Rocky Mountains. Another parallel has to do with the rejection of multilateralism: the isolationists, along with many Americans, felt that existing international organizations did not accurately reflect the role of the US in the world, and were indeed intended to constrain US influence.

There are two principal lessons of the first era of globalization and its collapse after 1918. First, an open international economy requires collaboration among the major economic powers, especially during periods of economic stress. The 19th-century fiction of self-equilibrating international markets may have applied to particular markets; but it did not apply to the world economy as a whole. For a globalized economy to persist, especially in the face of periodic crises, the principal financial centres need to cooperate to stabilize markets and safeguard openness.

The second lesson of the collapse of the classical version of globalization is that national governments cannot undertake the measures needed to sustain an open economy if they do not have the support of their constituents. Policymakers must answer to their constituents and if constituents are hostile to the world economy, policymakers who ignore this hostility will cease to be making policy.

The stability of the classical gold-standard era in the 19th century and early 20th century was due in part to the fact that the major member states gave few political rights, and little political power, to the middle and working classes and poor farmers. The failures of the interwar period were largely due to the inability of political leaders to sustain classical policies in newly democratic nations. Indeed, by the 1920 almost every industrial country was democratic, and attempts to subject these political economies to gold-standard austerity measures led to a powerful backlash — both against the government, and often against the rest of the world.

The post-World War Two international economic order, planned in broad outlines at Bretton Woods, attempted to find a middle ground between classical gold-standard stability and interwar confusion, while allowing room for more flexible national macroeconomic and social policies. Trade was liberalized, but gradually and with exceptions and escape clauses where liberalization would have been politically difficult. Exchange rates were stabilized, but capital controls limited the degree of financial integration. Social safety nets and the welfare state were accepted as part of the post-war compromise (Lamoreaux and Shapiro, eds. 2019). This system worked well for 25 years. However, economic integration eventually caught up with some of the contradictions in the Bretton Woods order, symbolized by the extent to which the gradual rebirth of international finance undermined the Bretton Woods monetary system.

The march toward globalization started in earnest in the early 1980s, as the Reagan and Thatcher administrations led the developed countries toward greater engagement with global markets. Over the late 1980s and early 1990s, many developing countries jettisoned their previous economic nationalism. When the Soviet Union collapsed and it and most of its former allies embraced economic integration — as China and Vietnam had done long before — it seemed that globalization had triumphed for good.

However, the second age of globalization faced problems parallel to those of the first: international economic forces increasingly bumped up against domestic political pressures. As we have seen, the crisis of 2007–2009 and its aftermath brought these tensions to the fore, as political movements rejected past patterns of economic and political integration — and, in some cases, took power on anti-integrationist platforms. It remains to be seen whether this reflects the end of the second era of globalization, or merely a pause in its onward march.

6. What the future might hold

The future of global trade, and more broadly global economic openness, is in doubt. There are considerable geopolitical headwinds: the Russian invasion of Ukraine has disrupted world trade, while the rise of China has raised questions in many quarters about the wisdom of relying upon China as the world's workshop. However, in my view the principal source of doubt about the future has to do with the extent of domestic political opposition to the measures necessary to secure cooperative international economic and political relations. The roots of this opposition are broad and deep, and they cannot be wished or persuaded away. Progress in addressing global problems depends on progress in addressing the domestic problems that underlie the current upsurge of pessimism about, and hostility to, globalization.

A first step in this direction requires recognizing the legitimacy of many of the concerns that populist nationalists have seized upon. Major regions of our economies, and major segments of our populations, have faced and continue to face serious economic difficulties. What started with the decline of manufacturing industries in these areas typically has led to broader economic distress, and eventually to grim social problems (Feler and Senses 2017). In the United States, social mobility has declined to alarmingly low levels, especially in the distressed regions (Chetty *et al.* 2014). Inter-regional mobility has also fallen dramatically, largely due to rapidly rising housing prices in prosperous areas, which makes it difficult or impossible for people to move from areas where good jobs are scarce to areas with more opportunities (Ganong and Shoag 2017).

Both short-term and long-term measures are needed to address the problems of those left out of globalization's prosperity. In the short run, troubled regions need help in pulling themselves out of what is often a downward spiral. Central governments need to consider "place-based policies" that can address immediate problems effectively (Shambaugh and Ryan 2018). In the longer run, more structural policies to address regional differences will be important, especially those aimed at improving the economic and social infrastructure, and the educational institutions, in regions that have been struggling.

The contours of effective short- and long-term policies are not necessarily clear. Regions differ, as do countries; what works in one may not work in another. Nonetheless, if the needs of troubled regions, sectors, and people are not addressed, we can reliably expect a continuation and deepening of the current scepticism about international economic and political integration. Those with the most at stake in globalization need to find ways to address the valid concerns of those who regard it with scepticism and fear.

Theory and history demonstrate that an open international economy requires cooperation among the major economic centres. That cooperation in turn requires domestic political support for the measures necessary to help keep the world economy functioning smoothly. Support for globalization and integration has eroded continually over the course of the 21st century. A reversal of this erosion depends on the willingness and ability of supporters of international economic and political integration to demonstrate to their compatriots, with deeds rather than words, that its benefits can be distributed much more broadly than they have been to date.

REFERENCES

Autor, David H., David Dorn, and Gordon H. Hanson (2013), "The China Syndrome: Local Labor Market Effects of Import Competition in the United States", *American Economic Review* 103, No. 6, pp. 2121-68

Broz, J. Lawrence, Jeffry Frieden, and Stephen Weymouth (2019), Populism in Place: The Economic Geography of the Globalization Backlash, *International Organization* 75, no. 2 (Spring 2021).

Chetty, Raj, Nathaniel Hendren, Patrick Kline, and Emmanuel Saez (2014), "Where is the Land of Opportunity? The Geography of Intergenerational Mobility in the United States", *Quarterly Journal of Economics* 129, No. 4, pp. 1553–1623.

Chinn, Menzie and Jeffry Frieden (2011), *Lost Decades: The Making of America's Debt Crisis and the Long Recovery*, New York: W W Norton.

Colantone, Italo and Piero Stanig (2018), "The Trade Origins of Economic Nationalism: Import Competition and Voting Behavior", *Western Europe, American Journal of Political Science* 62, 4 (October), pp. 936-953.

Colantone, Italo and Piero Stanig (2019), "The Surge of Economic Nationalism in Western Europe", *Journal of Economic Perspectives* 33, No. 4 (Fall), pp. 128-51.

Dal Bo, Ernesto, Fred Finan, Olle Folke, Torsten Persson and Johanna Rickne (2018), *Economic Losers and Political Winners: Sweden's Radical Right*, Working paper.

Eichengreen, Barry (1992), *Golden Fetters: The Gold Standard and the Great Depression, 1919-1939*, New York: Oxford University Press.

Feler, Leo, and Mine Z. Senses (2017), "Trade Shocks and the Provision of Local PublicGoods", *American Economic Journal: Economic Policy* 9 (4), pp. 101-43.

Freeman, Richard B. (1995), "Are Your Wages Set in Beijing?" *The Journal of Economic Perspectives*, 9, No. 3 (Summer), pp. 15-32.

Frieden, Jeffry (2019), *The political economy of the globalization backlash: Sources and implications. In Meeting Globalization's Challenges*, Princeton: Princeton University Press.

Frieden, Jeffry (2021), "International Cooperation in the Age of Populism", in Maria Eugenia Mata, Miguel Rocha de Sousa and Luis Brites Pereira (eds.) *Economic Globalization & Governance: Essays in Honor of Jorge Braga de Macedo*, New York: Springer.

Frieden, Jeffry, Michael Pettis, Dani Rodrik, and Ernesto Zedillo (2012), *After the Fall: The Future of Global Cooperation Geneva Report 14*, London: Center for Economic Policy Research.

Frieden, Jeffry and Stefanie Walter (2017), "Understanding the Political Economy of the Eurozone Crisis", *Annual Review of Political Science*, Vol. 20, pp. 371-390.

Ganong, Peter and Daniel Shoag (2017), "Why Has Regional Income Convergence in the U.S. Declined?" *Journal of Urban Economics* 102, pp. 76-90.

Heino, A. J. (2019), "Authoritarian populism index", available at: https://populism index.com.

Krugman, Paul (2008), "Trade and Wages, Reconsidered", *Brookings Papers on Economic Activity* Vol. 2008 (Spring 2008), pp. 103-137.

Lamoreaux, Naomi and Ian Shapiro (eds.) (2019), *The Bretton Woods Agreements*, New Haven: Yale University Press.

Mody, Ashoka (2018), *EuroTragedy: A Drama in Nine Acts*, Oxford: Oxford University Press.

Moretti, Enrico (2012), *The New Geography of Jobs*, New York: Houghton Mifflin Harcourt.

Rodrik, Dani and Charles Sable (2019), "Building a Good Jobs Economy", Working paper.

Sawhill, Isabel V. and Christopher Pulliam (2019), "Six facts about wealth in the United States", Brookings blog Up Front, available at https://www.brookings.edu/blog/up-front/2019/06/25/six-facts-about-wealth-in-the-united-states/. (Accessed January 3, 2020.)

Shambaugh, Jay and Ryan Nunn (eds.) (2018), *Place-Based Policies for Shared Economic Growth*. Washington, DC: Brookings Institution.

Wolff, Edward N. (2017), "Household Wealth Trends in the United States 1962 to 2016: Has Middle Class Wealth Recovered?", NBER Working Paper number 24085, Cambridge: NBER.

PART II
ON LESSONS FROM THE EU'S BLUEPRINT DEEP TRADE AGREEMENT (CETA) FOR EU TRADE POLICY

Summary

The EU has increasingly adopted deep trade agreements, the Comprehensive Economic and Trade Agreement (CETA) with Canada serving as a blueprint for later ones. The lessons that CETA offers are hence of particular interest for a better understanding of EU deep trade agreements. This bilateral new generation trade agreement, which had been signed in 2016, is in force since 2017 (albeit provisionally), still awaiting ratification by all member states and some regions. **Chapter 5** (Guimarães) argues that efficiency reasons underlie the expansion of policy areas (and EU competences) and trade agreements in the EU. Competence creep became limited by member state or sub-state competences. As a result of the engagement of subnational entities in trade policy and the CJEU's Singapore decision, there have been transformative shifts in the locus of trade policymaking from centralized competences to divided sovereignty with national and subnational entities. **Chapter 6** (Coutinho) explains why there had been a grey zone with respect to EU trade competences and its clarification by the CJEU (Singapore decision). CETA's qualification as a mixed agreement determines that its application is limited and provisional, and under a permanent threat until all member states and some regions have ratified the agreement (reasoning applicable to all mixed agreements). The separation of such a mixed agreement in two, in line with the competence distribution in the EU, could facilitate and speed up ratification. **Chapter 7** (Leblond and Viju-Miljusevic) analyse whether CETA, the EU's first third-generation trade agreement, has been effective in liberalizing trade. Those agreements focus above all on beyond-the-border impediments to international trade (*e.g.*, rules and regulations) rather than at-the-border barriers (*e.g.*, tariffs). The case of CETA allows for studying the effectiveness of facilitating trade through regulatory and administrative cooperation in a five-year period.

CHAPTER 5

EU FTAs AND DIVIDED SOVEREIGNTY: TRANSFORMATIVE SHIFTS IN TRADE AUTHORITY

Maria Helena Guimarães

Abstract: EU trade policy has evolved on the scope of its remit through what can be framed as "creeping competence" (Pollack 1994, 2000). Since the Treaty of Rome to the Lisbon Treaty the EU has consolidated its sovereignty over trade by broadening its competences. However, the enlarged scope of EU FTAs has pushed subnational units to demand shared sovereignty over trade issues to protect the *status quo* on their regulatory competences. In turn, the 2017 Court of Justice ruling that the EU-Singapore Agreement could only be concluded with the consent of the EU and its member states has led the Commission to propose the splitting of trade deals into EU-only and "mixed" agreements. While the EU holds to its exclusive competences in the former, mixed agreements require divided sovereignty with the member states. Both the engagement of subnational entities in trade policy and the impact of the Court decision represent transformative shifts in the locus of trade policymaking from centralized competences to divided sovereignty with national and subnational entities. The ensuing difficulties in ratifying EU trade agreements have prompted stop-gap solutions that raise questions as to where the pattern of "creeping competence" is applicable. These political and legal challenges highlight that "creeping competence" may have unintended consequences unleashed by the dynamics of the policy itself. In trade policy the notion of "creeping competence" has to capture the legal challenges, the efforts to claw back centralization, as well as the pushback by subnational entities to protect their regulatory sovereignty.

Keywords: creeping competence; divided sovereignty; EU trade policy; subnational engagement; failing forward.

1. Introduction

In the last two decades there has been an increase in the number of EU FTAs (Free Trade Agreements), with a progressive widening and expansion of the trade agenda, addressing issues that go beyond the conventional scope of trade policy focused on reducing tariffs and quantitative restrictions. These deeper FTAs include provisions on environmental protection, labour rights, health issues or public procurement, and have been raising issues of competence over trade policy, and changing the nature of the politics of trade. This chapter analyzes how EU trade policy has evolved since its inclusion in the Treaty of Rome as a common EU policy, to the Treaty of Lisbon, which expanded EU competences over trade issues in a progressive pattern of "competence creep" (Pollack 1994, 2002), to the present transformative shifts towards divided sovereignty between the EU and its member states. I argue that the centralization of EU trade policy has been challenged by the very expanding scope and depth of the EU trade agreements. EU FTAs increasingly include new issue-areas that often impinge upon national and subnational competences, and they have pushed subnational entities to demand shared sovereignty over trade policy-making. As a consequence, the negotiation and conclusion of recent EU trade deals, such as with Canada and Mercosur, have become more difficult and contentious. The effort to improve the efficiency of trade negotiations by consolidating investment and intellectual property under EU competence in the Treaty of Lisbon had significant consequences, namely the difficulties to ratify trade agreements not only by national but also by subnational parliaments (Freudlsperger 2021). Therefore, the broader and deeper trade agenda brought to the fore the challenges to the expansion of EU competence beyond core trade issues, as further centralization of trade-related policies in the Treaty of Lisbon led to the increasing contestation of FTAs (Broschek 2021, Egan and Guimarães 2022, Bollen, de Ville, and Gheyle 2020).

On the other hand, the 2017 Court of Justice of the EU (CJEU) ruling that some issues included in the new generation FTAs (non-direct foreign investment and investor-state dispute settlement regime) are not of exclusive competence of the EU (Court Opinion 2/15 on the EU-Singapore Agreement), has also challenged the centralization in the EU of further trade-related issues. Following the CJEU ruling, having to face subnational entities claims for further involvement in trade policy decision-making and the increasing difficulty in the ratification of trade agreements, the Commission decided to split trade deals into EU-exclusive and mixed-competences agreements. Thus, the continual expansion of competences over trade-related issues has led the EU to address the shortcomings of the existing institutional arrangements, and to adjust to the new political and legal challenges.

Drawing on Pollack's notion of "creeping competence" (1994, 2000), I argue that while in the Treaty of Rome the EU took responsibility for trade policy, and the Treaty of Lisbon further expanded the scope of the EU trade powers to new areas, the centralization of trade policy is presently experiencing a backlash. The Commission's previous "creeping competence" is now challenged by the consequences of a more ambitious EU trade agenda, which has pushed demands for shared sovereignty in the negotiation and signing of EU FTAs, particularly by subnational authorities. The increasing engagement of subnational entities in trade policy and the CJEU decision on shared powers in specific trade-related issues, represent transformative shifts in the in the pattern of EU "creeping competence" in trade policy. Thus, "creeping competence" needs to account for the attendant political risks of the push-back by subnational entities to protect the *status quo* on their regulatory competences, and for the legal constraints to the Commission's efforts to claw back its original authority on trade policy. These changes in the locus of trade policy-making raise questions as to where the pattern of "creeping competence" is applicable and where it is not, as well as to the use of stop-gap solutions to address the challenges of sovereignty claims by national and subnational entities. The recent developments regarding the EU-Mercosur agreement illustrate the political efforts to adapt to the new trade agenda and to avoid stalling the ratification of EU FTAs and the pace of EU treaty-making. This highlights that "creeping competence" may have unintended consequences due to the dynamics unleashed by trade policy itself.

In assessing the evolution of trade authority with the "creeping competence" concept, I sustain that the latest evolution of EU trade policy fits the "failing forward" argument of European integration (Freudlspeger 2021, Jones, Keleman and Meunier 2021). The adjustments the EU is seeking by splitting trade agreements, and the recent stop-gap measures to try to move trade policy forward, are rooted in the difficulties to ratify broad-agenda FTAs, and in the Court ruling on EU-exclusive competences.

The chapter addresses the following questions: As subnational entities increasingly demand a 'voice' in FTAs negotiations and the ratification of trade agreements is ever more difficult, how is subnational mobilization impacting centralized sovereignty over EU trade agreements? How does the

Court ruling on the EU-Singapore FTA impact the Commission's creeping competence on trade? The chapter is divided into 3 sections. The first section shows how the increasing scope and depth of EU trade agreements is challenging the EU competences over trade agreements. Section 2 addresses the evolution of competences over FTAs, from centralization to retrenchment, and stop-gap measures to address political challenges and legal constraints. The third section uses Pollack's notion of "creeping competence" in the realm of trade policy to argue that the increasingly diversified scope and depth of EU trade agreements is leading to transformative shifts in trade authority, from consolidated undivided EU competences to divided sovereignty with member states over specific trade-related issues.

2. The EU expanding trade agenda and subnational competences

The EU has currently 41 trade agreements with 72 countries. Out of these deals, 31 are FTAs or have an FTA component (Conconi *et al.*, 2021). Striking these trade agreements is getting ever more challenging for the EU, as they no longer are merely about decreasing or eliminating tariffs, and enlarging or abolishing quotas, to ease access to foreign markets. These first-generation trade agreements gave way to second-generation deals that furthered economic integration by tackling non-tariff barriers, and by including trade-related issues such as intellectual property, labor and environmental standards that are closely inter-related with trade. By addressing these behind-the-border measures and restrictive governmental policies, trade agreements became increasingly politicized. Not only civil society and NGOs campaigned in opposition to specific trade deals (De Ville and Siles-Brügge 2016, Buonanno 2017, Eliasson and García-Duran 2017), as indeed national and subnational governments became more vigilant on the impact of FTAs on their economic interests and public policy competences on social rights, consumer protection, or public procurement (Tatham 2018, Kersschot, Kerremans, and De Bièvre 2020, Egan and Guimarães 2022). While first- and second-generation trade deals aimed at increasing market access for physical goods, the third generation deals now encompass trade in services and digital trade, as well as add new dimensions to trade-related issues on human rights (slave labor, for example) or on environmental performance (Leblond and Viju-Miljusevic 2019). Therefore, trade agreements are increasingly "living agreements" (Meunier and Morin 2015) that respond to technological changes and advancements (artificial intelligence), to new society concerns (data protection), and to the transformations in the global economy and in trade patterns, particularly those relating to the restructuring of global supply chains in a post pandemic world. These are all factors that propel the expansion of the international trade agenda into ever more multidimensional trade agreements (Guimarães 1995).

With their deeper and ever-larger scope provisions, trade agreements increasingly call the attention of subnational authorities, as they address trade-related issues that intrude on their constitutional and regulatory competences. Consequently, subnational entities progressively "establish themselves as stakeholders in trade politics" (Broschek 2021, 2), and subnational parliaments emerge as "sounding boards for public contestation" (Freudlsperger 2020, 45), and gain 'actorness' in EU politics of trade. This was paramount in the Wallonia Parliament *ex post* veto of Comprehensive Economic Trade Agreement with the EU (CETA) in 2016. The Wallonia saga, with the regional parliament refusal to ratify the agreement, put on hold its signature until a clarification instrument regarding compliance with socio-economic issues, environmental regulations, and the safeguard of public interest in the dispute resolution mechanism was included in its annexes. The influence of Belgium's sub-federal parliament on the EU ability to conclude CETA epitomizes the rise in regional attention and participation in EU trade policy, as subnational governments seek to preserve their autonomous policies, competences and prerogatives against the supranational encroachment brought up by the expanding agenda of EU trade agreements (De Bièvre and Poletti 2020, Van Loon 2020, De Ville and Siles-Brügge 2016, Young 2019). One can then expect that regional actors make 'political statements' on their subnational constitutional rights, and that they mobilize for shared sovereignty on trade policy issues, contesting EU exclusive powers. These constraints and incursions on policy realms to which subnational authorities are sensitive (public procurement, social policies), trigger the involvement of sub-central entities in the politics of trade, raising calls for shared sovereignty with the EU, which is problematic not only for the central governments but in particular for the EU.[46] As deeper trade agreements

[46] A recent survey of European citizens' views towards trade policy shows their apprehension regarding these policy incursions. Many believe that the bilateral trade agreements signed with Canada, Japan and Mexico will limit the autonomy of national governments to pass their own laws, namely those relating to environmental and health standards – two main priorities of trade policy for Europeans – and also limit their policy autonomy to protect workers and education policies (Eurobatometer 2019).

increasingly expose subnational jurisdictions to international trade rules, and subnational authorities, in turn, hold competences of relevance to EU trade policy-making (Freudlsperger 2020, 1–2), the centralization of trade policy is called into question (D'Erman 2020). The demands for devolution become more audible as subnational entities mobilize to participate in the negotiation of trade agreements, and require their consent in the signing of the trade deals. Trade agreements have also distributional effects across subnational territories, with some economic sectors in specific regions being more negatively affected by EU trade liberalization. As such, the most impacted regions will demand shared decision-making powers in an attempt to protect their interests. These distributive issues across regional units contribute to the politicization of EU trade policy, and add to the governance challenges in EU treaty-making.

Subnational ratification challenges arise in federal systems, where subnational parliaments have legislative powers. Despite that these challenges are bigger where regions have veto powers on trade policy, such as in Belgium, in Germany states also have ratification powers within the second chamber (the Bundesrat), where the federal government and the Länder traditionally seek consensus, sometimes after the federal level makes concessions to the states' demands. German states increasingly take part in trade debates, which include parliamentary motions against EU trade deals, namely regarding investor-state dispute settlement provisions. In other EU states, such as in Spain, there is mounting attention to the impact of EU deals on regional economic interests, namely in the agricultural sector. In Ireland and France, regional economic agents have voiced their concerns and pressured the national government not to ratify the Mercosur agreement, due to its impact, respectively, on the import-competing beef sector and on the protection of geographical indications. In sum, there is growing subnational engagement regarding the consequences of EU trade deals on regional competences and autonomy, but also on their effects on regional economic and sectoral interests.

As the multiple trade-related dimensions of trade liberalisation impact sub-central regulatory authority, subnational economic interests, and social policy preferences, multilevel governance issues become key elements of EU trade politics. EU trade treaty-making, which takes place at different levels of governance, is increasingly about competence distribution and sovereignty partition between the subnational and the supranational level – and not only across the supranational/national divide – and thus authority over trade is becoming more fluid (Egan and Guimarães 2022). This brings challenges to the multilevel politics of trade and to the effective cross-cutting governance of trade policy (Garben 2019).

In this context, the comprehensive and multidimensional trade agenda of the EU is generating an increasing difficulty to conclude trade agreements. Ratification problems in member states delay the entry into force of trade agreements as national and subnational entities seek to safeguard their sovereign rights and socio-economic preferences. These are not new issues in the EU trade policy process, as ratification conflicts began in the 1980s, but they are now exacerbated by the effects of the multidimensional trade agenda across levels of governance. Indeed, the time needed for ratification of trade agreements has been lengthening, and is presently of about three years since the agreement signature (Freudlsperger 2021), highlighting the increasing sovereignty-salience of various provisions of the deep trade agreements.

3. EU FTAs: from delegated competence to divided sovereignty

3.1 From Rome to Lisbon

Trade policy is one of the EU's core Treaty-delegated competences, as established by Art. 3 (1) TFEU. With the Treaty of Lisbon (2007), the Commission has extended its exclusive competences by bringing more dimensions of trade policy under Article 207 TFEU, namely foreign direct investment and the commercial aspects of intellectual property rights. In doing so, the EU enlarged the scope of its exclusive competences on trade and reinforced internal cohesion to speak with 'one voice' in global trade negotiations, (Conceição-Heldt and Meunier 2017). This centralization in the scope of competences would streamline trade negotiations by improving their efficiency and effectiveness in face of the diversity of member states' interests and preferences, and the constraints of constitutionally divided powers (Garcia 2020). The Treaty kept the Commission policy entrepreneurship on trade 'at the wheel' of EU treaty-making, but it would have to consult the Council and inform the European Parliament. The member states determine the Commission's negotiating mandates (the negotiating directives) and oversee the Commission's negotiation of the trade agreements. The role of the European Parliament was bolstered as it has to give its consent to trade agreements before the Council can adopt a decision by qualified majority to conclude a trade deal, by authorizing its signature. Therefore, while trying to improve inter-institutional coordination, and providing for more effective and legitimate institutional scrutiny (Bollen, de Ville, and Gheyle 2020), the Lisbon Treaty also transferred competences to the supranational level to cover new areas of trade, enlarging the scope of the Commission's competences.

The expansion of European trade policy competences with the Lisbon Treaty has led to significant pushback from national parliaments, as well as from subnational parliaments and regional governments. In face of the expansion of the EU trade agenda and its impact on their constitutional rights, the "creeping competence" of the Lisbon Treaty over trade policy has ultimately generated demands for increased participation in trade negotiations, and the advocacy of subnational direct involvement in the EU trade decision-making process.

3.2. The Court ruling on the EU-Singapore FTA

In the aftermath of the Treaty of Lisbon, the Commission assumed that trade agreements that did not include political cooperation issues could be considered of "EU-exclusive" competence, while the Council had a different view on the exclusive competence of the EU to conclude trade agreements (Conconi *et al.*, 2021). Thus, the Commission requested the Court of Justice to decide on its competence to conclude the EU-Singapore Agreement (EUSFTA). In doing so, it demanded a clarification from the Court on the division of competences regarding EU trade agreements, and hence on the scope of the Common Commercial Policy. The request of the Commission was made at a time when contestation in member states to CETA and TTIP (Transatlantic Trade and Investment Partnership) was on the rise, including in subnational parliaments (Egan and Guimarães 2022). In this context, CETA was officially denominated a "mixed agreement" by the Council, under pressure from some member states, particularly the German government. This opened a window of opportunity for subnational influence and engagement to demand a say in the negotiation of the agreement.[47]

In its Opinion 2/15 (delivered in May 2017) regarding the division of competences between the EU and its member states, the CJEU ruled that provisions on portfolio investment and the regime on dispute settlement

[47] The Namur Declaration (2016) and the Trade Together Declaration (2017) reflect, at the academic level, the dilemma on the division of authority over EU trade policy, with the signatories of the former Declaration defending shared competences with the national and subnational levels, while the Trading Together document argued for "EU-only" competences.

between investors and states were not of EU-only competence, but rather of shared competence between the Commission and the EU member states, thus requiring national ratification. In response to the Commission request to the CJEU (in the context of the EU FTA with Singapore) the Court ruled that EU competence is still "incomplete", as some trade issues require both EU and member states consent (Freudlsperger 2021), and as such the EU has not complete authority over trade. And while the competence issues in the EU tend to be solved with Treaty revisions, the Court ruling is having a significant effect in the present dynamics of EU trade policy, as it set limits to competence creep (Garben 2017, 210).

This meant that deals with similar provisions needed to be ratified by member states' national parliaments and in some EU federal states by sub-national parliaments as well, according to their national constitutional provisions (Woolcock 2010, Eschenbach 2015).[48] In Belgium, sub-federal parliaments may even use their individual veto over federal foreign policy, as happened with the CETA (Bursens and De Brièvre 2021). The Commission then decided to split the EUSFTA in two distinct agreements — an "exclusive-competence" FTA, and a separate "mixed agreement" to address investment liberalization issues not covered by EU-exclusive competence (namely investment protection). Eventually, the EU signed two EU-Singapore agreements in October 2018 — a free trade agreement, and an investor protection agreement (AIP) of shared competence that still needs to be ratified by 16 EU member states.

Following the CJEU ruling, the Commission recommended to split future agreements. 'EU-only' agreements would include all trade provisions except portfolio investment and investor-state dispute settlement, so that they would not require member state approval. Mixed agreements are subject to approval and ratification by both the EU and its member states, and include provisions of shared competence with member states. In this new trade policy scenario, the EU-Vietnam Agreement (signed by the Council in 2020) was also split into a trade agreement and an AIP, and the negotiations with New Zealand and Australia followed the same strategy.[49] The full range of trade policy issues is no longer of the exclusive competence of the EU, as it has to share powers in select trade policy issues. By splitting the trade agreements,

[48] National parliaments of all member states but Malta, and all regional parliaments in Belgium, must ratify "mixed" trade agreements.

[49] At the time of writing, the negotiation of the FTAs with New Zealand, Chile and Mexico are concluded but the agreements have not yet been signed.

the Commission tried to take hold of (part) of its former exclusive powers on trade policy-making, a centralized competence that it enjoyed since the Treaty of Rome and was expanded with the Treaty of Lisbon.

However, in May 2018, the Council adopted a new approach on negotiating and concluding EU trade agreements, resulting mainly from the Court of Justice ruling, but also wary of the increasing engagement of new players in trade policy-making — not only civil society and NGOs, but also subnational entities. While the Commission tried to hold on to its authority and entrepreneurship on trade policy by splitting the agreements, the Council is reluctant to concede authority to the Commission, and insists it must establish what is covered in the EU-only deals. As such, in 2018 it decided that according to their content, the agreements with Mercosur, Mexico, and Chile should be "mixed", to abide by the 2017 CJEU ruling and to contain national and subnational contestation.

Despite that the Court ruling can be interpreted as distinguishing between core-trade liberalization issues and trade-related provisions as a criterion to assign EU-only competence and EU and member states 'mixed competence', a "grey area" on the distribution of competences remains (Conconi *et al.*, 2021), preventing the establishment of a clear pattern in the division of authority over trade. As mentioned above, the living nature of trade agreements suggests that future deals may have an even larger scope, incorporating new trade-related issues (such as in the area of culture), and encompassing new dimensions of human rights and labour standards, or new aspects of investment flows. This more encompassing agenda will further the dilemmas and debate over exclusive versus shared sovereignty.

3.3 Stop-gap solutions

Despite that in the EU-Mercosur Agreement member states, led by France, pushed for a mixed agreement to share trade sovereignty with the EU[50], the deal is being strongly contested by national and regional parliaments due to deforestation and environmental concerns, as well as trade protection issues. In a stance that is reminiscent of the 2016 rejection of CETA, Wallonia's Parliament already unanimously adopted a resolution rejecting the EU-Mercosur agreement (The Brussels Times 2020). In face of the apparent ratification difficulties, as the Agreement's 'mixity' may lengthen the

[50] France also wanted the EU Mexico agreement to be mixed (Politico 2022b).

ratification process in national and subnational parliaments, the EU Commission is now proposing to redesign and split the agreement, as it has been on hold since 2019. This suggests that the Commission is taking the opportunity to claw back its competence on the core trade issues of the Agreement, and to re-take into its hands its EU-exclusive competences. In the agreement with Mexico, the Commission is also proposing a split solution, to avoid national and subnational parliaments' shared sovereignty in core trade parts of the deal. These discussions mirror a 'tug of war' between the Commission and the member states on their sovereignty over the EU trade policy agenda, as it progressively expands beyond trade.

As progress on getting EU trade agreements into force has been stalled[51], the option for separate deals with a 'fast track' model of approval for core trade issues is gaining traction among member states (Politico 2022a). This is a move that deviates from the 2018 Council stated preference for mixed agreements, as key member states like Germany are now aligning with the Commission intention of drafting separate negotiating directives for EU-exclusive competences and for mixed investment agreements.[52] More importantly, these latest developments illustrate how the continual expansion in the scope of the Commission trade competences has led the EU to confront the shortcomings of its institutional arrangements, by adjusting to the new challenges through stop-gap measures, to address the evolving legal and political challenges of EU treaty-making. As Jones, Keleman and Meunier (2021, 1528) argue, as the nature of EU FTAs broadens, the issues of institutional competence on trade policy remain. The new plan of the Commission to create an additional protocol to the EU-Mercosur agreement containing supplementary environmental (non-binding) commitments, to satisfy national and subnational entities' concerns, are the latest example of those stop-gap measures trying to overcome the stalling free trade deal (Euractive 2022).

[51] The EU-Vietnam Agreement still needs to be ratified by 17 member states. CETA awaits ratification by 12 member states. Just recently the Irish Parliament did not ratify CETA as it considered that the agreement was unconstitutional on the grounds that the provisions on investor tribunals breached the judicial sovereignty of the state (The Irish Times, Nov. 2022).

[52] The Council Conclusions on the negotiation and conclusion of EU trade agreements state that it is for the Council to decide case by case whether to open negotiations on the basis of separate agreements, and that association agreements, depending on their content, should be mixed. They add that when separate agreements are necessary, investment agreements should be negotiated in parallel with FTAs.

One may argue that the expansion of trade agreements provisions beyond purely-trade issues highlights that sovereignty over trade agreements is actually different between the beginning and the end of the trade policy process. The Commission has delegated and centralized competence to negotiate trade agreements, and the member states have the competence to approve and ratify them. Put in other words, the Commission has the capacity and the entrepreneurial ability to initiate new trade agreements, but the authority to decide lies with the member states. This is a challenge for EU trade policy making and for the timely entry into force of trade agreements. As the German chancellor O. Scholz recently acknowledged, "it is a somewhat complicated idea that the EU has the competence for FTAs, and then all the parliaments of member states — sometimes regional governments — have to agree in order for a FTA to come into force" (Politico 2022a).[53]

In traditional trade agreements, with provisions that did not encroach on national and subnational competences, this divided authority did not entail legal or political risks at the subnational level, nor did it cause inter-institutional clashes (D'Erman 2020).[54] They are the "lowest level" of preferential trade agreements and do not raise issues of sovereignty, nor multilevel governance challenges (Bongardt and Torres 2017). The enlarged scope of second and third generation trade deals, with provisions that intrude on national and subnational competences, brings to the fore how these two types of competence over FTAs hamper the signature of trade deals and stall EU treaty-making, leading to stop-gap solutions often on a case by case basis

4. The end of EU "competence creep" over trade agreements?

Pollack's notion of EU "creeping competence" (1994, 2000) is particularly useful to interpret these two key changes in the multilevel politics of politics of FTAs. In his work Pollack argues that since the Treaty of Rome (1957) until the Maastricht Treaty (1992) the EU has substantially expanded its activities and the range of issue-areas over which it has competences. Then, he points out that this creeping centralization has slowed in the Maastricht era: while the EU retained active regulatory competences over an increasing

[53] Olaf Scholz's speech at the 13th German Mechanical Engineering Summit in Berlin, on state-business relations, in 11 Oct 2022. (Available at https://www.youtube.com/watch?v=eGnEBe9-bNE).

[54] Most past EU FTAs were mixed-competence agreements.

range of issue-areas, its competences over budgetary policies retrenched. Looking at EU policy-making in the area of trade, namely the EU's treaty--making competences, the evolution of EU competences over trade can be compared with Pollack's findings.

In the realm of commercial negotiations the locus of trade policy decisions transitioned from the national to EC level with the Treaty of Rome, and the Treaty of Lisbon expanded the EU authority to new trade policy issues, reinforcing its grip over other aspects of international trade, namely services, the commercial aspects if intellectual property and foreign direct investment. Therefore, the Treaty of Rome is a milestone in the delegation of trade competences to the EU, and the EU "creeping competence" over trade policy continued after Maastricht, with the Lisbon Treaty of 2007 actually expanding the scope of EU authority.

In the post-Lisbon era, the 2017 CJEU ruling on the EUSFTA regarding EU competences, which established shared competence between the Commission and the EU member states in specific issues, represents a transformative shift in the EU "creeping competence", as it cuts back EU exclusive trade competences. The ruling came at a time when subnational entities were already demanding a say in trade negotiations, and making the case for divided sovereignty with national authorities. They demanded participation in trade negotiations, and were also calling for national and subnational parliamentary ratification, given their concerns that the new provisions of trade agreements would increasingly constrain their constitutional powers. The increasingly comprehensive nature of trade agreements, with provisions on trade-related areas impinging upon national and subnational regulatory competences (environment, public health, public procurement), are the backdrop for the Court decision and the demands of subnational authorities, both pointing to a retrenchment in the EU trade centralized powers. The consequences of the CJEU ruling, coupled with the increased engagement of subnational authorities in trade policy emerge as two key factors underlying the change in the "creeping competence" of the EU over FTAs. Legally, the 2017 CJEU decision – the most recent legal landmark on the division of sovereignty over trade – shifts the "locus" of trade policy-making, as part of the deep trade agenda becomes subject to divided competences. Politically that shift is supported by subnational mobilization demanding shared competences.

Building on Pollack's (2000, 522) levels of autonomy progress across issue--areas, Table 5.1 pinpoints the evolution in authority between the EU and member states over trade policy since Rome to the Treaty of Lisbon, and the latest shift in trade sovereignty produced by the 2017 CJEU decision. While prior to the establishment of the EU integration project all trade policy decisions were taken in the national sphere (level of authority 1), the Treaty of Rome gave the Commission exclusive privilege on trade policy (level 4). This formal power of the EU, however, was only gradually transferred to the Commission — policy decisions on commercial negotiations were still taken both at national and European Community level (2) in 1968, and mostly at EC level (3) in 1970. According to the author, the Single Market Act (SMA) of 1992 brings increased powers to the EU. Given the implied exclusive external competences of the Commission, that gives it powers to conclude international agreements that include provisions that are already internally binding, the Single Market programme for deeper regulatory convergence indirectly contributed to the Commission's creeping trade authority (level 4). The Lisbon Treaty marks a defining institutional change in the Commission's external trade competences as it formally widens those competences to new issue-areas (level 5, the largest scope ever of trade authority under the Commission's remit). The CJEU Singapore verdict, in turn, represents a cutback in the Commission's trade authority (level 3), whereby most trade competences remain at the EU-level, but there is partial "decentralization" to national and subnational entities of the existing Commission authority to manage EU trade policy (*cf.* Pollack 2000).

The legal constraints but also the political backlash against trade centralization since the 2010's, though not threatening a complete retrenchment in the scope of centralized trade authority, is shifting the 'locus' of trade policy by relocating sovereignty over specific trade-related issues to the intersection between the Commission and the member states' authority.

Table 5.1 Levels of authority in trade policy[55]

Before 1957	1957	1968	1970	1992	2007	2017
	Treaty of Rome			Single Market Programme	Treaty of Lisbon	CJEU ruling on EU-Singapore FTA
1	4	2	3	4	5	3

Key: 1 = all competences at national level; 2 = competences at both national and EU level; 3 = most competences at EU level (EU-exclusive FTAs and mixed agreements on select issues); 4 = all competences at EU level; 5 = extended competences to EU level due larger scope of FTAs.
NB: Adapted from Pollack (2000) and updated by the author.

Furthermore, while in Pollack's (2000) findings the EU has retained its competences and is an active regulator in a wide range of regulatory issue-areas after Maastricht (Pollack 2000), in the realm of agreements on trade such creeping regulatory authority faces the resistance of subnational units. Taking the case of public services such as health or transport, in which subnational units preserve their competences, the EU regulatory powers are subject to the political and economic backlash by subnational entities. The expansion of trade-related regulatory provisions in the second and third generation agreements seems to have slowed the pace of the regulatory activeness of the EU in trade-related issues, as national and subnational entities question, and often contest, the regulatory approximation aims of these agreements, namely on social policies in which they have constitutionally granted competences.

Following the Court of Justice ruling, the Commission proposal to split trade agreements into EU-exclusive and 'mixed agreements' speaks of the Commission's efforts to hold on to its creeping trade competences in core trade liberalization measures, while it had to concede authority on selected trade-related issues. This move was intended to limit the contentiousness of deep trade agreements and avoid national and subnational vetoes to the ratification of all-inclusive trade deals. The stop-gap solutions that are being experimented by the Commission speak of the EU efforts to adjust to the

[55] Pollack's (2000) six level taxonomy considers also the category "only some competencies at EU level". As trade policy does not fit in this score, the levels of authority in trade policy were adapted to a 1-5 taxonomy.

deeper trade agenda, and to move trade liberalization forward, grounded on its dynamism and capacity for adaptability (Garben 2017). The bilateral non--legally binding and merely declaratory text negotiated with Brazil to address member states' environmental concerns with the Mercosur Agreement, best illustrate these efforts.

In the same line of Freudlsperger's (2021) "failing forward" argument, the difficulties at the subnational level to accept deeper trade agreements — stemming from the expansion of the EU trade agenda — lead to the necessity of "mixed" agreements. This shows that there are gaps in the EU-exclusive trade competence, as the CJEU judicial decision on the EUSFTA laid bare. The problems and (sometimes) the impossibility to ratify trade agreements in national and subnational parliaments may have lasting implications for EU trade policy-making (Jones, Keleman and Meunier 2022). While the splitting of trade agreements has implied a division of sovereignty between the EU and its member states (in mixed agreements) and, thus, a retrenchment in the EU "creeping competence" over trade, it may also be an opportunity for the EU to move its trade agenda forward. Similarly, ratification issues may create opportunities to negotiate agreements with deeper integration provisions (Freudlsperger 2021). This research confirms the "failing forward" conceptual framework by applying the argument to the latest evolution in the EU "creeping competence" over the trade policy agenda. Indeed, the splitting of trade agreements and the stop-gap measures, which respond to the increasing complexities in the ratification of trade deals, represent the EU legal adjustments and political adaptations to move the EU trade agenda forward.

5. Conclusion

The expansion of the scope and the deepening of EU trade agreements is an important driving force behind the transformative shifts in the locus of competences over trade policy. It brings to light the new nature and challenges of today's multilevel politics of trade, and the complexities of the split-level functioning of modern EU trade policy, where not only the national and supranational levels of government interact, but where the involvement of the subnational tier becomes key to ensure the implementation of ever more deep trade agreements.

While there are economic benefits from the trade liberalization and market-access provisions of FTAs, there are costs for EU trade policy-making of pursuing non-economic objectives (on human rights and forced labour, sustainable development, and in the future, due diligence). While EU market liberalization competences do not bring up debates on division of competences, the expansion in the scope of trade agreements to a plethora of trade--related dimensions is raising issues of sovereignty that *per se* are politically sensitive as they challenge sub-central competences. This has led subnational entities to demand to be part of the governance structure of EU trade policy, calling into question the EU delegated powers over trade policy.

In turn, both the CJEU decision stipulating that not all trade policy issues are under EU-exclusive competences, and the Commission response suggesting to separate deals in shared competence and EU-exclusive power agreements, have concurred for a backlash in the creeping powers of the EU over trade policy enshrined in the Treaty of Lisbon. The legal, as well as the political challenges to EU trade policy centralization, have led to stop-gap and case by case measures, which put to test the pattern of EU trade policy--making — that the Treaty of Rome had delegated to the EU and the Treaty of Lisbon had reinforced.

Drawing on Pollack's concept of EU "creeping competence", and bridging that notion with the "failing forward" argument, I conclude that in the realm of trade policy the continual expansion of competences has led the EU to confront the shortcomings of its institutional arrangements and to adjust to the new challenges. It does so by the splitting of trade agreements and by resorting to stop-gap measures, which facilitate the pursuit of its trade agenda. Therefore, the ongoing shifts in trade authority and its consequences for EU trade policy fit the "failing forward" framework of institutional change.

"Creeping competence" in trade has encountered legal constraints in the 2017 CJEU ruling, and involves political risks stemming from subnational entities' pushback to protect their competences, highlighting the unintended consequences unleashed by the dynamics of trade policy itself. In sum, both the ruling by the Court and the pushback of competences from subnational entities are constraining the expansion of the EU creeping centralization over the trade agenda 'beyond Lisbon', and are calling into question the future of EU-only trade agreements. Furthermore, the legal restraint imposed by the CJEU and the potential that the subnational contestation of the EU trade agenda will remain, will have a lasting impact on the EU's prospects of concluding deeper trade agreements at a time when trade deals are key elements of the EU's geopolitical interests, and trade policy is a crucial instrument to increase its global influence.

REFERENCES

Bollen Y., De Ville, F., and Gheyle, N. (2020), "From Nada to Namur: National Parliaments' Involvement in EU Trade Politics and the Case of Belgium", in: Broschek, J. and Goff, P. (eds.) *The multilevel politics of trade* (Vol. 59), pp. 256-78, Toronto: University of Toronto Press.

Bongardt, A. and Torres, F. (2017), "Comprehensive Trade Agreements: Conditioning Globalisation or Eroding the European Model?" *Intereconomics*, 52(3), pp. 165-170.

Broschek, J. (2021). "The federalization of trade politics in Switzerland, Germany and Austria", *Regional and Federal Studies* 33(1), pp. 91-112 doi: 10.1080/13597566.2021.1932829

Buonanno, L. (2017), "The New Trade Deals and the Mobilization of Civil Society Organizations: Comparing EU and US Responses", *Journal of European Integration*, 39(7), pp. 795-809.

Bursens, P. and De Bievre, D. (2021), "Seizing the moment: Regional opportunity structures and Wallonia's temporary veto of the EU – Canada bilateral trade agreement", *Regional and Federal Studies*, 33 (1), pp. 113-132, doi: 10.1080/13597566.2021.2007477

Carolan, M. (2022), "Ireland's proposed ratification of EU-Canada trade deal unconstitutional as Irish law stands, Supreme Court rules", *The Irish Times*, 11 November, available at https://www.irishtimes.com/search/?query=mercosur%20ratification

Court of Justice of the European Union (CJEU) (2017), Opinion 2/2015, Luxembourg City: CJEU.

Conceicao-Heldt, E. and Meunier, S. (eds.) (2017), *Speaking With a Single Voice: The EU as an effective actor in global governance?* New York: Routledge.

Conconi, P., Herghelegiu, C. and Puccio, L. (2021), "EU trade agreements: To mix or not to mix, that is the question", *Journal of World Trade*, 55(2), pp. 231-260.

De Brieve, D. and Poletti, A. (2020), Towards Explaining Varying Degrees of politicization of EU Trade Agreement Negotiations, *Politics and Governance*, 8(1), pp. 243-253.

De Ville, F. and Siles-Brugge, G. (2016), *TTIP: the truth about the transatlantic trade and investment partnership*, New York: Polity Press.

D'Erman, V. J. (2020), "Mixed competences and 'second generation' trade agreements: a consideration of EU disintegration", *Political Research Exchange*, 2:1, 1806003, doi:10.1080/2474736X.2020.1806003

Egan, M. and M.H. Guimarães (2022), "Trade contestation and regional politics: The case of Belgium and Germany", *Frontiers in Political Science*, doi: 10.3389/fpos.2022.962617

Eliasson, L.J. and Garcia-Duran, P. (2017), "Why TTIP is an unprecedented geopolitical game-changer, but not a Polanyian moment", *Journal of European Public Policy*, 24(10), pp.1522-33

Eschbach, A. (2015), *The Ratification Process in EU Member States*, Cologne: Institute for Comparative Public Law.

Eurobarometer (2019), "European's attitudes on trade and trade policy", *Report on the Special Barometer 491*, Brussels: European Comission.

Freudlsperger, C. (2021), "Failing forward in the Common Commercial Policy? Deep trade and the perennial question of EU competence", *Journal of European Public Policy* 28(10), pp. 1650-1668.

Freudlsperger, C. (2020), *Trade Policy in Multilevel Government*: Organizing Openness, Oxford: Oxford University Press.

Garben, S. (2019), Competence Creep Revisited, *Journal of Commons Market Studies*, 57(2), pp. 205–222.

Garcia, M. (2020), "Multilevel Politics of Trade in the European Union in the Aftermath of the Lisbon Treaty", in Jorg Broschek and Patricia Goff (eds.) *The Multilevel Politics of Trade: Configurations, Patterns and Dynamics*, Toronto: University of Toronto Press.

Guimaraes, M.H. (1995), *Policymaking in Multidimensional Trade Negotiations: Testing a 'Modified Liberal Model', Trade-Related Aspects of Intellectual Property Rights in the Uruguay Round*, PhD Dissertation, University of Cincinnati, USA.

Hope, Alana (2020), "Wallonia votes against EU trade pact with Mercosur countries", *The Brussels Times*, 6 February, available at https://www.brusselstimes.com/93770/wallonia-votesagainst-eu-trade-pact-with-mercosur-countries-brazil-argentina-uruguay-paraguayagriculture-environment.

Jones, E., Kelemen R. D. and Meunier, S. (2021), Failing forward? Crises and patterns of European integration, *Journal of European Public Policy*, 28(10), pp. 1519-1536.

Kersschot, M., Kerremans, B. and De Bievre, D. (2020), "Principals and transceivers: regional authorities in EU trade negotiations", *Political Research Exchange* 2 (1) 1714454, doi: 10.1080/2474736X.2020.1714454.

Leblond, P. and Viju-Miljusevic, C. (2019), "EU trade policy in the twenty first century: change, continuity and challenges", *Journal of European Public Policy*, 26(12), pp. 1836-1846.

Meunier, S. and Morin, J.F. (2015), "No agreement is an island: Negotiating TTIP in a dense regime complex", in J.F. Morin, T. Novotna, F. Ponjaert, and M. Telo, *The Politics of Transatlantic Trade Negotiations, TTIP in a Globalized World*, New York: Routledge, pp. 196-209.

Politico (2022), "Brussels looks to evade EU capitals to get Mercosur deal done", available at: https://www.politico.eu/article/brussels-eu-commission-grab-trade-power-mercosur-deal.

Politico (2022a), "Brussels launches power grab to fast-track EU trade deals", available at: https://www.politico.eu/article/eu-tries-to-grab-power-back-on-trade-deals.

Pollack, M. A. (2000), "The end of creeping competence? EU policy-making since Maastricht", *JCMS: Journal of Common Market Studies, 38*(3), pp. 519-538.

Pollack, M. A. (1994), Creeping Competence: The Expanding Agenda of the European Community, *Journal of Public Policy*, 14(2) pp. 95-14.

Struna, Hugo, Messad, Paulo (2022), "Brazilian Elections: Lula's victory to revive EU--Mercosur agreement", *Euractive*, available at https://www.euractiv.com/section/economy-jobs/news/brazilian-elections-lulas-victory-to-revive-eu-mercosur-agreement/.

Tatham, M. (2018), "The Rise of Regional Influence in the EU — From Soft Policy Lobbying to Hard Vetoing", *Journal of Common Market Studies*, 56(3), pp. 672–686.

Van Loon, A. (2020), The Selective Politicization of Transatlantic Trade Negotiations *Politics and Governance*, 8(1), pp. 325–335, doi: 10.17645/pag.v8i1.2608.

Woolcock, S. (2010), "The Treaty of Lisbon and the European Union as an actor in international trade", ECIPE Working Paper, No. 01/2010, Brussels: ECIPE.

Young, A. (2019), "Two wrongs make a right? The politicization of trade policy and European trade strategy", Journal of European Public Policy, 26(12), pp. 1883-1899. doi: 10.1080/13501763.2019.1678055.

CHAPTER 6
THE LEGAL NATURE OF NEW GENERATION FREE TRADE AGREEMENTS: LESSONS FROM THE CETA SAGA[56]

Francisco Pereira Coutinho

Abstract: The Comprehensive Economic and Trade Agreement (CETA) is a "new generation" bilateral "mixed" free trade agreement signed on 30 October 2016 between Canada and the European Union alongside its Member States. In the European Union, "mixed" trade agreements follow an adoption procedure that determines, in the best-case scenario, a substantial delay to their entry into force, and, in the worst, a veto by Member States that damages the international standing of the European Union. The European Commission bowed to Member States' pressure and decided to qualify CETA as a "mixed agreement" instead of an "EU-only agreement". That the "guardian of the Treaties" had no constitutional leeway on the choice of CETA's approval form became clear after the decision of the Court of Justice on the free trade agreement negotiated between the European Union and Singapore (Opinion 2/15). CETA's "mixed" nature determines that its application is limited and provisional, and under a permanent Damocles sword existential threat.

Keywords: Canada; CETA; Court of Justice; European Union; Mixed Agreements.

1. Heading Towards a Vetocracy?

The European Union emerged in the middle of the twentieth century as an economic federal union of States (Forsyth 1982, 5). Negotiating and

[56] This article builds on Pereira Coutinho (2018). All websites accessed on 1 November 2022. Judicial rulings referred without indication of source should be presumed as originating from the Court of Justice (of the European Union).

adopting free trade agreements remains one of its *raisons d'être*. Contrary to Boris Johnson's claim that the post-Brexit United Kingdom would be easily "striking free trade deals around the world" (Rayner 2020), the negotiating power of a State, even a G7 member, is pale in comparison to the world largest economy. Ever since the Rome Treaty (1957) granted the European Economic Community *ius tractandi* (Article 113), dozens of international agreements were concluded with third countries and international organisations.[57] The importance of international agreements for the European economy cannot be overstated: about 31 million jobs in the Union (1/7 of the total) are, directly or indirectly, linked to external commerce (Rueda-Cantuche and Sousa 2016, 1).

The Lisbon Treaty substantially enlarged the legal capacity of the Union to adopt "new generation" bilateral free trade agreements (Cremona 2017); *i.e.* "a trade agreement which contains, in addition to the classical provisions on the reduction of customs duties and of non-tariff barriers to trade in goods and services", provisions that reflect new trends of contemporary international law, "such as intellectual property protection, investment, public procurement, competition and sustainable development" (Court of Justice 2017, §17).[58]

The Comprehensive Economic and Trade Agreement (CETA) is an example of a "new generation" bilateral free trade agreement signed on 30 October 2016 between Canada, on one part, and the European Union and the Member States, on the other part. It is estimated to increase bilateral trade by more than 23 per cent and an annual growth of 12 billion Euro of the Union's GDP.[59]

In stark contrast with the political bonhomie that usually encircles the conclusion of free trade agreements, CETA is being fiercely challenged by anti-globalization movements, which contend that it promotes a dilution of social, environmental, and public health standards in Europe, and is a trojan horse for big corporations to forfeit the jurisdiction of national

[57] The complete list can be found here: https://eur-lex.europa.eu/browse/directories/inter-agree.html.

[58] Opinion 2/15, 16 May 2017, *Free Trade Agreement between the European Union and the Republic of Singapore*, ECLI:EU:C:2017:376, §17.

[59] European Commission, "EU-Canada agree deal to boost trade and investment", *Memo*, 26 September 2014, available at http://europa.eu/rapid/press-release_MEMO-14-542_en.htm. Since September 2017, CETA's provisional application triggered a substantial increase in the trade of goods and services between Canada and the EU. See https://carleton.ca/tradenetwork/an-overview-of-canada-eu-trade-performance/.

courts (Foodwatch 2022). Such a public outcry transformed the negotiation, approval, and ratification of CETA into an unprecedented saga of the Union's Common Commercial Policy (CCP).

On 28 June 2017, the President of the European Commission, Jean-Claude Juncker, informed the Heads of State and Government of the Member States that it would be seeking CETA's approval as an "EU-only agreement" (Vicenti 2017) — *i.e.*, an agreement to be adopted solely by the Union and Canada, as its provisions fell under legal basis granting exclusive external competence to the Union.

This initiative met staunch resistance. Several representatives of European affairs national parliament commissions declared, under the political dialogue mechanism, that CETA needed national ratification, as it "contains provisions that concern policy areas which are within the competences of the Member States".[60] The same perspective was taken by national ministers for commerce in the Council.[61]

The pressure paid off with the Commission announcing on 5 July 2017 that CETA would after all be submitted to the Council as a "mixed agreement".[62]According to Commissioner Cecilia Malmström, this was a political stance:

> From a strict legal standpoint, the Commission considers this agreement to fall under exclusive EU competence. However, the political situation in the Council is clear, and we understand the need for proposing it as a «mixed» agreement, in order to allow for a speedy signature.[63]

[60] "Letter to Mr De Gucht — Role of national Parliaments in free trade agreements", 26 June 2014, available at http://www.ipex.eu/IPEXL-WEB/scrutiny/COM20140153/huors.do. See also the position of the German *Bundestag* [*Drucksache* 18/8072, 12 April 2016, "Die transatlantischen Beziehungen zukunftsfest weiterentwickeln", available at http://dip21.bundestag.de/dip21/btd/18/080/1808072.pdf, §9], or the French National Assembly [Résolution Européenne sur le projet d'accord économique et commercial entre l'Union européenne et le Canada", Texto No 428 ("Petite Loi"), Ordinary Session 2014/2015, 23 November 2014, available at http://www.assemblee--nationale.fr/14/ta/ta0428.asp, §1].

[61] Foreign Affairs Council (Commerce), 8737/16, Meeting No. 3463, 13 May 2016, available at http://www.consilium.europa.eu/pt/meetings/fac/2016/05/12-13/.

[62] *Proposal on the signing on behalf of the European Union of the Comprehensive Economic and Trade Agreement between Canada of the one part, and the European Union and its Member States, of the other part,* 5 July 2016, COM (2016) 444 Final, at 4.

[63] European Commission — Press Release, *European Commission proposes signature and conclusion of EU-Canada trade deal,* 5 July 2016, available at https://ec.europa.eu/commission/presscorner/detail/en/IP_16_2371.

"Mixed agreements" are international agreements which, for legal or political reasons, are jointly adopted by the Union and by all or some of its Member States with one or several third States and/or international organisations (Schermers 1983, 25). They serve pragmatic purposes:[64] beyond avoiding constitutional questions related to the delimitation of vertical external competences (Maresceau 2010, 12–13; Eeckout 2011, 221; Möldner 2011, §5), "mixed agreements" provide Member States greater visibility in the international relations (Rosas 2000, 201; Schütze 2011, §17), preventing at the same time the "freezing" of the Union's competences.[65]

Taking the "mixed path" for the approval of an international agreement is not without consequences. While a "EU-only agreement" is ratified, usually in a few months, after being approved by a simple majority in the European Parliament and by a qualified majority in the Council,[66] the entry into force of a "mixed agreement" requires national ratification. It is estimated that CETA requires the approval of thirty-eight national and regional parliaments (Kleimann and Kübek 2016, 1; Silva Pereira 2017, 187). Even referenda cannot be excluded: a consultative referendum was called in the Netherlands on the ratification of the (mixed) association agreement between the EU and Ukraine.[67]

[64] Advocate-General Eleanor Sharpston, C-240/09, 15 July 2010, *Lesoochranárske zoskupenie VLK*, ECLI:EU:C:2010:436, §56.

[65] Baere (2014, 738), which argues that a precise delimitation of competences between the Union and the Member States could hinder the development of the Union's constitutional order.

[66] Article 218(8)(§1) TFEU. Unanimity is necessary: *i)* when the agreement covers a field for which unanimity is required for the adoption of a Union act (Article 218(8)(2§) TFEU); *ii)* in association agreements (Articles 217 and 218(8)(2§) TFEU); *iii)* in agreements that establish an economic, financial and technical cooperation with accession candidate countries (Articles 212 and 218(8)(2§) TFEU); *iv)* in the agreement on accession of the Union to the European Convention for the Protection of Human Rights and Fundamental Freedoms (Article 6(2) TEU and Article 218(8)(2§) TFEU); *v)* in agreements in the fields of trade in services and the commercial aspects of intellectual property, as well as foreign direct investment, whenever such agreements include provisions for which unanimity is required for the adoption of internal rules (Article 207(4)(2§) TFEU); *vi)* in agreements in the field of trade in cultural and audiovisual services, where these agreements risk prejudicing the Union's cultural and linguistic diversity (Article 207(4)(3§)(a) TFEU); *vii)* in agreements in the field of trade in social, education and health services, where these agreements risk seriously disturbing the national organization of such services and prejudicing the responsibility of Member States to deliver them (Article 207(4)(3§)(b) TFEU).

[67] On 6 April 2016, 61,1% of voters rejected the agreement. Although the electoral turnout of 32% was less than what it was required for a binding result (30%), the Dutch Parliament ratified the agreement after the Dutch Government obtained clarifications on its interpretation from the other Member States (Van der Loo 2017a).

CETA showcases that the spectre of the Union becoming a vetocracy in what regards the approval of "mixed agreements" is all but real. Although subjected to qualified majority under Article 207(4)(§1) TFEU,[68] CETA's signature approval by the Council was threatened by Bulgaria and Romania for domestic reasons related to visa entry requirements of their citizens into Canada (Gotev 2017),[69] and more notoriously in Belgium, by the veto of the Walloon parliament.[70] By October 2022, six years after signature and five years after a provisional application which began on 21 September 2017 (Article 30.7.3), CETA had been ratified by only sixteen Member States.[71] CETA's current application is limited to the parts of the agreement falling within the competence of the Union,[72] and (indefinitely) pending on the completion of national ratification procedures. CETA must be ratified by every Member State before it will come fully and permanently into force. In another words, *definitive* failure of ratification in one Member State determines the termination of the agreement:

> If the ratification of CETA fails permanently and definitively because of a ruling of a constitutional court, or following the completion of other

[68] See, however, Kempen (2016, 11), which contends that CETA had to be approved by the Council by unanimity, as it constitutes "a step backwards in Union Law as regards the liberalisation of the movement of capital to or from third countries" (Article 64(3) TFEU), and because it discriminates against EU citizens.

[69] The threat paid off with the Canadian Government promising to implement a visa waiver by December 2017 (Novinite, 2017).

[70] In the Byzantine Belgium constitutional system, the federal Government requires consent from five regional parliaments to decide on the signature and approval of international agreements in the Council (Economist, 2016a). On 14 October 2016, the Parliament of Wallonia rejected granting federal authorization for the signature of CETA ("Projet de motion déposé en conclusion du débat sur les projets de Traité CETA et de Déclaration interprétative du traité, en application de l'article 70 du Règlement, par Mmes Zrihen, Simonet et Ryckmans (Doc. 605 (2016-2017) n.° 1), C.R.A. No 3 (2016-2017), 14 October 2016, available at http://nautilus.parlement-wallon.be/Archives/2016_2017/CRA/cra3.pdf]. This stance was reversed two weeks later after the federal Government's pledge of submitting a request to the Court of Justice on the validity of CETA's Investor-State dispute settlement system ["Motion déposée en conclusion du débat sur l'Accord économique et commercial global (AECG-CETA)", 633 (2016-2017), No. 3, 28 October 2017, available at http://www.dirittounioneeuropea.eu/images/Mozione_Parlamento_Vallone.pdf].

[71] See CETA ratification tracker, available at https://carleton.ca/tradenetwork/research-publications/ceta-ratification-tracker/.

[72] Recital 4 of Council Decision (EU) 2017/38 of 28 October 2016. The provisional application of CETA does not include matters listed in the "Notice concerning the provisional application of the Comprehensive Economic and Trade" (*JO*, 16 September 2017, L 238/9).

> constitutional processes and formal notification by the government of the concerned state, provisional application must be and will be terminated.[73]

This chapter aims at ascertaining whether CETA *had* to be adopted as a "mixed agreement", or whether the European Commission was entitled to present it for approval as an "EU-only agreement". I will argue that this is a constitutional question pertaining to the division of competences between the Union and the Member States not subjected to the political will of the "guardian of the Treaties" (section two). In light of the case law of the Court of Justice, CETA had to be approved as a "mixed agreement" as it includes subject-matters falling within shared competences of the Union and the Member States (section three). Adopting CETA as a "mixed" bilateral free trade agreement determines, at best, a substantial delay on its entry into force, and, at worst, a veto to its ratification that will severely damage the international standing of the European Union. I will finish with an analysis of the solutions that could be pursued to prevent and mitigate a definitive refusal of ratification of CETA by a Member State (section four).

2. The European Union's *Ius Tractandi*

2.1. General Remarks

The European Union participates in international relations through the conclusion of agreements with third States and international organisations. The principle of conferral restricts the legal capacity of the Union to the adoption of agreements based on external competences bestowed upon it by the Member States (Article 5(2) TEU). According to Article 216(1) TFEU, the European Union may pursue international agreements in four

[73] Declaration 20 (Statement of the Council regarding the Termination of Provisional Application of CETA), *Comprehensive Economic and Trade Agreement (CETA) between Canada, of the one part, and the European Union and its Member States, of the other part — Statements to the Council minutes*, 13463 REV 1, 27 October 2016, Brussels, at 14. See also the German Federal Constitutional Court decision of 13 October 2016, 2 BvR 1368/16, 2 BvR 1444/16, 2 BvR 1823/16, 2 BvR 1482/16, 2 BvE 3/16, triggered by a constitutional complaint of 193.086 citizens, that declared that Germany has the power to terminate provisional application in its territory of CETA's provisions covered by the sphere of competences of the Member States through the written notification referred to in Article 30.7(3)(c) CETA.

circumstances: i) where the Treaties so provide; ii) where the conclusion of an agreement is necessary in order to achieve, within the framework of the Union's policies, one of the objectives referred to in the Treaties; iii) where it is provided for in a legally binding Union act; iv) where it is likely to affect common rules or alter their scope.

The *ius tractandi* of the Member States remains intact concerning external competences not conferred upon the Union (Article 4(1) TEU). This means that an international agreement concluded by the Member States and/or by the Union with third States and/or with other international legal persons may either be: i) an "EU-only agreement", when adopted solely by the Union; ii) a "national-only agreement", when adopted solely by Member States; iii) a "mixed agreement", when adopted jointly by the Union and its Member States. Ascertaining whether the EU may conclude an international agreement or whether it needs its Member States is thus a constitutional question related to the nature of a given external competence (2.2.), and to the scope of the treaty legal basis chosen for the conclusion of the international agreement (2.3.).

2.2. The External Competence of the Union

2.2.1. Exclusive Competence

Whenever the Union is granted an exclusive competence, Member States are, in the domestic realm, prevented from unilaterally enacting binding legal instruments, and, externally, from concluding international agreements without the Union's approval (Article 2(1) TFEU).

Article 3(1) TFEU portrays an exhaustive list of exclusive competence domains of the Union. Among them is the CCP, which is a rare example of a purely external competence of the Union.[74]

The exclusivity of an external competence conferred upon the Union may stem explicitly from Article 3(1) TFEU (*a priori* exclusive competences) or from the fulfilment of one of the conditions set forth in Article 3(2) TFEU: the Union has an (implicit) exclusive external competence to adopt international agreements when the conclusion of an international agreement is provided for in a legislative act of the Union, is necessary to enable the Union to

[74] General-Advocate Eleanor Sharpston, Opinion 2/15, 21 December 2016, *Free Trade Agreement between the European Union and the Republic of Singapore*, ECLI:EU:C:2016:992, §63.

exercise its internal competence, and so far as such a conclusion may affect common rules or alter their scope.

The Union has an exclusive competence to conclude international agreements in four circumstances: i) when such a possibility is provided for in the Treaties (first situation provided for in Article 216(1) TFEU); ii) when, according to the principle of complementarity, the conclusion of the international agreement "is necessary in order to achieve, within the framework of the Union's policies, one of the objectives referred to in the Treaties" (second situation provided for in Article 216(1) TFEU) in one of the Union's exclusive competences set forth in Article 3(1) TFEU, or when an internal competence cannot be exercised by the Union without the recognition of an external competence (second situation provided for in Article 3(2) TFEU); iii) when the *ius tractandi* of the Union is provided for in a legislative act of the Union (third situation provided for in Article 216(1) TFEU and first situation provided for in Article 3(2) TFEU);[75] iv) when the conclusion of an international agreement affects common rules or alters their scope (fourth situation provided for in Article 216(1) TFEU and third situation provided for in Article 3(2) TFEU).

The exclusivity of the Union's *ius tractandi* frequently stems from the internal exercise of a shared competence. According to Article 4(1) TFEU, the Union shares competences with the Member States where the Treaties confer upon it a competence which does not relate to an exclusive (Article 3 TFEU) or supporting (Article 6 TFEU) competence. The shared nature of the competence implies that it may be exercised either by the Union or by the Member States. The principle of pre-emption determines, however, that if the Union decides to exercise a shared competence, Member States can no longer exercise that competence (Article 2(2) TFEU). This means that from that moment on, the Union acquires a *de facto* exclusive competence.

Pre-emption covers the elements governed "by the Union act in question and therefore does not cover the whole area".[76] Pre-emption is, moreover, temporary: Member States shall again exercise their competence to the extent that the Union has decided to cease exercising its competence concerning a specific part of a shared competence (Article 2(2) TFEU).

[75] A legislative act is, according to Article 289(3) TFEU, a legal act adopted through a legislative procedure.

[76] Protocol No. 25 TFEU on the Exercise of Shared Competence (*OJ*, 115, 9 May 2008, at 307).

The recognition to the Union of an implicit exclusive external competence to conclude international agreements derives directly from the principles of primacy and sincere cooperation, as an independent external action of the Member States could affect the application of common rules adopted internally by the Union. To avoid the latter scenario, the Court of Justice developed the "ERTA doctrine": the exercise by the Union of an exclusive internal competence determines the automatic recognition of an external competence (parallelism of competences principle (*in foro interno, in foro externo*)).[77] The "ERTA effect" is triggered whenever there is a risk that common EU rules might be adversely affected by international commitments adopted by the Member States.[78] Such a finding does not presuppose that the areas covered by the international commitments and those covered by the EU rules coincide fully, being enough that those commitments fall within an area which is already largely covered by such rules.[79] Such an assessment must be based not only on the scope of the rules in question but also on their nature and content, as well as take into account not only the current state of EU law in the area in question but also its future development, insofar as that is foreseeable at the time of that analysis.[80]

2.2.2 Shared Competence

Beyond shared competences subjected to pre-emption (*stricto sensu* shared competences), the TFEU recognizes as *latu sensu* shared competences: i) parallel or irregular competences, which cover the fields of research,

[77] 22/70, 31 March 1971, *AETR*, ECLI:EU:C:1971:32, §§12-19.

[78] C-114/12, 4 September 2014, *Commission v. Council*, EU:C:2014:2151, §68; Opinion 1/13, 14 October 2014, *Convention on the civil aspects of international child abduction*, EU:C:2014:2303, §71; or Opinion 3/15, 14 February 2017, *Marrakesh Treaty to Facilitate Access to Published Works for Persons who are Blind, Visually Impaired or Otherwise Print Disabled*, EU:C:2017:114, §105.

[79] Opinion 2/91, 19 March 1993, *Convention Nº 170 of the International Labour Organization concerning safety in the use of chemicals at work*, ECLI:EU:C:1993:106, §§25-26; Opinion 1/03, 7 February 2006, *Competence of the Community to conclude the new Lugano Convention on jurisdiction and the recognition and enforcement of judgments in civil and commercial matters*, EU:C:2006:81, §126; C-114/12, *Commission v. Council*, EU:C:2014:2151, §§69-70; Opinion 1/13, 14 October 2014, *Convention on the civil aspects of international child abduction*, §§72-73; or Opinion 3/15, 14 February 2017, *Marrakesh Treaty to Facilitate Access to Published Works for Persons who are Blind, Visually Impaired or Otherwise Print Disabled*, EU:C:2017:114, §§106-107.

[80] Opinion 2/91, *Convention Nº 170 of the International Labour Organization concerning safety in the use of chemicals at work*, ECLI:EU:C:1993:106, §25; Opinion 1/03, 7 February 2006, *Competence of the Community to conclude the new Lugano Convention on jurisdiction and the recognition and enforcement of judgments in civil and commercial matters*, ECLI:EU:C:2006:81, §126.

technological development and space, development cooperation and humanitarian aid (Article 4(3) and (4) TFEU), in which the Union lacks pre-emption; ii) supporting competences listed in Article 6, in which the Union can only carry out actions to support, coordinate or supplement the action of the Member States, which can take the form of legal binding acts as long as they do not affect the competence of the Member States, and do not entail harmonisation of Member States' laws or regulations (Article 2(5) TFEU); iii) the competence to define and implement a common foreign and security policy, including the progressive framing of a common defence policy (Article 2(4) TFEU), which does not include the adoption of legislative acts (Article 24 (2)(2§) TEU), and does not affect the competences of each Member State to formulate and conduct its own external policy.[81]

The shared nature of a competence subjected to pre-emption (*stricto sensu*) which has not yet been exercised internally by the Union pursuant to Article 3(2) TFEU cannot be used to base the adoption of an "EU-only agreement". The same does not hold true regarding shared external competences not subjected to pre-emption, which cover domains that do not prevent the Union nor the Member States from exercising in tandem their *ius tractandi*, as long as they respect the reciprocal obligations stemming from the principle of sincere cooperation (Klamert 2014, 163–171).

The exercise of a shared external competence by the Union can be based: i) on Treaty provisions that foresee such a competence (first situation provided for in Article 216(1) TFEU);[82] ii) be "necessary in order to achieve, within the framework of the Union's policies, one of the objectives referred to in the Treaties" in shared competence domains (second situation provided for in Article 216(1) TFEU); or iii) be based in a legally binding act of a non-legislative nature (third situation provided for in Article 216(1) TFEU)

[81] Declarations 13 and 14 concerning the common foreign and security policy mention, in this regard, that the provisions in the TEU covering the Common Foreign and Security Policy "do not affect the responsibilities of the Member States, as they currently exist, for the formulation and conduct of their foreign policy nor of their national representation in third countries and international organisations", and "do not prejudice the specific character of the security and defence policy of the Member States".

[82] E.g., in the domains of: i) the common foreign and security policy (Article 37 TEU); *ii)* the cooperation with third countries and the competent international organisations in the field of education and sport, in particular the Council of Europe (Article 166(3) TFEU), culture, in particular with the Council of Europe (Article 167(3) TFEU), and public health (Article 168(3) TFEU); *iii)* research, technological development and space (Article 186 TFEU), cooperation (Article 209(2) and 212(3) TFEU) and humanitarian aid (Article 214(4) TFEU).

or a legislative act that foresees the conclusion of international agreements in parallel competence domains (research, technological development and space, development cooperation and humanitarian aid) (third situation provided for in Article 216(1) TFEU and Article 4(3) and (4) TFEU).[83]

2.3. Choosing a Legal Basis

The principle of conferral mandates the Union to explicitly base the exercise of a competence to conclude an international agreement in a Treaty provision (legal basis).[84] Determining the scope of a Treaty legal basis is, therefore, a condition to ascertain whether the Union alone has the competence to conclude an international agreement or whether such competence is shared with the Member States.[85]

According to the Court of Justice, the choice of a legal basis for the conclusion of an international agreement must rest on objective factors that are amenable to judicial review, including the aim and content of the agreement.[86] Whenever doubts arise on which treaty legal basis should be adopted, the Luxembourg court follows the "centre of gravity" theory: if the examination of the agreement reveals that it pursues more than one purpose or that it includes two or more components, and if one of those is identifiable as the main or predominant purpose or component, whereas the other is merely incidental, that agreement must be based on a single legal basis, namely that required by the main or predominant purpose or component.[87] If the international agreement includes, both as regards the aims pursued and its

[83] Advocate-General Eleanor Sharpston, Opinion 2/15, 21 December 2016, *Free Trade Agreement between the European Union and the Republic of Singapore*, ECLI:EU:C:2016:992, footnote 24.

[84] Opinion 2/00, 6 December 2001, *Cartagena Protocol*, EU:C:2001:664, §22.

[85] Opinion 1/08, 30 November 2009, *Conclusion of agreements in the context of the General Agreement on Trade in Services (GATS)*, EU:C:2009:739, §112.

[86] C-137/12, 22 October 2013, *Commission v. Council*, EU:C:2013:675, §52; C-263/14, 14 June 2016, *Parlament v. Council*, ECLI:EU:C:2016:435, §43.

[87] C-137/12, *Commission v. Council*, EU:C:2013:675, §53. In this case, the Court of Justice declared that the decision to approve the international agreement on the legal protection of services pursued "an objective that has a specific connection to the common commercial policy, which means that, for the purposes of the adoption of that decision, Article 207(4) TFEU, together with Article 218(5) TFEU, must be cited as the legal basis and which also means that the signing of the Convention on behalf of the European Union falls within the exclusive competence of the European Union, pursuant to Article 3(1)(e) TFEU. By contrast, the improvement of the conditions for the functioning of the internal market is an ancillary objective of that decision that provides no justification for its adoption on the basis of Article 114 TFEU" (idem, §76).

contents, two indissociably linked purposes or components, neither of which can be regarded as secondary or indirect as compared with the other, the decision of the Union approving that agreement should be based on the corresponding legal basis.[88]

3. The Competence of the European Union to Approve CETA

3.1. The Common Commercial Policy

The CCP is an exclusive external competence of the Union based on the "conclusion of tariff and trade agreements relating to trade in goods and services" (Articles 3(1)(e) and 207(1) TFEU). The Lisbon Treaty broadened the scope of the CCP through the inclusion, in Article 207(1) TFEU, of references to the protection of foreign direct investment and to commercial aspects of intellectual property. This material enlargement had immediate effects in the case law of the Court of Justice: if before the entry into force of the Lisbon Treaty, the European Community was not entitled to adopt TRIPS (*Trade Related Aspects of Intellectual Property*) as an "EU-only agreement",[89] afterwards that agreement was considered to fall within the CCP.[90]

May then Article 207(1) TFEU be exclusively invoked for the conclusion of CETA? If not, can CETA still be approved as an "EU-only agreement" based also on exclusive implicit competences?

Since CETA "has identical objectives and essentially the same contents as the Free Trade Agreement with Singapore (EUSFTA)", and therefore the Union's competence is the same in both cases,[91] the answer to these questions can be found in the opinion of the Court of Justice concerning the bilateral free trade agreement concluded with Singapore (Opinion 2/2015).[92]

[88] C-94/03, 10 January 2006, *Commission v. Council*, EU:C:2006:2, §51; C-263/14, 14 June 2016, *Parlament v. Council*, ECLI:EU:C:2016:435, §44.

[89] Opinion 1/94, 15 November 1994, *Competence of the Community to conclude international agreements concerning services and the protection of intellectual property*, ECLI:EU:C:1994:384, §§98 and 105.

[90] C-414/11, 18 July 2013, *Daiichi*, ECLI:EU:C:2013:520, §61.

[91] *Proposal on the signing on behalf of the European Union of the Comprehensive Economic and Trade Agreement between Canada of the one part, and the European Union and its Member States, of the other part*, 5 July 2016, COM (2016) 444 Final, at 4.

[92] Opinion 2/15, 17 May 2017, *Free Trade Agreement between the European Union and the Republic of Singapore*, ECLI:EU:C:2017:376.

Although it did not use of the "centre of gravity" theory (3.1.1.), the Court of Justice considered that almost the entirety of EUSFTA provisions were comprised within the exclusive competence of the Union (3.1.2.). In the shared competence with the Union were only included the provisions regarding portfolio investments and the investor-State dispute settlement mechanism (3.1.3).

3.1.1. The "Centre of Gravity" Theory

Without surprise, as even the European Commission recognized that provisions concerning cross-border transport services and non-direct foreign investment do not fall within the CCP,[93] the Court of Justice did not apply the "centre of gravity" theory in Opinion 2/2015, thereby assuming that EUSFTA is an agreement that pursues several purposes and has multiple components, neither of which can be identifiable as the main or predominant and the others merely as incidental or having a very limited scope.

The Luxembourg court recognized as autonomous components of EUSFTA: i) the provisions falling within the CCP; ii) the provisions that liberalize transport services between the EU and Singapore, which fall within the transport policy; iii) the provisions concerning non-direct foreign investment, which fall within the free movement of capital provisions of the TFEU.

3.1.2. Exclusive Competence of the European Union

The main conclusion to draw from Opinion 2/15 is that the Union is competent to negotiate and adopt "new generation" free trade agreements as "EU-only agreements".

The Court of Justice considered that almost the entirety of EUSFTA provisions fall within the CCP, and therefore are included in the exclusive competence of the Union (Article 3(1) TFEU and first situation provided for in Article 216 (1) TFEU). This is the result of the amendments introduced in Article 207(1) TFEU by the Lisbon Treaty, and from a broad jurisprudential interpretation of the exclusive CCP's external competence of the Union, according to which an international agreement provision falls within the CCP whenever it relates specifically to international trade, "in that it is essentially intended to promote, facilitate or govern trade and has direct and

[93] Idem, §§14 and 16.

immediate effects on trade", not being enough the mere fact that "is liable to have implications for international trade".[94]

A specific connection to international trade was found in provisions of EUSFTA concerning: i) market access for goods[95] (Chapters 3 to 6); ii) non--tariff barriers to trade and investment in renewable energy generation[96] (Chapter 7); iii) trade in services (Chapter 8), with the exception of supply of services in the field of transport, which is excluded from the CCP by Article 207(5) TFEU;[97] iv) the protection of foreign direct investment (section A of Chapter 9);[98] v) public procurement (Chapter 10);[99] vi) intellectual property (Chapter 11);[100] vii) competition (Chapter 12);[101] viii) sustainable development (Chapter 13),[102] thereby proving that the CCP is not confined

[94] C-414/11, *Daiichi*, ECLI:EU:C:2013:520, §51; C-137/12, 22 October 2013, *Commission v. Council*, EU:C:2013:675, §57; Opinion 3/15, 14 February 2017, *Marrakesh Treaty to Facilitate Access to Published Works for Persons who are Blind, Visually Impaired or Otherwise Print Disabled*, EU:C:2017:114, §61.

[95] Opinion 2/15, 17 May 2017, *Free Trade Agreement between the European Union and the Republic of Singapore*, ECLI:EU:C:2017:376, §§40-48.

[96] Idem, §§72-74.

[97] Idem, §53-57. The Court upheld the case law according to which provisions that cover the four modes of supply of services that follow the classification used by the World Trade Organization (WTO) fall within the CCP (Opinion 1/08, 30 November 2009, *Conclusion of agreements in the context of the General Agreement on Trade in Services (GATS)*, EU:C:2009:739, §§4, 118 and 119).

[98] Opinion 2/15, 17 May 2017, *Free Trade Agreement between the European Union and the Republic of Singapore*, ECLI:EU:C:2017:376, §§78 and 110. The Court pursued a declarative interpretation of Article 207(1) TFEU, considering that the use, by the framers of the TFEU, of the words "foreign direct investment" "is an unequivocal expression of their intention not to include other foreign investment in the common commercial policy" (§83), and rejected the restrictive interpretation of the concept of "foreign direct investment" proposed by the Council and by some Member States, according to which the CCP includes the admission but not the protection of foreign direct investment (idem, §§85-87). It also declared that the EU/Singapore agreement does not include any compromise governing the system of property ownership, which is an exclusive competence of the Member States according to Article 345 TFEU, considering that Article of 9.6. EUSFTA "seeks solely to make any nationalisation or expropriation decisions subject to limits which are intended to guarantee investors that such a decision will be adopted under equitable conditions and in compliance with general principles and fundamental rights, in particular with the principle of non-discrimination" (idem, §107).

[99] Idem, §§75-77. Excluded from the CCP but subjected to an implicit exclusive external competence of the Union, are the commitments concerning public procurement in the field of transport (idem, §§219-224).

[100] Idem, §§111-130.

[101] Idem, §§131-138.

[102] Idem, §§139-167. According to the Court of Justice, the provisions concerning sustainable development "govern trade between the European Union and the Republic of Singapore by making liberalisation of that trade subject to the condition that the Parties comply with their international

to the pursuit of economic objectives related to the gradual liberalization of trade (Van der Loo 2017b, 4).

The "ERTA doctrine" (fourth situation provided for in Article 216(1) TFEU and third situation provided for in Article 3(2) TFEU) was invoked to include provisions of EUSFTA concerning cross-border transport services (Chapters 8 and 10) within the implicit exclusive external competence of the Union. Although the conclusion of international agreements in the field of transports is based in the transports common policy (Article 207(5) TFEU), which is a shared competence (Article 4(2)(g) TFEU), the Court considered that the compromises assumed in EUSFTA concerning the transport sector could affect, or even alter, the common rules laid down in EU secondary law which apply to the supply of those services in that domain.[103]

In the exclusive external competence of the Union were, finally, included: i) institutional provisions, namely those concerning exchange of information, notification, verification, cooperation, mediation, decision-making power and transparency (Chapters 14, 16 and 17), which have an ancillary nature, and thus fall within the same competence as the provisions they support;[104] ii) provisions that institute the dispute settlement mechanism between the parties on the interpretation and application of Chapters 2 to 12 EUSFTA (Chapter 15), since the competence of the European Union to conclude international agreements necessarily entail the power to submit itself to the decisions of a body which, whilst not formally a court, essentially performs

obligations concerning social protection of workers and environmental protection" (§166). This conclusion is based on the obligation to pursue the CCP according to the principles and objectives of the Union's external action (Article 21(3) TEU and 205-207(1) TFEU), which include sustainable development linked to the preservation and improvement of the quality of the environment and the sustainable management of global natural resources (Article 21(1)(f) TEU) (§147). The possibility of Article 21 TEU broadening the material scope of the CCP was rejected by General-Advocate Eleanor Sharpston (C-240/09, 15 July 2010, *Lesoochranárske zoskupenie VLK*, ECLI:EU:C:2010:436, §495) with the argument that such provision serves only the purpose of obliging the Union to contribute to certain objectives in its policies and activities.

[103] Opinion 2/15, 17 May 2017, *Free Trade Agreement between the European Union and the Republic of Singapore*, ECLI:EU:C:2017:376, §193 (services of international maritime transport), 202 (rail transport services), §211 (road transport services) and §224 (public procurement in the transport domain). The Court considered that the provisions concerning internal waterways transport were accompanied, at most, by commitments of extremely limited scope that had no relevance when examining the nature of the competence (idem, §§216-217).

[104] Idem, §§275 and 282.

judicial functions, such as the Dispute Settlement Body created within the framework of the WTO Agreement.[105]

3.1.3. Shared Competences

The only material domain of EUSFTA which the Court of Justice considered not to be included in the exclusive competence of the Union concerned non-direct investment (Chapter 9, section A), namely portfolio investment, which is an investment that takes place in the form of the acquisition of company securities with the intention of making a financial investment without any intention to influence the management and control of the undertaking.

The European Commission argued that EUSFTA provisions concerning portfolio investment fall within the exclusive competence of the Union through the "ERTA doctrine" (fourth situation provided for in Article 216(1) TFEU and third situation provided for in Article 3(2) TFEU), as they "affect" TFEU provisions on free movement of capital (Article 63 TFEU). The argument that "common rules" (Article 3(2) TFEU) also include primary law was, however, rejected by the Court of Justice:

> (...) in the light of the primacy of the EU and FEU Treaties over acts adopted on their basis, (...) agreements concluded by the European Union with third States, derive their legitimacy from those Treaties and cannot, on the other hand, have an impact on the meaning or scope of the Treaties' provisions. Those agreements accordingly cannot «affect» rules of primary EU law or «alter their scope», within the meaning of Article 3(2) TFEU.[106]

This conclusion does not prevent an overlap between commercial and investment policies. According to the Court of Justice, the provisions that cover portfolio investment fall in the shared competence, as an international agreement concerning such investment may be necessary to achieve, "within the framework of the Union's policies, one of the objectives referred to in the Treaties" (second situation provided for in Article 216(1) TFEU). Since the free movement of capital and payments between Member States and third States, laid down in Article 63 TFEU, is not formally binding on third States, the conclusion of international agreements which contribute

[105] Idem, §299.
[106] Idem, §235.

to the establishment of such free movement on a reciprocal basis may be classified as necessary in order to fully achieve such free movement, which is one of the objectives of Title IV ('Free movement of persons, services and capital'), which fall within the shared competence relating to the internal market (Article 4(2)(a) TFEU).[107]

Also covered by the shared competence between the Union and the Member States is the EUSFTA Investor-State Dispute Settlement mechanism (Chapter 9, Section B). Arbitration is an exclusive discretionary prerogative of an investor conditioned to the withdrawal of any pending similar claim submitted to a domestic court (Article 9.17.1(f) EUSFTA). Since Member States cannot oppose the investor submission of arbitration, the mechanism removes disputes from the jurisdiction of national courts, and cannot, therefore, be established without the Member States' consent.[108]

3.2. CETA's Typology

"Mixed" agreements can be theoretically by classified as: i) *mandatory*, when they include provisions falling within the exclusive competence of the Union *and* the Member States; ii) *facultative*, when they include provisions falling under the exclusive competence of the Union *and* the shared competence, *or* only under shared competence; iii) *false*, when they include provisions falling under the exclusive competence of the Member States *or* under the exclusive competence of the Union;[109] iv) *incomplete*, when they are concluded by the Union with only some of the Member States (Schermers 1983, 23-33; Rosas 1998, 129–132; 2000, 203–206; Maresceau 2010; Möldner 2011, §§7–15; Klamert 2014, 183–185).

[107] Idem, §§239-241.

[108] Idem, §§288-293. To bypass the severe criticism of EUSFTA's Investor-State Dispute Settlement mechanism, CETA created an innovative institutionalized arbitration system that involved the establishment of a permanent investment dispute settlement tribunal, the *Investment Court System* (ICS). The procedural condition regarding the withdrawal or discontinuance of "any existing proceeding before a tribunal or court under domestic or international law" [Article 8.22 (1)(f)] remains untouched. See Diogo (2018).

[109] Article 2(1) TFEU mentions that Member States, when empowered by the Union, may legislate and adopt legally binding acts in the Union's exclusive competence domains. The Union may thus authorize Member States to adopt jointly international agreements in its external exclusive competence domains (Baere 2014, 720), which means that, in practise, an exclusive competence of the Union is not exercised as such (Rosas 2013, 33).

In Opinion 2/15, the Court of Justice declared that every provision of the agreement with Singapore fell under the exclusive competence of the Union, with the exception of those concerning investment portfolio and the Investor-State Dispute Settlement mechanism, which fell under the shared competence. Since no provision of EUSFTA was considered to fall under Member States exclusive competence, could CETA then be approved as an "EU-only agreement"? Or the fact that it included provisions falling under shared competences mandated its approval as a "mixed" agreement?

According to Advocate-General Juliane Kokott:

> Individual aspects of an agreement for which the (Union) has no competence internally «infect» the agreement as a whole and make it dependent on the common accord of the Member States. The picture created by the Commission itself in another context is also absolutely true in relation (to Article 207 TFEU). Just as a little drop of pastis can turn a glass of water milky, individual provisions, however secondary, in an international agreement based on the first subparagraph of (Article 207 TFEU) can make it necessary to conclude a shared agreement.[110]

The pastis metaphor was never used by the Court of Justice. It is, however, impressive as it demonstrates that the existence of a provision not merely instrumental or ancillary *included in the Member States competence* is sufficient to force the approval of an international agreement as "mixed".

The possibility of the Union concluding as "EU-only agreements" international agreements that include provisions that fall under shared competence domains was endorsed by Advocate-Generals Whal and Sharpston.[111] This would entail broadening the scope of the typology of "facultative mixed agreements" or "facultative EU-only agreements". These are agreements which include provisions falling under the exclusive competence of the Union *and* shared competences *or* only shared competences, whose decision on approval form is political, and remains ultimately with

[110] C-13/07, 26 March 2009, *Commission v. Council*, ECLI:EU:C:2009:190, §121.

[111] Advocate-General Nils Whal, Opinion 3/15, *Marrakesh Treaty to Facilitate Access to Published Works for Persons who are Blind, Visually Impaired or Otherwise Print Disabled*, §§119-120, and Advocate--General Eleanor Sharpston, Opinion 2/15, *Free Trade Agreement between the European Union and the Republic of Singapore*, ECLI:EU:C:2016:992, §§73-75. See also Klamert (2014, 184).

the Council (Rosas 1998, 132).[112] Provisions falling under shared competences in EUSFTA or CETA would then be a variety of "pastis" (competence) which did not turn a glass of water (international agreement) *necessarily* milky (mixed).

In Opinion 2/15, the Court of Justice rejected, however, the possibility of EUSFTA taking the form of an "EU-only agreement" by declaring that it could not be concluded solely by the Union, as it includes provisions falling under shared competences.[113] The external shared competence *stricto sensu* (subjected to pre-emption) is thus, in practise, identical to an external exclusive competence of the Member States: both are "drops of pastis" whose inclusion in a trade agreement implies its conclusion as a "mixed agreement".[114] This means that the typology of "facultative mixed agreements" is limited to *latu sensu* shared competence domains (not subjected to pre-emption; i.e. parallel competences, supporting competences, and international agreements in the field of the common foreign and security policies).

In conclusion, the decision of the President of the European Commission to propose CETA as a "mixed agreement" was prescient, as a Council decision approving it as an "EU-only agreement" would be invalid.

[112] An example of a "facultative EU-only agreement" is, according to Van der Loo and Wessel (2017, 738), the Stabilisation and Association Agreement between the European Union and Kosovo. According to Recital 5 of the Council Decision (UE) 2015/1988, 22 October 2015, this is an "EU-only agreement", in which the commitments and cooperation to be entered into by the Union relate only to the areas covered by EU acquis or existing Union policies. Contrary to every other association agreements (Maresceau 2010, 17-20), the EU/Kosovo agreement is not "mixed", notwithstanding the fact that it is based on Article 37 TEU, concerning agreements concluded within the common foreign and security policy, and a report from a British parliamentary commission that labelled it as a unique case of a "EU-only agreement" that included shared competence provisions [European Scrutiny Committee of the House of Commons, *27. The EU and Kosovo: Stabilisation and Association Agreement (SAA)*, 21 July 2015, §27.9, available at https://publications.parliament.uk/pa/cm201516/cmselect/cmeuleg/342-i/34230.htm]. This was clearly a political decision aimed at preventing that, through ratification, some Member States (Cyprus, Spain, Slovakia, Greece and Romania) *de facto* recognized Kosovo as a sovereign State. See Duić (2015, 17) or Van der Loo and Wessel (2017, 738).

[113] Opinion 2/15, 17 May 2017, *Free Trade Agreement between the European Union and the Republic of Singapore*, ECLI:EU:C:2017:376, §§243-244 and 292.

[114] Before the entry into force of the Lisbon Treaty, this was the legal framework applicable in the shared competence domains foreseen in Article 133(6)(§2) (trade in cultural and audio-visual services, educational services, and social and human health services), which required common accord of the Member States for negotiation, and also mandated that the conclusion of an agreement to be made jointly by the Community and the Member States.

4. Consequences and solutions for CETA's ratification refusal by a Member State

CETA's parties are, on the one side, Canada, and on the other side, the Union and each Member State. It is a bilateral "mixed" agreement, in which both the Union and the Member States are contracting parties that assume jointly one of the sides of the treaty legal relationship.[115]

The entry into force of CETA will happen "on the first day of the second month following the date the Parties exchange written notifications certifying that they have completed their respective internal requirements and procedures" (Article 30.7 (2)). The conclusion of ratification procedures in twenty-nine legal orders — Canada, the European Union and each of the twenty-seven Member States — is required. A ratification refusal in a single Member State prevents the entry into force of CETA, being irrelevant whether the agreement was already ratified by Canada, the European Union, and every other Member State (Kleimann and Kübek 2016, 23) (Van der Loo and Wessel 2017, 743).

The Union usually binds itself to a "mixed" agreement through a Council Decision only after the Member States have deposited their ratification instruments, thus following the rule set forth in Article 102 of the Treaty on the European Atomic Energy Community (Euratom) (1957), which states that "agreements or contracts concluded with a third State, an international organisation or a national of a third State to which, in addition to the Community, one or more Member States are parties, shall not enter into force until the Commission has been notified by all the Member States concerned that those agreements or contracts have become applicable in accordance with the provisions of their respective national laws" (Rosas 2000, 208) (Eeckout, 2011, 260) (Klamert, 2014, 202) (Baere, 2014: 739).[116]

A definitive refusal of ratification by a Member State entails a *de facto* veto to the conclusion of a "mixed" agreement by the Union. Kleimann and Kübek

[115] In a bilateral "mixed agreement", the Union and the Member States declare, in a single legal instrument, their will to be bind to a third party, while the latter simultaneously accept the Union and the Member States as contracting parties (Marescеau 2010, 12).

[116] Van der Loo and Wessel (2017, 746), mention as the sole exception the "Agreement between the European Union and its Member States, of the one part, and Iceland, of the other part, concerning Iceland's participation in the joint fulfilment of commitments of the European Union, its Member States and Iceland for the second commitment period of the Kyoto Protocol to the United Nations Framework Convention on Climate Change" [Council Decision (UE) 2015/1340, 13 July 2015].

(2016, 24) argue, however, that such a veto would be tantamount to a breach of the principle of sincere cooperation. Member States are thus obliged to sign and ratify the components of a "mixed agreement" that fall under the exclusive competence of the Union; if they wish not to be bound by other provisions, they must formulate a reservation.

Beyond suggesting that the formulation of a reservation could have the effect of withdrawing a party from obligations stemming from a bilateral treaty,[117] Kleimann and Kübek's proposal would neutralize the sovereign prerogative of ratification of international agreements. Member States do not enter "mixed agreements" as "a mere appendage of the European Union",[118] and retain the sovereign power to refuse ratification.[119] From the requirement of unity in the international representation of the Union and from the principle of since cooperation,[120] stems merely an "obligation of means" to proceed without undue delay to ratification[121] — *e.g.*, it would breach good faith obligations to suspend CETA's ratification to extract commercial benefits from Canada (Eeckout, 2011: 260; Klamert 2014, 202–203).[122]

[117] In bilateral treaties, disagreements between the parties should be discussed during negotiations and settled in the text of the treaty (Bacelar Gouveia 2017, 247). For that reason, Article 20(2) of the Vienna Convention of the Law of the Treaties (VCLT) (1969) — which, although not ratified by every Member State, codifies international customary law — states that "when it appears from the limited number of the negotiating States and the object and purpose of a treaty that the application of the treaty in its entirety between all the parties is an essential condition of the consent of each one to be bound by the treaty, a reservation requires acceptance by all the parties".

[118] Advocate-General Eleanor Sharpston, General-Advocate Eleanor Sharpston, Opinion 2/15, 21 December 2016, *Free Trade Agreement between the European Union and the Republic of Singapore*, ECLI:EU:C:2016:992, §77, which adds that the fact that the Union may have played the leading role in negotiating the "mixed" agreement is, for these purposes, irrelevant.

[119] Member States are also free to vote against the adoption of a "mixed agreement" by the Council, even if they had previously approved its signature.

[120] Opinion 1/94, *Competence of the Community to conclude international agreements concerning services and the protection of intellectual property*, ECLI:EU:C:1994:384, §108; C-246/07, 20 April 2010, *Commission v. Sweden*, ECLI:EU:C:2010:203, §73.

[121] See Van der Loo and Wessel (2017, 762), which derive this obligation from Article 18(a) VCLT that states that a "State is obliged to refrain from acts which would defeat the object and purpose of a treaty when it has signed the treaty or has exchanged instruments constituting the treaty subject to ratification, acceptance or approval, until it shall have made its intention clear not to become a party to the treaty".

[122] Rosas (2010, 368-369) gives as an example the cases of Italy and Greece, which conditioned the provisory entry into force and ratification of the EU/South Africa trade agreement to the protection of the designations of origin "grappa" and "ouzo".

"Mixed" agreements ratification must also respect the vertical repartition of competences between the Union and the Member States. Although national parliaments frequently address "mixed" agreements in its entirety,[123] in the absence of any delegation of competences by the Union, their competence is restricted to the approval of provisions falling under shared competences, which means that they cannot refuse ratification based on motives related to provisions that fall under the exclusive competence of the Union.[124]

A veto threat to CETA's ratification could be prevented in several ways. One would be to follow the path taken to solve the "Walloon veto" crisis: the adoption of an interpretative instrument of CETA by the parties to the agreement. This is a document which, according to Article 31(2)(b) VCLT,[125] has a binding nature concerning the interpretation of several provisions of the agreement, namely those related to investment protection and dispute resolution.[126]

Another possibility would be to adopt the solution found to prevent the ratification refusal of the Netherlands stemming from the popular rejection of the EU/Ukraine association agreement: on the margin of a European Council meeting, the Heads of State and Government of the Member States, using their "intergovernmental hats", adopted a Decision which reflects their "common understanding" of that association agreement.[127] This Decision is an executive international agreement between the Member States which

[123] See the Portuguese parliament's resolution proposal 49/XIII/2 ("Aprova o Acordo Económico e Comercial Global entre o Canadá, por um lado e a União Europeia e os seus Estados-Membros, por outro, assinado em Bruxelas, em 30 de outubro de 2016"), available at https://www.parlamento.pt/ActividadeParlamentar/Paginas/DetalheIniciativa.aspx?BID=41344.

[124] Advocate-General Eleanor Sharpston, General-Advocate Eleanor Sharpston, Opinion 2/15, 21 December 2016, *Free Trade Agreement between the European Union and the Republic of Singapore*, ECLI:EU:C:2016:992, §568.

[125] Which states that the context "for the purpose of the interpretation of a treaty shall comprise, in addition to the text, including its preamble and annexes, any instrument which was made by one or more parties in connection with the conclusion of the treaty and accepted by the other parties as an instrument related to the treaty".

[126] See §1(e) of the Joint Interpretative Instrument on the Comprehensive Economic and Trade Agreement (CETA) between Canada and the European Union and its Member States (*OJ*, 2017, L 11/3, 14 January 2017).

[127] European Council conclusions on Ukraine, *Decision of the Heads of State or Government of the 28 Member States of the European Union, meeting within the European Council, on the Association Agreement between the European Union and the European Atomic Energy Community and their Member States, of the one part, and Ukraine, of the other part*, 15 December 2016, available at https://www.consilium.europa.eu/en/press/press-releases/2016/12/15/euco-conclusions-ukraine/

does not affect the other parties (Ukraine and the Union).[128] According to the Council's legal services it limits itself to:

> exclude, as among the Member States of the EU, certain interpretations that could be given to the language of the agreement and certain forms of action that could be considered on its basis. In case the EU Court of Justice would have to interpret the provisions of the association agreement in the future, the draft Decision could also be used in its reasoning to assess the intentions of the EU Member States as to the scope of the commitments undertaken when becoming parties.[129]

If CETA's ratification refusal by a Member State in the end is not overcome, two possibilities could be ultimately pursued: i) CETA's approval by the Council as an "EU-only agreement" after securing Canada's approval of the extraction of provisions not supported by legal basis granting exclusive competence to the Union; ii) the transformation of CETA into an "incomplete mixed agreement", through the conclusion of a new agreement by the Union, Canada and the other Member States. In both cases, except for the provisions concerning portfolio investment and the investor-State dispute settlement mechanism, the remaining provisions would be applicable in the Member State that initially refused to ratify CETA (Mayer 2016; Kleimann and Kübek 2016, 24; Van der Loo and Wessel 2017, 746–749).

5. Conclusion

The European Union's external competences are exercised within a complex multilevel federal system that comprises sovereign States vested with *ius tractandi* (Baere 2014, 749). Opinion 2/15 of the Court of Justice introduced

[128] The European Council stated that the Decision "is legally binding on the 28 Member States of the European Union, and may be amended or repealed only by common accord of their Heads of State or Government. It will take effect once the Kingdom of the Netherlands has ratified the agreement and the Union has concluded it. Should this not be the case, the Decision will cease to exist" (ibid.).

[129] Opinion of the Council Legal Service, *Draft Decision of the Heads of State or Government, meeting within the European Council, on the association agreement between the European Union and the European Atomic Energy Community and their Member States, of the one part, and Ukraine, of the other part*, EUCO 37/16, 12 December 2016, §7.

some order into the system's "jungle" of external competences through a broad interpretation of the exclusive competence of the Union under the CCP. Although this jurisprudential stance clearly allows for the conclusion of "new generation" free trade agreements as "EU-only agreements", it is unlikely that agreements so contentious as CETA will take such a path. Member States can still request the inclusion of provisions falling within their exclusive competence, or in the shared competence, forcing the conclusion of such an agreement as "mixed"[130], or request its approval as a "false mixed agreement". Either possibility requires unanimity to amend the Commission's proposal,[131] and may trigger a conflict with the "guardian of the Treaties", which can retaliate by using the "nuclear option" of withdrawing its proposal,[132] thereby blocking the Council's approval of the agreement.

CETA is an advanced indicator of the level of risk of the Union becoming a vetocracy regarding the approval of "new generation" free trade agreements. If it fails, Commissioner Cecilia Malmström's prophecy that if the European Union cannot make a deal with Canada, it will most likely not make one with the United Kingdom (Economist 2016b), could ultimately be fulfilled regarding any relevant State or international organization in the current dire context of economic globalization.

[130] CETA's negotiating mandate provided by the Council to the Commission in April 2009 implicitly assumes the "mixed" nature of the agreement when it authorizes the Commission to negotiate, on behalf of the European Community and *its Member States*, an Economic Integration Agreement with Canada (European Council, 9036/09, 24 April 2009, "Recommendation from the Commission to the Council in order to authorize the Commission to open negotiations for an Economic Integration Agreement with Canada", available at http://data.consilium.europa.eu/doc/document/ST-9036-2009-EXT-2/en/pdf).

[131] Article 293(1) TFUE. This procedure was followed, for instance, in free trade agreements concluded with Peru and Colombia, which were proposed by the Commission as "EU-only agreements" and approved by the Council as "mixed" agreements. See European Commission, 16 October 2016, C(2014) 7557 final, p. 2, available at http://ec.europa.eu/transparency/regdoc/rep/3/2014/EN/3-2014-7557-EN-F1-1.pdf.

[132] C-409/13, *Comissão c. Conselho*, 14 April 2015, ECLI:EU:C:2015:217. The Commission also has, *a fortiriori*, the power to withdraw the recommendation concerning the opening of negotiations of an international agreement (Article 218(3) TFEU), if does not want to follow the directives of the Council that mandate the modification of the nature of the agreement.

REFERENCES

Bacelar Gouveia, Jorge (2017), *Direito Internacional Publico*, Coimbra: Almedina.

Baere, Geert De (2014), "EU external action", in Barnard, Catherine and Peers, Steve, *European Union Law*, pp. 704-750, Oxford: Oxford University Press.

Cremona, Marise (2017), "A Quiet Revolution: The Common Commercial Policy Six Years after the Treaty of Lisbon", in *SIEPS* 2, available at: http://www.sieps.se/sites/default/files/Sieps%202017_2%20web.pdf.

Diogo, João Francisco (2018), "Resolução de Litígios de Investimento no CETA: uma resposta aos críticos?", in Coutinho, Francisco Pereira, Feteira, Lúcio Tomé and Santos, Ruth (eds.), *O Acordo Economico Global entre a União e o Canada (CETA)*, Lisboa: CEDIS/FDUNL, pp. 159-185.

Duić, Dunja (2015), "What is the Future of Stabilization and Association Agreement with Kosovo (risk of incoherence in the EU law)?", *Review of European Law* 2-3, pp. 5-23.

Eeckout, Piet (2011), *EU External Relations*, 2nd Edition, Oxford: Oxford University Press.

Foodwatch (2022), "CETA. An Attack on Health, the Environment, Consumer Protection and Democracy", in *Report 22*, July 2022, avaliable at: https://www.foodwatch.org/en/news/2022/ceta-a-trojan-trade-agreement/.

Forsyth, Murray (1982), *Unions of States: The Theory and Practice of Confederation*, New York: Leicester University Press.

Gotev, Georgi (2017), "Bulgaria and Romania maintain reservations on CETA", in *Euroactiv.com*, 19 October, available at: https://www.euractiv.com/section/trade-society/news/bulgaria-and-romania-maintain-reservations-on-ceta/.

Kempen, Bernhard (2016), *Legal Opinion on the majority requirements in the Council of the European Union* [pdf], available at: https://www.mehr-demokratie.de/fileadmin/pdf/2016-10-14_Kempen_Legal_Opinion_CETA.pdf.

Klamert, Marcus (2014), *The Principle of Loyalty in EU Law*, Oxford: Oxford University Press.

Kleimann, David and Kubek, Gesa (2016), "The Signing, Provisional Application, and Conclusion of Trade and Investment Agreements in the EU, The Case of CETA and Opinion 2/15", *Robert Schuman Centre for Advanced Studies Research Paper No. RSCAS 2016/58*, http://dx.doi.org/10.2139/ssrn.2869873.

Maresceau, Marc (2010), "A Typology of Mixed Bilateral Agreements", in Hillion, Christophe and Koutrakos, Panos, *Mixed Agreements in EU Law Revisited — The EU and its Member States in the World*, pp. 11-29, Oxford: Hart.

Mayer, Franz C. (2016), "European Vetocracy? How to Overcome the Wallonian CETA Problem", in *VerfBlog*, 24 October, available at: http://verfassungsblog.de/european vetocracy-how-to-overcome-the-wallonian-ceta-problem/.

Moldner, Mirka (2011), "European Community and Union, Mixed Agreements", in (ed.) Wolfrum, Rudiger, *Max Planck Encyclopedia of Public International Law*, Oxford: Oxford University Press.

Novinite (2016), "Canada Officially Confirms Visa Waiver for Bulgaria, Romania as of Dec 2017", *Novinite.com*, 1 November, available at: http://www.novinite.com/articles/177134/Canada+Officially+Confirms+Visa+Waiver+for+Bulgaria%2C+Romania+as+of+Dec+2017.

Pereira Coutinho, Francisco (2018), "A Natureza Juridica do Acordo Economico e Comercial Global (CETA)", *Themis* 6, pp. 295-331.

Rayner, Gordon (2020), "Boris Johnson hails «new chapter» as MPs prepare to back Brexit deal", *The Telegraph* 29 December, avaliable at: https://www.telegraph.co.uk/politics/2020/12/29/boris-johnson-hails-new-chapter-mps-prepare-back-brexit-deal/.

Rosas, Allan (1998), "Mixed Union-Mixed Agreements", in Koskenniemi, Martti (ed.), *International Law Aspects of the European Union*, pp. 125-148, The Hague: Kluwer.

Rosas, Allan (2000), "The European Union and Mixed Agreements", in Dashwood, Alan and Hillion, Christophe, *The General Law of EC External Relations*, London: Sweet & Maxwell, pp. 200-220.

Rosas, Allan (2013), "Exclusive, Shared and National Competence in the Context of EU External Relations: do such distinctions mattter?", in Govaere, Inge, *The European Union in the World — Essays in Honour of Marc Maresceau*, Leiden: Martinus Nijhoff Publishers, pp. 17-43.

Rueda-Cantuche, Jose M. and Sousa, Nuno (2016), "EU Exports to the World: Overview of Effects on Employment and Trade", in *Chief Economist Note*, availabe at: http://trade.ec.europa.eu/doclib/docs/2016/february/tradoc_154244.pdf.

Schermers, Henry G. (1983), "A Typology of Mixed Agreements", in O'Keeffe, David and Schermers, Henry G. (eds.), *Mixed Agreements*, Boston: Kluwer Law. pp. 23-33.

Schutze, Robert (2011), "European Community and Union, Party to International Agreements". In Wolfrum, Rudiger, *Max Planck Encyclopedia of Public International Law*, Oxford: Oxford University Press.

Silva Pereira, Pedro (2017), "Acordo CETA: o Parlamento Europeu fez a diferenca", *Análise Europeia* 3, pp. 183-197.

Unknown author (2016), "Tears over the colapse of the EU-Canada trade deal", *The Economist*, 21 October, available at https://www.economist.com/news/europe/21709145-grumpy-insular-mood-european-union.

Unknown author (2016), "Wallonia is adamantly blocking the EU's trade deal with Canada", in *The Economist*, 22 October.

Van der Loo, Guillaume (2017), "The Dutch Referendum on the EU-Ukraine Association Agreement: What's Next?", *Netherlands Yearbook of International Law 2016* 47, pp. 337-350.

Van der Loo, Guillaume (2017), *The Court's Opinion on the EU-Singapore FTA: throwing off the schakles on mixity?*, Brussels: CEPS.

Van der Loo, Guillaume, and Ramses A. Wessel (2017), "The Non-Ratification of Mixed Agreements: Legal Consequences and Solutions", in *Common Market Law Review* 54, pp. 735-770.

Vicenti, Daniela (2017), "EU leaders on collision course with Commission over CETA", in *Euroactiv.com*, 29 June, available at: https://www.euractiv.com/section/trade-society/news/eu-leaders-on-collision-course-with-commission-over-ceta/.

CHAPTER 7
CETA AS THE EU'S FIRST THIRD-GENERATION TRADE AGREEMENT: DOES IT ACT LIKE ONE?[133]

Patrick Leblond and Crina Viju-Miljusevic

Abstract: The Comprehensive Economic and Trade Agreement (CETA) between Canada and the European Union (EU) has been hailed as the trend-setter for third-generation trade agreements, which focus predominantly on beyond-the-border impediments to international trade (*e.g.*, rules and regulations) than at-the-border barriers (*e.g.*, tariffs). CETA formed the basis for subsequent EU trade agreements, which are a key element of the EU's trade policy. It also provided inspiration for third-generation trade agreements outside the EU. The big question for trade policy, in the EU and beyond, is whether third-generation trade agreements achieve their intended objectives with respect to beyond-the-border obstacles to trade. In other words, are they effective instruments in liberalizing international trade? After all, facilitating trade through regulatory and administrative cooperation is much more difficult than eliminating or lowering tariffs on imported goods. Having been in force (provisionally) for five years, CETA offers the best case to study the effectiveness of third-generation trade agreements.

Keywords: third generation trade agreements; CETA; regulatory cooperation; procurement; movement of people.

[133] The authors would like to express their gratitude to Mengxue Peng and Jake Rooke for their able research assistance. They would also like to thank the anonymous reviewer for their useful comments on an earlier draft of this chapter and the Jean Monnet Centre of Excellence at Carleton University under the European Union's Erasmus+ program for providing funding in support of this chapter's preparation.

1. Introduction

The Comprehensive Economic and Trade Agreement (CETA) between Canada and the European Union (EU), which entered into force provisionally in September 2017,[134] was hailed at the time of its negotiation as a "landmark" agreement (Dendrinou and Verlaine, 2016). According to Fahey (2017), the CETA was "heralded as the best, the most ambitious and the most progressive form of trade agreement by leading European Union actors that the EU has ever concluded" (293). Allee *et al.* (2017) found that the CETA was a novel trade agreement, with only seven percent of its language copied from 49 previous agreements that the authors analysed. It was also seen as a "forerunner" or "template" for the Transatlantic Trade and Investment Partnership (TTIP) agreement between the EU and the United States before it was abandoned by the Trump administration (Fahey, 2017; Goff, 2014). The CETA also served as a model for the Trade and Cooperation Agreement between the EU and the United Kingdom following the latter's "Brexit" (Neuwahl, 2021).

Along with the Trans-Pacific Partnership (TPP) agreement, which was negotiated at the same time, the CETA was considered the first "deep" trade agreement. Mattoo *et al.*(2020) define deep trade agreements (DTAs) as "reciprocal agreements between countries that cover not just trade but additional policy areas, such as international flows of investment and labour, and the protection of intellectual property rights and the environment, among others" (3). DTAs such as the CETA are considered third-generation trade agreements. As they go deeper than first and second-generation ("free") trade agreements,[135] they usually also include more extensive institutional mechanisms to facilitate cooperation between the parties, because a significant amount of work to remove existing or potential barriers to trade is

[134] As a "mixed" or "shared" competence trade agreement, the CETA must be ratified not only by the European Parliament but also by the national (and sometimes regional) parliaments of all 27 EU member states. Until this process is completed, the CETA is in force provisionally with some provisions pertaining to mixed competencies being suspended temporarily.

[135] The literature often uses the terms free trade agreements (FTAs) and preferential trade agreements (PTAs) interchangeably; however, as Rodrik (2018) argues, DTAs are not as free or even preferential as first- and second-generation trade agreements, because they deal increasingly with standards, rules and regulations rather than traditional market access issues such as tariffs and quotas. Third-generation policy issues can open up cross-border economic exchanges as well as restrict them. Consequently, we use the term "trade agreements" herein to refer to FTAs, PTAs, customs unions, and economic partnership agreements.

expected to occur after the agreement has entered into force. Therefore, DTAs are often referred to as "living" agreements.

Now that the CETA has been in force for over five years, it provides us with enough time to make an initial assessment of the agreement's effectiveness as the flagship third-generation trade agreement. During this period, trade in goods and services between Canada and the EU has grown significantly more rapidly than before. But is this positive outcome due to provisions pertaining to third-generation trade issues or is it just the result of tariff reductions/elimination (i.e., first-generation trade provisions)? The short answer to this question is that we do not know (yet), because the CETA's third-generation provisions and their impact have not been measured so far. This contribution provides a first step towards such measurement by examining the qualitative (or institutional) progress that has been achieved on the CETA's third-generation commitments. Based on such an assessment, does the CETA act as the third-generation trade agreement that it was designed to be? The short answer is yes; however, progress is taking longer than originally anticipated or hoped for, which should limit the impact of third-generation measures on the agreement's economic impact. To develop the argument, this contribution first makes the case that the CETA is a third-generation trade agreement. Then, it examines the CETA's performance during its first five years of operation, looking specifically at the following DTA policy areas: public procurement, movement of people, certification of goods and regulatory cooperation, with a particular focus on the CETA's Regulatory Cooperation Forum.

2. The CETA as a third-generation EU trade agreement

Over recent decades, trade agreements have been major impetuses for economic growth. They have played a significant role in opening markets and creating framework conditions beneficial to trade and investment. They have evolved in time, expanding their scale and scope. They can be categorized into three generations (see Table 7.1).

Table 7.1. Three generations of trade agreements

	1st Generation	2nd Generation	3rd Generation
Background	• Development of regionalism	• Rise of trade in services • Emergence of global value chains (GVCs)	• Digitization of the economy: increasing deterritorialization of trade • Growing dematerialized world trade • Interconnected world economy
Characteristics	• Focus on tariff barriers • Easy to implement	• Focus on non-tariff barriers • Internationalization of firms • A regulation and integration model based on contractual approach	• Attempt to liberalize other policy issues that affect trade in goods and services (*e.g.*, investment, people, ideas, sustainability, data) • Non-trade objectives (*e.g.*, human rights, gender equality, climate change) • Necessity of wider and deeper cooperation • A renewal of economic regulation
Examples	• EEC • EU-Switzerland • EU-Mexico	• NAFTA • EU-Switzerland • EU-Colombia-Peru-Ecuador	• CETA • Updated EU-Mexico
Innovations	• FTAs • Custom unions	• Inclusion of social clause • Protection of intellectual property rights • Dispute settlement mechanism • Institutions to assist implementation • Government procurement provisions • Provisions on labour and the environment	• Mixed agreements • Precautionary principle • New "Regulatory Cooperation Forum" • Deepening and widening of regulatory cooperation (issue-specific committees) • Investment court system • Enhanced protection of intellectual property rights • Adoption of negative list approach • Updated public procurement processes

2.1 First-generation trade agreements

Rioux *et al.* (2020) argue that the European model as the ideal model of multidimensional regional integration has laid the foundation of the first generation of trade agreements. The EU's first-generation trade agreements were concluded before the 2006 European Commission's "Global Europe" Communication and Stabilisation and Association Agreements (SAAs) with Western Balkan countries, concluded between 2009 and 2016 (European Commission, 2017a; 2018). Since first-generation trade agreements focus on the reduction or elimination of tariff barriers, the implementation process is easy. Specifically, the customs administrations only need to release the new tariffs when agreements enter into force (Leblond and Viju-Miljusevic, 2019). Besides, these agreements typically cover industrial goods, with agricultural products added to their scope at a later stage.

Two examples of first-generation trade agreements signed by the EU are the ones with Switzerland and Mexico. The agreement signed between the EU and Switzerland dates back to 1972. The bilateral agreement aimed to remove barriers to trade for industrial and some agricultural products: import and export customs duties, discriminatory taxation, and quantitative restrictions and measures with equivalent effect (Katunar *et al.*, 2014). The trade agreement between the EU and Mexico, concluded in 2000, focused on the progressive liberalization and ultimate elimination of tariffs as well as the establishment of preferential tariff quotas (European Commission, 2018). The EU-Mexico FTA includes 11 chapters: market access, rules of origin, technical standards, sanitary and phytosanitary standards, safeguards, investment and related payments, trade in services, public sector procurement, competition, intellectual property, and dispute settlement (Caballero, 2022). The agreement covered all industrial goods and a small proportion of agricultural and fishery products. Nonetheless, EU-Mexico trade agreement is considered modest because non-tariff barriers are barely covered. Additionally, it did not address new emerging issues in trade and investment, such as environmental and social provisions (European Commission, 2017b).

2.2 Second-generation trade agreements

As international trade has embraced several structural changes since the 1990s, trade agreements had to expand their focus (Leblond and Viju-Miljusevic, 2019; Rioux *et al.*, 2020). The first key development was the growth of trade in services, which has expanded more swiftly than trade in goods since the 1990s to become the most active component of world trade (WTO, 2015). The second significant development is the emergence of global value chains (GVCs), which led to intermediate goods and services being traded globally (Leblond and Viju-Miljusevic, 2019; Rioux *et al.*, 2020). GVCs are a result of multinational firms establishing subsidiaries and dividing up their manufacturing processes and activities across the world. Against this background, second-generation trade agreements were shaped by the North American Free Trade Agreement (NAFTA), which adopted a decentralized, market-led model based on national laws and a contractual approach (Rioux, 2022; Rioux *et al.*, 2020; Rioux *et al.*, 2015). It entered into force in 1994.

The NAFTA was the first trade agreement signed by two developed countries with a developing/emerging country. As a consequence, it incorporated a social clause (Rioux *et al.*, 2020). Broadly, the agreement sought to remove barriers to trade in goods and services as well as the movement of capital across the three North American economies. It also aimed to advance fair competition as well as promote and secure cross-border investments between the parties (Harbine, 2002). Notably, the NAFTA was the first trade agreement to include obligations to protect intellectual property rights. The NAFTA's Free Trade Commission, consisting of cabinet-level representatives who meet annually, was set up to supervise the agreement's implementation. Working groups were also established to help with implementation, such as reviewing rules of origin and proposing modifications. In his review of the NAFTA, Gantz (2004) argues that the agreement is evolutionary rather than revolutionary in terms of investment provisions. By introducing a formal investor-state dispute settlement mechanism, NAFTA allowed US companies to seek arbitration outside Mexico by an independent body. Apart from establishing a new pattern for trade agreements in terms of services, investment, intellectual properties and business-related mobility, the NAFTA was the first trade agreement to include labour and environment provisions (Lester *et al.*, 2017).

The EU's bilateral agreements with Switzerland and the EU-Colombia-Peru-Ecuador trade agreement are examples of second-generation trade agreements. Due to the limited scope of the 1972 EU-Switzerland trade agreement, the two parties signed a series of bilateral agreements known as 'Bilaterals I' in 1999. These agreements cover areas such as free movement of people, technical barriers to trade, public procurement, agriculture, transport, and research. In 2004, the two parties signed 'Bilaterals II', which expanded the areas of cooperation to include processed agricultural products, statistics and combating fraud (European Commission, 2022a). For its part, the EU-Columbia-Peru-Ecuador trade agreement has been provisionally applied in Peru since March 1, 2013, in Columbia since August 1, 2013, and in Ecuador since January 1, 2017. In addition to partial or full elimination of tariffs, the agreement focuses on non-tariff barriers. Additionally, it addresses some of the new areas of importance such as trade in services, government procurement and intellectual property rights, including geographical indicators. A social clause commits the parties to respect human and labour rights as well as environmental protection (European Commission, 2022b).

2.3 Third-generation trade agreements

With the development of the Internet, electronic commerce and new information and communications technologies such as electronic data interchange, enterprise resource planning software, radio-frequency identification, artificial intelligence, the world economy has become even more interconnected and interdependent. Consequently, international trade agreements have evolved and adapted to these changes (Leblond and Viju-Miljusevic, 2019; Rioux *et al.*, 2020). Third-generation trade agreements not only aim to reduce and eliminate conventional tariff and non-tariff barriers, but include so-called "WTO-plus" provisions (*i.e.*, not covered by WTO agreements): *e.g.*, competition policy, data protection, environmental laws, investment, labour market conditions and human rights (González *et al.*, 2017; Śliwińska, 2019). Owing to the wide-ranging issues included in third-generation agreements, their implementation requires wider and deeper cooperation when compared to trade agreements from previous generations (González *et al.*, 2017).

The CETA is the world's first third-generation trade agreement to come into force. Apart from establishing a free trade area for goods and services, the CETA also aims to minimize regulatory and administrative barriers that hinder trade and investment flows (González *et al.*, 2017). In recognition of digital trade's increasing importance, the CETA includes a separate chapter on electronic commerce. It recognizes the importance of transnational regulatory cooperation to ensure the agreement's effective implementation, which is why it offers an extensive institutional framework to facilitate such cooperation (Leblond, 2016; Rioux *et al.*, 2020). It is also the first agreement involving only developed countries to include provisions related to sustainable development, the movement of people and the protection of labour and the environment.

The CETA's investment court system (ICS) is remarkably different from traditional investor-state dispute-settlement mechanisms, such as the NAFTA's chapter 11 (Gantz, 2022). Unlike other agreements, the ICS allows for the formation of a tribunal with fifteen members: five respectively appointed by both the EU and Canada and the rest of five appointed by third-party countries. It also includes an appellate tribunal. Furthermore, the CETA sets out from previous trade agreements by increasing the scale and scope of intellectual property rights' protection (*e.g.*, covering the patent protection of seeds and medicines) (Couvreur, 2015; Śliwińska, 2019). Another noteworthy enhancement in this area is the expanded protection of the EU's geographical indications, which are applied in the EU (González *et al.*, 2017). CETA has also extended public procurement obligations to sub-regional entities in both jurisdictions, including not only provincial and regional governments but also municipal governments (Rioux *et al.*, 2020). In regard to sectoral coverage, the CETA is the first trade agreement to adopt a negative list approach (Madner, 2016). This means that products that are not explicitly excluded are up for liberalization.

3. The CETA's economic performance

From an economic perspective, the CETA seems to be working as intended. Despite the Covid-19 pandemic, which disrupted international trade flows and investments, economic activity between Canada and the EU remains higher than before the agreement came into force: in 2021, two-way trade in goods was 34 percent higher than before 2016 (Global Affairs Canada, 2022a). On average, the annual rate of growth for Canada-EU bilateral trade was 7.9 percent in 2018-2019, compared to 4.4 percent for the period 2011-2016 (Global Affairs Canada and European Commission, 2021). Agricultural products, which represented 9.3 percent of total bilateral trade between the two economies in 2019, increased by 35 percent between 2016 and 2020 (see Figure 7.1). For non-agricultural products, the increase was 10 percent over the same period, but with a significant decline in machinery, mineral fuels and motor vehicles and parts between 2019 and 2020 because of the Covid-19 pandemic (see Figure 7.1).

Figure 7.1. Total Canada-EU Goods Trade, sectors with largest growth (million Euro)

Sector	2016	2019	2020	Growth 2016-2019 (%)	Growth 2016-2020 (%)
Total Canada-EU Trade					
Agricultural products	5,399	6,200	7,274	14.8	34.7
Non-agricultural products	47,167	60,470	51,884	28.2	10
Machinery	9,204	11,864	9,769	28.9	6.1
Pharmaceutical products	4,790	6,845	6,899	42.9	44
Ores, slag and ash	1,766	3,483	3,625	97.2	105.3
Mineral fuels	2,912	4,219	2,100	44.9	–27.9
Motor vehicles and parts	5,187	6,025	4,363	16.2	–15.9

Source: Global Affairs Canada and European Commission, 2021.

Among Canadian merchandise exports to the EU, the products that enjoyed the largest tariff reductions (more than 10 percentage points) registered the highest growth rate between 2016 and 2021: 54.5 percent on average. In total, products that received tariff reductions under CETA recorded a growth rate of 24.6 percent over the period 2016–2021. Canadian imports from the EU grew at 46.2 percent during the same period; however, there was little variation in growth rates across products with different levels of tariff reductions (Global Affairs Canada, 2022a).

Canada-EU trade in services shows a similar trend, with a total growth rate of 39 percent over 2016–2019 period. Canadian services exports to the EU increased by 37 percent while EU services exports to Canada grew by 41 percent. The Canadian services exports to the EU that registered the most increase post-CETA are other business services, transportation and travel services. They accounted for 70 percent of total services trade in 2019. The three main categories of EU services exports that recorded the most growth post-CETA are commercial services, transportation and travel services (Global Affairs Canada and European Commission, 2021). Canada's services exports started to recover from the Covid-19 pandemic in 2021, mainly within the category of commercial services, travel and transportation. Thus, Canada's services exports to the EU grew by 4.2 percent while Canada's services imports from the EU rose by 11.7 percent (Global Affairs Canada, 2022b).

From an economic perspective, the CETA appears to have had a positive impact on trade between Canada and the EU in its first five years of existence, for both goods and services. At its third meeting, held in Brussels in early December 2022, the CETA's Joint Committee (ministerial level) issued a statement that said the same: "Following five years of provisional application, Canadian and European businesses are reaping the benefits of CETA two-way trade having increased by over 30%. CETA has boosted job creation for both partners. The Joint Committee received a comprehensive assessment of the strong economic outcomes of the Agreement over the last five years."[136] The big question for this chapter's purpose is what portion of the CETA's positive economic impact is due to provisions that pertain to third-generation trade issues when compared to tariff reductions (or elimination). It is telling that Global Affairs Canada's (2022a) assessment of the CETA's performance in its first five years is devoted solely to goods and tariff reductions, with particular attention paid to utilization rates of the agreement's preferences. There is no mention of the impact of regulatory cooperation, government procurement or the mobility of persons. In another report published shortly after the CETA's assessment, Global Affairs Canada (2022b) acknowledges that "[t]raditionally, analyses of FTAs have focused primarily on the economic and welfare impacts of reducing tariffs on goods" and that other (non-tariff) commitments should be evaluated to determine if they are achieving their intended outcomes. However, while summarizing "a selection of existing empirical analyses regarding key areas of FTAs beyond tariffs," the report concludes that "it is too early for the impact of these newly introduced, non-tariff commitments to be reliably measured." So, although a proper economic assessment of the CETA's third-generation trade provisions remains elusive, it is still possible to examine the qualitative progress that has been achieved on these commitments. This is what the analysis in the next sections is about, focusing on a selection of key commitments undertaken by Canada and the EU in the CETA.

[136] https://policy.trade.ec.europa.eu/news/joint-statement-ceta-five-years-cornerstone-canadaeu-economic-relations-2022-12-02_en.

4. Institutional and regulatory cooperation in the CETA

The scope of regulatory cooperation within trade agreements has expanded in the last two decades to include intellectual property, public procurement, telecommunications, electronic commerce, professional qualifications, and environment and green industries. The WTO and OECD have struggled in their efforts at regulatory transparency and international standards. Consequently, bilateral or regional trade agreements have come to be perceived as major venues for regulatory cooperation so that further trade liberalization might be achieved (Hoekman and Sabel, 2019). The reason for the interest in international regulatory cooperation (IRC) is that differences in regulatory standards can act as barriers to trade (Hobbs, 2007). They can either lead to an import ban if the exporting firm cannot satisfy the importing country's regulatory requirements or, in a similar fashion to a tariff, to additional costs in order to meet the importing country's standards (Gaisford and Kerr, 2001). The OECD (1994) defines IRC "as the range of institutional and procedural frameworks within which national governments, sub-national governments, and the wider public can work together to build more integrated systems for rule-making and implementation, subject to constraints of democratic values, such as accountability, openness and sovereignty" (15). The OECD has outlined eleven forms of IRC mechanisms, which range from higher levels of cooperation such as harmonization or mutual recognition of technical regulations to very low levels of cooperation such as dialogue and informational exchanges.

Regulatory differences are often the result of the isolated development of domestic regulations which, while they vary in specifics, yield similar regulatory outcomes. Thus, if harmonization were to be achieved in trade agreements, the potential gains from trade could be reaped with minimal loss in regulatory benefit. This notion underlies the commitment to reducing regulatory barriers to trade in the WTO (James and Anderson, 2005), the extensive regulatory harmonization in the EU (Gaisford *et al.*, 2003) and the commitments to regulatory cooperation in most major trade agreements such as the NAFTA, the Asia Pacific Economic Cooperation (APEC) and the Association of South East Asian Nations (ASEAN) (Yeung *et al.*, 1999). However, in general, there are strong assumptions underlying the process of regulatory harmonization: (1) the differences in regulations do not accurately reflect actual differences in societies' preferences; (2) that preferences are not strongly held in the societies (Kerr, 2006). Harmonization is feasible depending on the degree of divergence in standards — as divergence increases, the costs of adjustment are likely to rise — and the degree to which the existing standards reflect the preferences of a country's population. If there is a strong attachment to an existing standard, then considerable utility may be lost by moving to an alternative standard (Sawyer, 2004). Harmonization can also be achieved by accepting existing international standards, a method that is often used in current trade agreements. Another form of high IRC is mutual recognition. Through mutual recognition, parties mutually recognize some parts of their regulatory regimes. Mutual recognition is based on sufficient trust in the equivalence of regulations and the process of conformity led by regulatory bodies. In this situation, parties can keep distinct domestic regulations, with no trade restrictiveness impact. In general, cooperation is easier between parties that have similar regulatory approaches and are at a similar level of development.

Traditionally, trade agreements dealt with purely economic interests. In the case where requests for protection come not from producers with a vested interest but rather consumers, environmentalists or other civil society groups, the issues likely lack an economic motivation — although, as with any rule-making, there may be significant economic ramifications. In cases where standards differ substantially between countries, trade agreements provide only a limited set of feasible outcomes. If standards differ in minor ways, then an agreement on mutual recognition can be attempted. Trade agreements are negotiated by diplomats while devising standards, whether based on science or not, requires considerable technical expertise. What can, however, be accomplished in a trade agreement is the establishment of an institutional forum (or fora) where cooperation negotiations can be mandated. Also, as most IRC activities occur outside of trade agreements, the latter still provide the institutional framework, context and impetus to initiate and advance cooperation.

In EU's case, it has been successful in achieving harmonization to its rules with countries that are preparing for EU accession or in trade agreements with developing countries. In these cases, the burden of adjustment falls on the partner countries (Goldberg, 2019). However, with highly developed economies, the approach to IRC is different. The CETA is a good example of such an approach for the EU. It includes several chapters that address regulatory cooperation. It also establishes a long list of specialized committees (in article 26.2) to manage various regulatory and administrative aspects affecting trade and investment between Canada and the EU. These specialized committees are mandated to meet at least once per year. Finally, the CETA also devotes a specific chapter on regulatory cooperation (chapter 21), whose objectives are outlined in article 21.3 and include building trust, facilitating bilateral trade and investment as well as contributing to the protection of human, animal or plant life, health and the environment. Chapter 21 clearly mentions that cooperation is voluntary and policy-makers and regulators from Canada and the EU are not constrained from adopting new legislation. The CETA also includes one regulatory sectoral annex that focuses on regulatory cooperation in motor vehicles. This is the only sector where harmonization of regulations is envisioned by committing Canada to adopt international standards defined by the United Nations. Additionally, two new protocols are part of CETA: "protocol on the mutual acceptance of the results of conformity assessment" and "protocol on the mutual recognition of the compliance and enforcement programme regarding good manufacturing practices for pharmaceutical products." These protocols allow for mutual recognition for a list of specified product categories.

The CETA's institutional framework is quite unique given the need to engage stakeholders, including businesses and civil society organizations, in negotiating, among others, regulatory issues pertaining to human and social rights and the environment (Deblock, 2022). Institutional coordination is, therefore, crucial to the CETA's effective implementation as a third-generation trade agreement (Camilleri, 2022; Leblond, 2016). A comprehensive assessment of the CETA's institutional and regulatory cooperation to implement the agreement's third-generation provisions and address beyond-the-border barriers to trade and investment is beyond the scope of this chapter. So, this chapter focuses its analysis on three key, third generation innovations provided by the CETA: the Regulatory Cooperation Forum, government procurement and the movement of persons. The analysis is sufficient to offer a preliminary conclusion on the CETA's behaviour as a third-generation trade agreement.

4.1 The CETA's Regulatory Cooperation Forum

The CETA, through article 21.6, has created a Regulatory Cooperation Forum (RCF) to perform a variety of tasks, including being a discussion platform for regulatory policy, consultations with stakeholders, assistance to regulators, review of regulatory initiatives and encouragement of bilateral cooperation (Deblock, 2022). Despite not having decision-making power, the RCF enables and encourages further discussion on bilateral regulatory cooperation between Canada and the EU.

The RCF met four times since its inception, in December 2018, February 2020, February 2021 and May 2022. Based on stakeholders' submissions,[137] the parties adopted a work plan that is updated regularly with new opportunities for regulatory cooperation (Global Affairs Canada, 2022c). At the first meeting, the parties identified five fields of cooperation: cybersecurity and the Internet of things, animal welfare (transportation of animals), "cosmetic-like" drug products, pharmaceutical inspections, and safety of consumer products through exchange of information between the EU RAPEX (rapid alert system for dangerous products) alert system and Canada's RADAR (consumer product incident reporting system). The parties decided to work on the first four topics during the following year. For the last topic, an administrative arrangement for information exchange had already been established in November 2018 (Global Affairs Canada, 2018). At the RCF's second meeting, three additional fields of cooperation were added to the workplan: wood pellet boilers, Standards Council of Canada and CEN-CENELEC Agreement, and paediatric medicines (Global Affairs Canada, 2020).

The outcomes of RCF's discussions on these issues range from regular technical exchange of information and joint communication initiatives (consumer product safety, animal welfare, wood pellet boilers) to mutual recognition of compliance and enforcement programmes (pharmaceutical inspections) to increased regulatory harmonization ("cosmetic-like" drug products, pediatric medicines). For pharmaceutical products, the parties agreed, under the CETA Protocol, on the "mutual recognition of the compliance and enforcement programme regarding good manufacturing practices" (Global Affairs Canada, 2022c). The RCF initiative focused on expanding the existing framework to include extra-jurisdictional inspections. The discussions were successful and the new decision was launched on 1 April 2021 in Canada and 15 April 2021 in the EU (Global Affairs Canada, 2022c). For "cosmetic-like" drug products, the goal was the elimination of quarantine and confirmatory re-testing for such products coming into

[137] The European Commission's call for proposals for regulatory cooperation activities in the RCF was issued on 18 January 2018, four months after the CETA came into force provisionally (https://ec.europa.eu/newsroom/growth/items/612647). Stakeholders had one month to send in their proposals. Global Affairs Canada's consultation with stakeholders with respect to their views on the RCF took place between February 10 and 11 April 2018 (https://open.canada.ca/data/en/dataset/c45c4cda-7134-4e65-8e99-5214eb07bcf3).

the EU from Canada. The discussions resulted in the elimination of the requirements for Canada for sunscreens, toothpastes and anti-dandruff shampoos starting in June 2021 (Global Affairs Canada, 2022d). In terms of pediatric medicines, Health Canada and the European Medicines Agency (EMA) are looking to increase regulatory harmonization for pediatric regulations based on existing models of collaboration. Owing to the Covid -19 pandemic, the priorities of the two agencies shifted and the process has been delayed. However, the RCF provided the necessary platform for exchanging information and for a better understanding of how the EMA implements its regulations in the EU (Global Affairs Canada, 2022d).

The CETA's RCF has clearly been an effective instrument in resolving some regulatory issues that acted as impediments to trade between Canada and the EU. It has also encouraged the sharing of information between Canadian and European regulatory authorities, which is the first step in finding solutions to regulatory obstacles to trade. However, it is difficult to determine how effective the CETA's RCF has been. Given that such institutional mechanisms are recent innovations in trade agreements (Deblock, 2022), the basis for assessing the RCF is still very thin. Nevertheless, it is possible to think that the RCF could have taken on more fields of cooperation if it met more often than once per year, which is the minimum set by the CETA. The challenge for the individuals involved in the CETA's RCF is that they may be involved in similar forums that are part of other third--generation trade agreements. This could make it difficult for them to meet more often and increase the scope of the fields or issues for cooperation that they take on. As a result, some issues must wait in the queue until they can make it on the RCF's work plan. The fact that not all proposed regulatory cooperation issues can make it on the RCF's work plan raises the question about how and when they make it on the work plan. The CETA offers no guidelines for such determination with respect to the RCF and other specialized committees (van Rooy 2022). Although van Rooy (2022: 121) calls the RCF's transparency on its work plan and what has been achieved "refreshing", she nevertheless argues in favour of oversight mechanisms (possibly by parliaments) and participatory rights for stakeholders based on explicit procedural rules for the RCF, and regulatory cooperation mechanisms in general (ibid: 132).

4.2 The CETA and government procurement

Chapter 19 defines the principles and rules that govern government procurement between Canada and the EU, at all levels of government (from the municipal to the federal/supranational).[138] Accessing provincial and municipal government procurement markets in Canada was one of the EU's major goals in negotiating the CETA (D'Erman, 2020; Leblond, 2016). When the CETA negotiations began (2008-09), the WTO's Agreement on Government Procurement (GPA) did not include Canadian provinces and municipalities; it covered only federal government procurement contracts. This situation changed with the revised GPA, which entered into force on 6 April 2014. In this revised agreement, the provinces accepted to be part of Canada's schedule. Nevertheless, chapter 19 goes beyond Canada's commitments under the GPA. According to Casier (2019: 13):

> CETA covers more entities, and the thresholds for goods and services procurement by sub-central entities is also lower than under the WTO GPA. CETA includes roughly twenty more central government entities and significantly more subnational entities, including most regional, local, district or other forms of municipal government, as well as all publicly funded academic, health and social-service entities.

In exchange, the EU agreed to open its access "to most of the utility sectors that it withholds under the GPA, namely: drinking water; electricity; transport by urban railways; automated systems; tramways, trolley bus, bus or cable; and transport by railways" (Grier 2020: 202).

Under the CETA, the Canadian federal government also committed to create a single platform (referred to as the "single point of access" [SPA]) for all government procurement in Canada by 2022 (Ruffat and Leblond, 2022: 148). The EU already had the Tenders Electronic Daily (TED), which provided firms with all procurement tenders offered by governments and public institutions in the EU, from the municipal to the supranational level.

To help with the chapter 19's implementation, the CETA established the Committee on Government Procurement (CGP). The CGP held its first meeting on 15 March 2018.[139] At the meeting, Canada and the EU discus-

[138] For a brief description of the CETA's chapter 19, see Ruffat and Leblond (2022).

[139] https://trade.ec.europa.eu/doclib/docs/2018/april/tradoc_156706.pdf.

sed the EU's legislative package on strategic public procurement. They also adjusted the CETA's threshold values (at which the agreement's provisions on government procurement apply) into domestic currency to reflect variations in the values of the Canadian dollar and the euro relative to special drawing rights (SDR).[140] The CETA's threshold values are expressed in SDR. At this first meeting, Canada updated the EU on the development of the SPA while the EU shared its experience with the TED. Government procurement opportunities, notably in the space sector, which the CETA opened for both sides, were also discussed, among other issues.

The CGP's second meeting occurred on 22 February 2019.[141] Again, Canada updated the EU on the progress with the SPA's development. Both parties shared information on promotional activities, including the publication of guidance documents. They also talked about the modalities for the exchange of statistics on procurement awards to suppliers located in the other jurisdiction. Finally, the EU shared information about its policies on green procurement.

The third CGP meeting took place on 25–26 November 2020.[142] Once more, the parties discussed the SPA's progress. They also reviewed and discussed suppliers' experience in taking advantage of the CETA's chapter 19 as well as issues raised by other stakeholders. They also agreed to continue the discussion on the systematic exchange of statistics on CETA-covered contracts awarded to Canadian and EU-based suppliers. The parties continued their discussion of the coverage of space-related procurement under the CETA. Finally, they shared information about legislative and regulatory developments in their respective jurisdictions that are related to public procurement (*e.g.*, the EU's Green Deal or Canada's Ethical Procurement of Apparel Initiative).

The CGP held its fourth meeting on 14 December 2021.[143] At the meeting, Canada announced that the SPA website, "CanadaBuys", was finally under development.[144] For its part, the EU informed Canada of a new online tool, "Access2Procurement", that allows suppliers to find out if a tender is covered by the CETA. Canada also updated the EU on the "state of play" regarding

[140] SDR are a synthetic unit of measure, derived from a basket of currencies, used by the International Monetary Fund for its financing and operations.

[141] https://trade.ec.europa.eu/doclib/docs/2019/april/tradoc_157845.pdf.

[142] https://trade.ec.europa.eu/doclib/docs/2020/november/tradoc_159079.pdf.

[143] https://www.international.gc.ca/trade-commerce/trade-agreements-accords-commerciaux/agr-acc/ceta-aecg/2021-12-14-summary_report-rapport_summaire.aspx?lang=eng.

[144] https://canadabuys.canada.ca/en.

procurement by the Canadian Space Agency and coverage under the CETA. Finally, the EU shared information with Canada about the proposed Foreign Subsidies Regulation and the International Procurement Instrument. The fifth and most recent meeting of the CGP happened on 3 October 2022. Regrettably, no report of the meeting was available at the time of writing (December 2022), only an agenda that covered, specifically, the following: Canada's SPA, the EU's International Procurement Instrument, and the Canadian Space Agency.[145]

In sum, the CGP has been consistent in the topics that it has covered in its first five meetings, notably the SPA and the coverage of space procurement by the CETA. Reports of the CGP's meetings demonstrate that a significant amount of information was shared between Canada and the EU with respect to legislative and regulatory developments relevant to government procurement. Discussions on statistics, supplier experience and other stakeholder concerns also took place. As such, the CGP appears to have played the role for which it was established. One can wonder if Canada's SPA would ever have seen the light of day without the need to provide updates on its development at every CGP meeting. Nevertheless, after five years of the CETA being in force provisionally, the SPA is still under development, even if the CanadaBuys website is functional with tenders from federal, provincial and municipal government entities.

4.3 The CETA and the movement of persons

The CETA aims to facilitate the movement of persons for business purposes between Canada and the EU in two ways: the temporary entry and stay of natural persons for business purposes (chapter 10) and the mutual recognition of professional qualifications (chapter 11). These two chapters' ultimate goal is to make trade in services and investment between Canada and the EU easier. For instance, in the case of professional services, a European engineer or an architect might have to spend a significant period of time in Canada to manage or supervise a project under a contract obtained by a European engineering firm. In such a case, the engineer or architect in question must be able to remain in Canada for more than the few months allowed for visitors. Moreover, this person may need to have his or her professional qualifications

[145] https://www.international.gc.ca/trade-commerce/trade-agreements-accords-commerciaux/agr-acc/ceta-aecg/2022-10-03-gp-agenda-ordre-jour-mp.aspx?lang=eng.

officially recognized in Canada to be able to sign statutory documents that may be required by the authorities. The same logic applies to the need to send one or several employees to oversee a new investment (*e.g.*, the building of a new factory or the acquisition of a company) in the other party.

According to the CETA's article 10.7.5, the "permissible length of stay of key personnel" is as follows: (a) intra-corporate transferees (specialists and senior personnel): the lesser of three years or the length of the contract, with a possible extension of up to 18 months at the discretion of the Party granting the temporary entry and stay; (b) intra-corporate transferees (graduate trainees): the lesser of one year or the length of the contract; (c) investors: one year, with possible extensions at the discretion of the Party granting the temporary entry and stay; (d) business visitors for investment purposes: 90 days within any six month period. For contractual service suppliers and independent professionals, the maximum length of stay that CETA allows them is 12 months, under certain conditions (see article 10.8). According to Mignon (2020), 635 work permits and 44 work permit extensions were issued under the CETA's provisions by Canadian immigration authorities in 2018. Unfortunately, no other statistics could be found on such CETA work permits. So, the provisions found in the CETA's chapter 10 appear to work in practice, with individuals having benefitted from them; we just do not know to what extent.

The CETA's second component with respect to the movement of persons concerns the mutual recognition of professional qualifications, which is necessary if business professionals want to offer their services in the other party's territory. Chapter 11 aims to get Canadian and EU authorities to negotiate and sign mutual recognition agreements (MRAs) that allow qualified professionals (or technicians) to provide services and act according to their formal qualifications and be legally recognized as such in both Canada and the EU. Concluding such MRAs is particularly challenging because professional qualifications are provincial competencies in Canada while they remain under the responsibility of member states inside the EU. In other words, the Canadian federal government and the European Commission, which are responsible for the CETA's implementation, can only encourage occupational regulatory bodies in Canada and the EU to propose and negotiate MRAs with each other; they have no legal authority to mandate such agreements. They are supposed to, through the so-called "MRA Committee"[146] to provide

[146] Formally, the MRA Committee is known at the Joint Committee on Mutual Recognition of Professional Qualifications.

a framework for negotiating and concluding MRAs under the CETA's chapter 11 (article 11.6 and annex 11-A offer guidelines for negotiations). The MRA Committee is also responsible for the final approval of MRAs between Canadian and European authorities.

According to the joint study conducted by the European Commission and the Government of Canada in 2008, there were more than 440 occupational and professional bodies in Canada alone (Brender, 2014: 15). After the France-Quebec agreement on labour mobility was signed in the fall of 2008, 70 MRAs had been signed between French and Quebec bodies at the end of 2014 (Doutriaux, 2015: 256). Therefore, there were high hopes for the CETA with respect to the mutual recognition of professional qualifications between Canada and the EU because of the CETA. Surprisingly, it is only in March 2022 that the first MRA was concluded (for architects); it is planned to come into effect in early 2023 (European Commission, 2022c). The first steps towards this MRA were taken by the Architects' Council of Europe and the Canadian Architectural Licensing Authorities in April 2019, when they submitted their proposal to the MRA Committee (Camilleri, 2022). Although it has taken many years to conclude these negotiations, they nevertheless represent an example of how the CETA can be an enabling tool for intensified regulatory cooperation and the mobility of professionals between Canada and the EU. According to the European Commission (2022c), this "MRA is the first of its kind which the EU has negotiated." It is now expected that other professional bodies will move forward with their own MRAs, using the successful template offered by Canadian and European architects.

5. Conclusion

What the analysis herein demonstrates is that so-called "beyond-the-border" issues dealing with standards and regulations can take a long time to be resolved, because they require the cooperation of several actors (*e.g.*, different levels of governments and/or different ministries or agencies as well as businesses and other organizations), with interests that do not always align perfectly, not to mention a certain degree of political or bureaucratic inertia. In other words, first- and second-generation provisions in trade agreements are quicker to be implemented and realized than third-generation ones. Deep trade agreements such as the CETA take time and effort to realize the benefits associated with third-generation elements.

Nevertheless, it is not a reason to give up on DTAs; third-generation benefits appear to materialize over time, at least based on regulatory cooperation, the monitoring of parties' commitments and the sharing of information. Consequently, the EU should make it a priority to collect non-trade data such as the number of people who apply and obtain work permits under the CETA's chapter 10. Similarly, statistics on government procurement tenders to which suppliers from the other party(ies) have bid on or won would be useful to assess the effectiveness of DTAs such as the CETA. In addition, building a database of regulatory cooperation (committee meetings, activities, agreements, shared information, etc.) in third-generation trade agreements would be helpful in assessing their effectiveness. Such a database would also serve to identify the factors that make regulatory cooperation successful or not. Finally, the EU's trade policy should plan for more human and financial resources for managing and implementing third-generation trade agreements. If such resources are not increased as regulatory cooperation fora and specialized committees multiply as more third-generation trade agreements come into force, there is a high risk that the effectiveness of regulatory cooperation decreases with each new or updated agreement as resources are stretched more thinly across more and more fora and committees. The implementation of third-generation provisions in trade agreements would suffer as a result, with the benefits of such agreements taking even longer to materialize than they have done with the CETA.

The analysis conducted herein tells us that the outcomes associated with third-generation trade agreements might take longer to develop due to the time and efforts needed to make third-generation provisions work effectively. This is an important characteristic of third-generation trade agreements that needs to be shared with the business community and the general public. Otherwise, by creating unrealistic expectations with respect to an agreement's economic benefits when it is signed or enters into force, there is a risk that businesses and individuals will end up concluding that DTAs are not worth it because they do not (or take too long to) deliver on their promises. Consequently, support for future DTAs could be jeopardized, which would undermine the EU's and other countries' trade policies with respect to trade agreements.

REFERENCES

Allee, T., Elsig, M. and Lugg, A. (2017), "Is the European Union Trade Deal with Canada New or Recycled? A Text-as-data Approach", *Global Policy* 8(2), pp. 246-252.

Brender, N. (2014), "Across the Sea with CETA: What New Labour Mobility Might Mean for Canadian Business", Briefing, July, Ottawa, ON: The Conference Board of Canada.

Caballero, E.S. (2022), "The modernization of the European Union-Mexico Association Agreement: between change and continuity", *EU-LAC Foundation*, Occasional paper FC/EU-LAC (7), available at https://eulacfoundation.org/sites/default/files/2022-06/Especial_FC_EULAC_7_EN.pdf.

Camilleri, M. (2022), "Regulatory Cooperation under CETA: Facing Up to the 'Gorilla in the Room' ", in R.G. Finbow (ed.) *CETA Implementation and Implications: Unravelling the Puzzle,* Montreal: McGill-Queen's University Press, pp. 97-115.

Casier, L. (2019), "Canada's International Trade Obligations: Barrier or Opportunity for Sustainable Public Procurement? Unpacking Canada's WTO GPA and CETA Commitments in Relation to Sustainable Procurement", IISD Report, International Institute for Sustainable Development, avaliable at: https://www.iisd.org/sites/default/files/publications/canada-international-trade-spp.pdf.

Couvreur, A. (2015), "New Generation Regional Trade Agreements and the Precautionary Principle: Focus on the Comprehensive Economic and Trade Agreement (CETA) between Canada and the European Union", *Asper Review of International Business and Trade Law* 15, pp. 265-292.

Deblock, C. (2022), "Canada and International Regulatory Cooperation: A Comparison of USMCA, CETA and CPTPP", in G. Gagné and M. Rioux (eds.) *NAFTA 2.0. From the First NAFTA to the United States-Mexico-Canada Agreement,* New York: Palgrave MacMillan.

Dendrinou, V. and Verlaine, J.-A. (2016), "EU, Canada Sign Landmark Free-Trade Agreement", *The Wall Street Journal,* October 30, available at: https://www.wsj.com/articles/eu-canada-prepare-to-sign-ceta-trade-deal-1477831000.

D'Erman, V.J. (2020), "The EU's Realist Power: Public Procurement and CETA Negotiations with Canada", *Journal of International Relations and Development* 23(1), pp. 1–23.

Doutriaux, Y. (2015), "La reconnaissance des qualifications professionnelles: Entente France-Québec et AECG", in C. Deblock, J. Lebullenger and S. Paquin (eds.) *Un nouveau pont sur l'Atlantique: L'Accord économique et commercial global entre l'Union européenne et le Canada,* Quebec, QC: Presses de l'Université du Québec, pp. 249-259.

European Commission (2017), *Report from the Commission to the European Parliament, the Council, the European Economic and Social Committee and the Committee of the Regions on implementation of free trade agreements 1 January 2016-31 December 2016,* Directorate--General for Trade, Publications Office, available at: https://data.europa.eu/doi/10.2781/085887.

European Commission (2017), *Ex-post evaluation of the implementation of the EU- Mexico Free Trade Agreement*, Directorate-General for Trade, available at: https://trade.ec.europa.eu/doclib/docs/2017/august/tradoc_156011.pdf.

European Commission (2018), *Report from the Commission to the European Parliament, the Council, the European Economic and Social Committee and the Committee of the Regions on implementation of free trade agreements 1 January 2017 - 31 December 2017*, Directorate--General for Trade, Publications Office, available at: https://trade.ec.europa.eu/doclib/docs/2018/october/tradoc_157468.pdf.

European Commission (2022), *Switzerland*. Directorate-General for Trade, available at: https://trade.ec.europa.eu/access-to-markets/en/content/switzerland.

European Commission (2022), *EU-Colombia-Peru-Ecuador Trade Agreement*, Directorate-General for Trade, available at: https://trade.ec.europa.eu/access-to-markets/cs/content/eu-colombia-peru-ecuador-trade-agreement.

European Commission (2022), *EU and Canada lay the foundations for free movement of architects*, 21 March, available at: https://policy.trade.ec.europa.eu/news/eu-and-canada-lay-foundations-free-movement-architects-2022-03-21_en.

Fahey, E. (2017), "CETA and Global Governance Law: What Kind of Model Agreement Is It Really in Law?", *European Papers* 2(1), pp. 293-302, available at: https://www.europeanpapers.eu/en/system/files/pdf_version/EP_EF_2017_I_007_Elaine_Fahey_00119.pdf.

Gaisford, J.D. and Kerr, W. A. (2001), *Economic Analysis for International Trade Negotiations*, Cheltenham: Edward Elgar Press.

Gaisford, J.D., Kerr, W.A. and Perdikis, N. (2003), *Economic Analysis for EU Accession Negotiations — Agri-Food Issues in the EU's Eastward Expansion*, Cheltenham: Edward Elgar Press.

Gantz, D.A. (2004), "The Evolution of FTA Investment Provisions: From NAFTA to the United States Chile Free Trade Agreement", *American University International Law Review* 19(4), pp. 679-768.

Gantz, D.A. (2022), "Canada's Approaches to Investor-State Dispute Settlement: Addressing Divergencies among CETA, USMCA, CPTPP, and the Canada-China FIPA", in R.G. Finbow (ed.) *CETA Implementation and Implications: Unravelling the Puzzle*, Montreal: McGill-Queen's University Press, pp. 183-209.

Global Affairs Canada (2018), *1st Meeting of the CETA Regulatory Cooperation Forum*, available at: https://www.international.gc.ca/trade-commerce/trade-agreements-accords-commerciaux/agr-acc/ceta-aecg/2018-12-14_rcf_report-rapport_fcr.aspx?lang=eng.

Global Affairs Canada (2020), 2nd *Meeting of the CETA Regulatory Cooperation Forum*, available at: https://www.international.gc.ca/trade-commerce/trade-agreements-accords-commerciaux/agr-acc/ceta-aecg/2020-02-RCF_report-FCMR_rapport.aspx?lang=eng.

Global Affairs Canada and European Commission (2021), "An Overview of Canada-EU Trade Performance under CETA", *Second Canada-EU CETA Joint Committee Meeting*, available at: https://www.international.gc.ca/trade-commerce/assets/pdfs/economist-economiste/statistics-statistiques/joint-ceta-statistics-report-ec_final-np-en.pdf.

Global Affairs Canada (2021), *2021 Canada's State of Trade, A Closer Look at Foreign Direct Investment*, Office of the Chief Economist, available at: https://www.international.gc.ca/transparency-transparence/assets/pdfs/state-trade-commerce-international/SoT-ENG.pdf.

Global Affairs Canada (2022), *CETA@5 Delivering trade benefits during unprecedented times*, Office of the Chief Economist, available at: https://www.international.gc.ca/trade-commerce/economist-economiste/analysis-analyse/benefits-ceta5-avantages.aspx?lang=eng.

Global Affairs Canada (2022), *2022 Canada's State of Trade, The Benefits of Free Trade Agreements*, Office of the Chief Economist, available at: https://www.international.gc.ca/transparency-transparence/assets/pdfs/state-trade-commerce-international/2022/sot-2022-eng.pdf.

Global Affairs Canada (2022), *Comprehensive Economic and Trade Agreement Regulatory Cooperation Forum - Work Plan*, available at: https://www.international.gc.ca/trade-commerce/trade-agreements-accords-commerciaux/agr-acc/ceta-aecg/2021-07-28-work-travail-plan.aspx?lang=eng.

Global Affairs Canada (2022), 4th *Meeting of the CETA Regulatory Cooperation Forum*, available at: https://www.international.gc.ca/trade-commerce/trade-agreements-accords-commerciaux/agr-acc/ceta-aecg/2022-05-03-rcf_summary-sommaire_fcr.aspx?lang=eng.

Goff, P. (2014), "Transatlantic Economic Agreements: Parsing CETA and TTIP", CIGI Papers No. 35, Centre for International Governance Innovation, July 21, available at: https://www.cigionline.org/static/documents/cigi_paper_35_0.pdf.

Golberg, E. (2019), *Regulatory Cooperation — A Reality Check*, M-RCBG Working Paper No. 115. available at https://www.hks.harvard.edu/sites/default/files/centers/mrcbg/img/115_final.pdf.

González, M., Gordo, E. and Manrique, M. (2017), "The EU's new-generation trade agreements: the CETA treaty", *Economic Bulletin, Banco de España*, issue SEP, pp. 1-7.

Grier, J.H. (2020), "Growing Significance of Regional Trade Agreements in Opening Public Procurement", in A. Castelli, G. Piga, S. Saussier and T. Tátrai (eds) *The Challenges of Public Procurement Reforms*. New York: Routledge, pp. 184-218.

Harbine, J. (2002), "NAFTA Chapter 11 Arbitration: Deciding the Price of Free Trade", *Ecology Law Quarterly* 29(2), pp. 371–394.

Hobbs, J.E. (2007), "Technical Barriers to Trade", in W.A. Kerr and J.D. Gaisford (eds.) *Handbook on International Trade Policy*, Cheltenham: Edward Elgar Press, pp. 394-403.

Hoekman, B. and Sabel, C. (2019), "Open Plurilateral Agreements, International Regulatory Cooperation and the WTO", *Global Policy* 10(3), pp. 297-312.

James, S. and Anderson, K. (2005), "On the Need for More Economic Assessment of Quarantine Policies", in K. Andersonn and T. Josling (eds.) *In the WTO and Agriculture, Vol. II,* Cheltenham: Edward Elgar Press, pp. 197-216.

Katunar, M., Maljak, M. and Martinić, S. (2014), "The Evolution of the EU's Foreign Trade Policy", available at: https://hrcak.srce.hr/file/216772

Kerr, W.A. (2006), "International Harmonization and the Gains from Trade", *Journal of International Law and Trade Policy* 7(2), 116-125.

Leblond, P. (2016), "Making the Most of CETA: A Complete and Effective Implementation Is Key to Realizing the Agreement's Full Potential", CIGI Papers No. 114, Centre for International Governance Innovation, October 30, available at: https://www.cigionline.org/publications/making-most-ceta-complete-and-effective-implementation-key-realizing-agreements-full-0/.

Leblond, P. and Viju-Miljusevic, C. (2019), "EU trade policy in the twenty-first century: change, continuity and challenges", *Journal of European Public Policy* 7(2), pp. 116-125.

Lester, S., Manak, I. and Ikenson, D. (2017), "Renegotiating NAFTA in the Era of Trump: Keeping the Trade Liberalization In and the Protectionism Out", *CATO Working Paper 46,* available at https://assets.realclear.com/files/2017/08/648_nafta.pdf.

Madner, V. (2017), "A New Generation of Trade Agreements: An Opportunity Not to Be Missed?", in S. Griller, W. Obwexer and E. Vranes (eds) *Mega-Regional Trade Agreements: CETA, TTIP, And TiSA: New Orientation for EU External Economic Relations,* Oxford: Oxford Academic, pp. 308-315.

Mattoo, A., Rocha, M. and Ruta, M. (2020), "The Evolution of Deep Trade", in Mattoo, A., Rocha, M. and Ruta, M. (eds), *Handbook of Deep Trade Agreements,* Washington, DC: The World Bank.

Mignon, N. (2020), "The CETA Report on Mobility of Professionals", EU Delegation to Canada, available at: https://trade.ec.europa.eu/doclib/docs/2020/december/tradoc_159158.pdf.

Neuwahl, N.A.E.M. (2021), "The 2020 EU-UK Trade and Cooperation Agreement as a Canada Style Agreement", May 19, EU3D Research Paper No. 4, avaliable at: https://ssrn.com/abstract=3633959.

OECD (1994), *Regulatory Cooperation for an Independent World,* Paris: OECD, available at: https://www.oecd-ilibrary.org/governance/regulatory-co-operation-for-an-interdependent-world_9789264062436-en.

Rioux, M., Ares, M. and Huang, P. (2015), "Beyond NAFTA with Three Countries: The Impact of Global Value Chains on an Outdated Trade Agreement", *Open Journal of Political Science* 5, pp. 264-276.

Rioux, M., Deblock, C. and Wells, G.-P. (2020), "CETA, an Innovative Agreement with Many Unsettled Trajectories", *Open Journal of Political Science* 10, pp. 50-60.

Rodrik, D. (2018), "What Do Trade Agreements Really Do?", *Journal of Economic Perspectives* 32(2), pp. 73-90.

Ruffat, A. and Leblond, P. (2022), "Public Procurement under CETA Chapter 1", in R.G. Finbow (ed.) *CETA Implementation and Implications: Unravelling the Puzzle,* Montreal: McGill-Queen's University Press, pp. 143-158.

Śliwińska, M. (2019), "New generation trade agreements as an economic challenge for the European Union and its Member States — the case of CETA", *Przeglad Europejski* 4(4), pp. 141–158.

Statistics Canada (2022), "International investment position, Canadian direct investment abroad and foreign direct investment in Canada, by industry and select countries, annual (x1,000,000)", Table 36-10-0659-01, available at: https://www150.statcan.gc.ca/t1/tbl1/en/tv.action?pid=3610065901.

Van Rooy, C. (2022), "A Cautionary Tale of Regulatory Cooperation in CETA: Executive Expertise and the Influence of Foreign Governments in Domestic Regulatory Processes", in R.G. Finbow (ed.) *CETA Implementation and Implications: Unravelling the Puzzle,* Montreal: McGill-Queen's University Press, pp. 116-140.

WTO (2015), "Trade in Services: The Most Dynamic Segment of International Trade", Geneva: World Trade Organization, available at: https://www.wto.org/english/thewto_e/20y_e/services_brochure2015_e.pdf.

Yeung, M.T., Perdikis, N. and Kerr, W. A. (1999), *Regional Trading Blocs in the Global Economy: The EU and ASEAN,* Cheltenham: Edward Elgar Press.

PART III

ON PUBLIC AND PRIVATE RESPONSES TO GLOBALIZATION CHALLENGES: EU TRADE POLICY AND GLOBAL VALUE CHAINS

Summary

With the EU's traditional free trade stance tested in recent times by a combination of crises and geopolitics, Part III focuses on reorientations of EU trade policy and on changing globalization patterns. The issue remains whether those will make trade more resilient and sustainable and bring it in line with the EU's sustainability objectives and the European Green Deal. **Chapter 8** (Couvreur, De Ville, Jacobs and Orbie) argues that the EU is still a defender of free trade and multilateralism but has been adjusting its trade policy since 2015. The EU now puts emphasis on defensive aspects against others (example: China, not domesticated by multilateral rules). The discursive justification goes that its stance had been naïve before. Yet, neither was EU trade policy naïve before nor is it entirely defensive now, as illustrated by sustainable development chapters or the carbon-border adjustment mechanism (CBAM). **Chapter 9** (Blot) reviews the new TSD Chapter approach and assesses its overall objective, which is to address sustainability concerns linked to international trade. It evaluates what this new approach entails and how effective it will be with respect to improving the monitoring and enforceability of the TSD chapters. It also discusses missed opportunities for enhancing sustainability in EU trade agreements and reflects what the new TSD approach could mean for newly concluded and ongoing trade agreements. **Chapter 10** (Della Posta) puts forward that global value chains might be more resilient than expected. The reason is that firms may also opt to switch some production (say from China) to a near-by location (with similar cost advantages but associated with a perceived lower geopolitical risk) rather than back home or to the same bloc.

CHAPTER 8
THE GOOD GEOPOLITICAL TRADE ACTOR? THE EUROPEAN UNION'S DISCURSIVE JUSTIFICATION OF THE ANTI-COERCION INSTRUMENT[147]

Sjorre Couvreur, Ferdi De Ville, Thomas Jacobs and Jan Orbie

Abstract: Traditionally, the EU has presented itself as a normative trade actor, as opposed to other geopolitical trading powers. However, today, it is increasingly recognized that the EU is undergoing a geopolitical turn which also manifests itself in its trade policy. Yet, confusion remains regarding what a 'geopolitical EU trade policy' entails and how the EU sells this new perspective in its trade policy. This chapter contributes to the ongoing debate on this topic by investigating how the European Commission discursively justifies its geopolitical turn in trade. Methodologically, we analyze EU trade discourse with particular attention for othering strategies. Empirically, we study a most-likely case of 'geopoliticization of trade', namely the Commission's initiative to launch an Anti-Coercion Instrument, by analyzing the most important EU documents covering the ACI so far and EU statements on the ACI in relevant media. We find that the Commission distinguishes a 'defensive' and 'offensive' variant of geopoliticization of trade, whereby the former is conceived as 'good' and pursued by the EU, while the latter is seen as 'bad' and employed by non-EU trading powers. This diverges from previous EU trade discourses since the 2000s, which portrayed the EU as transcending geopolitics — a normative power pursuing free trade and multilateralism — and other powers as essentially geopolitical — self-interested, protectionist, and regionalist. The EU's new othering strategy legitimizes the EU's geopolitical turn in trade, by simultaneously turning away from its previous, 'naively' normative trade discourse, while also contrasting the EU's trade policy to the 'offensive' geopolitical trade from 'bad' trade actors.

Keywords: EU trade policy; Geopolitics; Anti-Coercion Instrument; China; Othering

[147] We are grateful to the anonymous reviewers and editors of the journal and to all participants of the workshop on the (geo)politicization of EU trade and other external policies, ECPR Joint Sessions, Antwerp, 19-20 April 2022, for the useful feedback on an earlier version.

1. Introduction

The European Union is increasingly positioning itself as a geopolitical actor in international politics. Since the adoption of the EU Global Strategy of 2016, most observers agree that the EU has reached a turning point, moving towards a geopolitical union (Biscop 2018; Nicosia 2019; Rabinovych, and Novakova 2019). The mission statement of the European Commission President Von der Leyen in 2019 to lead a 'geopolitical commission' seemed to affirm this alleged shift in the EU's external posture (European Parliament 2020). Additionally, the EU High Representative for Foreign Affairs and Security Policy has repeatedly stated that Europe "must learn quickly to speak the language of power, and not only rely on soft power as we used to" (Weiler 2020). The EU's geopolitical turn also seems to increasingly manifest itself in the EU's trade policy, one of the EU's strongest external policy tools considering its exclusive legal competence, significant market power, and historical track record.

This emerging observation is peculiar, as, despite pressure from foreign policy circles in the past, most authors did not see the immediate use of trade as a foreign policy tool attainable within the EU context (Bossuyt *et al.*, 2020; De Ville and Silles-Brügge, 2018, Biscop, 2018). Indeed, ever since the EU obtained exclusive competence on trade policy in the Union's founding Treaty of Rome, EU trade policy has been seen as isolated from foreign and security policy concerns to pursue a technocratic and free trade-oriented trade policy course (Gebhard and Nordheim-Martinsen 2011; Pilegaard 2009). For a long time, the literature paid little attention to the possibility of geopolitical trade policy, reflecting the shielded nature of trade policy from geopolitical concerns. EU trade policymakers were seen as 'trade purists', who aim to use trade to defend and promote European economic interests, mainly through liberalization (Young and Peterson 2014, p. 186). Trade could, therefore, not act as an instrument to react to complex foreign policy and security issues. Yet, 'foreign policy specialists' still advocated for the use of trade as an instrument of the broader foreign policy objectives (Keukeleire 2001; 2003; 2004; Peterson 2007). Nonetheless, Bossuyt *et al.* (2020) argued that despite pressure from foreign policy circles, geopolitics through trade had not yet been achieved due to different structural and institutional factors at play. In other words, trade and foreign policy until recently still operated in separate policy worlds due to their different institutional settings. Ideologically, the EU's trade policy was still seen to be driven by neoliberal motives and the pursuit of free trade through the multilateral level of the WTO and different bilateral free trade agreements. Recent free trade agreements with Vietnam, Japan, Canada, Korea, and others justified this claim (De Ville and Siles-Brügge 2018; Orbie and De Ville 2020). Biscop (2018) also underscored the idea that a geopolitical EU trade policy had not been achieved, noting that although the EU Global Strategy of 2016 said a lot about trade compared to the European Security Strategy of 2003, a real commitment to integrating trade policy within the EU's broader foreign policy was still lacking.

Nevertheless, thinking on this matter has significantly changed in recent times and has particularly shifted in the context of increasingly tense US-China relations, the Covid-19 pandemic and Russia's war in Ukraine. Indeed, in the shadow of increasingly tense US-China relations, an increasingly vivid debate emerged on whether the EU's trade policy is also becoming more geopolitical and subordinated to foreign policy objectives (*e.g.* Beattie 2019; De Ville 2019; Felbermayr 2018; Meunier and Nicolaidis 2019). Meunier and Nicolaidis (2019) stated that trade policies are becoming essential geopolitical tools, coining the idea of the 'geopoliticization of EU trade policy'. Some observers even spoke about a 'Trumpian turn in EU trade policies' (Felbermayr 2018) and an 'economic battlefield and trade warfare' (Meunier and Nicolaidis 2019). The Covid-19 pandemic further accelerated policymakers' awareness of the dangers that come with interdependence and the need for more strategic autonomy. This consequently drove scholars to increasingly acknowledge the geopolitical turn EU trade policy has made since the pandemic (Jacobs, Gheyle, De Ville and Orbie 2022; Schmitz and Seidl 2022). Furthermore, Russia's invasion of Ukraine and the EU's swift reaction with unprecedented economic sanctions have led various authors to note the emergence of an 'EU Geoeconomic Power' (Postnikov and Adriaensen 2022; Biscop, Gehrke and Siman 2022; Helwig and Wigell 2022) or a 'geo-economic revolution' (Hackenbroich 2022). The EU's recent actions have thus suddenly sparked the previously unthinkable idea that 'Brussels is getting ready to dump its free trade ideals' or that 'the last big defender of rules-based open trade — the European Union — is about to fall' (Moens and von der Burchard 2022). Indeed, even though EU trade policy has for a long time been seen as isolated from foreign policy considerations, the trade-security nexus debate has increasingly accepted the idea of a geopolitical EU trade policy.

This shift seems particularly remarkable when contrasted with how the EU previously positioned itself toward the outside world. Throughout the past decades, various authors emphasized the *sui generis* nature of the European

Union's position in international affairs. These debates led to various perspectives on the EU's role in the world. Different concepts, such as Civilian Power Europe (Duchêne 1972); Normative Power Europe (Manners 2002); Europe as a 'post-modern' state (Cooper 2003) and Market Power Europe (Damro 2012) were developed to describe the EU's identity and, at the same time, to compare the EU to other actors in international politics. Particularly the idea of 'Normative Power Europe' (NPE) has continued to inspire scholarship (*e.g.* Wagnsson and Hellman 2018; Newman and Stefan 2019; Ahrens 2018), although a lively debate on its limitations and blind spots also emerged (Diez 2004, 2005; Diez and Manners 2007). Furthermore, normative discourses have been used extensively by officials from various EU institutions, including in the context of the EU's international trade policy. Many academic studies (*e.g.* Storey 2006; Manners 2009; Poletti and Sicurelli 2018) and much policy work engage with this more normative dimension of EU trade policy. Even in the year before the launch of the EU Global Strategy of 2016, the EU's Trade for All trade and investment strategy still noted that "the Commission must pursue a policy that benefits society as a whole and promotes European and universal standards and values alongside core economic interests, putting a greater emphasis on sustainable development, human rights, tax evasion, consumer protection, and responsible and fair trade" (European Commission 2015: 18). Furthermore, the recent EU Trade Policy Review (European Commission 2021a) stressed 'values' such as 'sustainability' and 'fairness' as key components of the EU's pursuit of open strategic autonomy (p.4) and aims to 'work with partners to ensure adherence to universal values, notably the promotion and protection of human rights' (p.6). Nonetheless, in light of the EU's broader geopolitical turn in trade described above, also the new trade strategy was commonly interpreted as a move towards a more strategic, interest-based approach. The EU Trade Policy Review indeed emphasized that trade policy should "support the EU's geopolitical interests" (pp.8–9) and that the EU should be more 'assertive' in enforcing its trade agenda (pp.19-20) (European Commission 2021a).

The remarkable and controversial nature of the EU's turn toward a more geopolitical view on trade, raises the question of how this pivot is justified and legitimized. Although the EU, over the past decades, has traditionally presented itself as a normative trade actor, opposing itself to other geopolitical trading powers, it has now increasingly come to position itself as a geopolitical trade actor in its own right. Given this remarkable development, it is fascinating from a strategic point of view to ask how the EU justifies this geopolitical turn discursively. This justification affects the internal and external legitimacy (and hence effectiveness) of the EU's policies, which is particularly important in the current turbulent times in which the old policy equilibrium is being destabilized. Concretely, this paper revolves around the research question: How does the European Commission discursively justify its geopolitical turn in trade?

Answering this question requires the adoption of a discursive perspective. Legitimation is after all a discursive process, which revolves around particular forms of language use, rhetoric, claims-making, and argumentation (Jiwani and Richardson 2011). As highlighted above, there is a notable shift in how the EU represents itself. Given how notable and remarkable this shift is, we can expect that it will be supported and given credence through auxiliary representations that effectively serve to legitimize the shift. Our goal in this chapter is to map, analyse and understand these auxiliary representations that strategically legitimize the shift in the EU's trade discourse. We will in particular be heeding the EU's use of so-called othering strategies as a way to discursively legitimize its actions. By answering the question of how the EU discursively legitimizes its geopolitical turn in trade policy, we can arrive at a better understanding of how the EU uses discourse to strategically justify a controversial policy turn which presumably goes against previously dominant ideas of free trade and multilateralism, while also improving our understanding of how the EU strategically positions its new trade rationale *vis-à-vis* other actors in international trade. From a policy perspective, this question allows us to assess possible contradictions and flaws within the EU's official trade discourse that, on a strategic level, could prove counterproductive in the long run.

Below, we first provide some context to our case study on the Anti-Coercion Instrument (ACI) that, as we argue, can be seen as the primary example of the geopoliticization of EU trade policy. Subsequently, we introduce the theoretical background and the methodology used in our analysis. We then put forward an empirical examination of how the EU's contemporary trade discourse contrasts with its previous rhetoric and practices, focusing on the rich case of the Anti-Coercion Instrument (ACI). This empirical analysis is based on a 132-page dataset that comprises six documents, as well as several official EU statements from relevant media outlets. We conclude with a discussion and a critical reflection on our findings.

2. The Anti-Coercion Instrument in context

The European Commission's official rhetoric around the launch of its Anti-Coercion Instrument provides a particularly useful dataset to get a more precise understanding of the shift in the EU's discourse. Indeed, the European Commission's proposal was recently referred to as the EU flexing its "geopolitical muscle with a new trade weapon" (Moens and Hanke Vela 2021) and "potentially the EU's most powerful gun" among the new defensive trade instruments (Allenbach-Ammann 2022). Given the controversy around the new instrument and its link with the EU's more assertive approach, it provides a most-likely case of the EU applying geopolitical trade. However, despite the Anti-Coercion Instrument being referred to as potentially the EU's most powerful new trade defence tool, the European Commission has not solely focused its attention on tackling economic coercion. Although this chapter focuses on this most-likely case of 'geopoliticization of trade', it is important to mention that in the context of an increasing acceptance of geopolitical EU trade policy, various other new instruments have also been created by the EU in the past years. Without going into detail, we will briefly mention these new instruments that reinforce the EU's traditional trade defence toolbox, before looking in-depth into the Anti-Coercion Instrument.

The European Union's trade defence toolbox has for decades only existed of three core tools: anti-dumping (AD), anti-subsidy (AS) and safeguard (SG) measures. These instruments aim at protecting European businesses against unfair or overwhelming import competition and need to maintain broad support for the EU's aim of trade liberalization (Hoekman and Kostecki 2001, p. 303; De Ville 2022). However, as the nature of trade in international politics changed, the EU's vision for its trade policy also diverted from a pure focus on 'liberalization' to a more pragmatic vision of 'open strategic autonomy'. While this new beacon for the EU's trade policy still holds on to the idea of liberalization and multilateralism, it also recognizes the need for more focus on the EU's geo-economic interests, which demands unilateral action when needed. In response, the EU has been introducing the following new unilateral instruments: a Foreign Subsidies Regulation (FSR); an updated Trade Enforcement Regulation (TER); a Foreign Investment Screening Mechanism (FISM); an International Procurement Instrument (IPI), a Carbon Border Adjustment Mechanism (CBAM) and 6) an Anti-Coercion Instrument (ACI). These various new instruments give the European Commission the ability to unilaterally restrict access to the European market based on certain policy decisions by third-country governments. Although we refer to other recent research to explain the motives behind this unprecedented unilateral turn in EU trade (*e.g.* De Ville 2022), it's worth underscoring that the geopoliticization of EU trade is taking place with various new policy tools that tackle different aspects of the increasingly geoeconomic rationale behind trade. Having mentioned the plethora of new trade defence instruments, this chapter focuses on what some pundits refer to as the "EU's most powerful gun" within this new arsenal: the Anti-Coercion Instrument (Allenbach-Ammann 2022).

The European Commission in December 2021 put forward a proposal for a Regulation to protect the Union and its Member States from economic coercion by third countries. The instrument comes after several EU Member States increasingly became a target of deliberate economic intimidation from third countries. The Commission defines economic coercion as "a situation where a third country is seeking to pressure the Union or a Member State into making a particular policy choice by applying, or threatening to apply, measures affecting trade or investment against the Union or a Member State" (European Commission 2021b). Consequently, the proposal addresses a legislative gap by creating a legal framework under the Union's Common Commercial Policy, allowing the Union to counteract coercion when necessary, by initiating a multi-step procedure which can lead the Union to impose countermeasures as a last resort. The stated aim of the instrument is primarily to avoid the necessity of countermeasures by encouraging engagement with the coercing country through negotiations, mediation, or adjudication (European Commission 2021b). The Anti-Coercion Instrument thus strengthens the EU's existing trade defence instruments, allowing for a stronger position on the global stage.

Concretely, the instrument would need to prevent previous situations in which the EU proved powerless against, for example, Beijing's trade embargo on Lithuania, after the country had pulled out of China's 17+1 diplomatic format and deepened its diplomatic ties with Taiwan (Lau and Moens 2021). However, the Commission proposal still needs to be agreed on by the European Parliament and the Council of the European Union under the Ordinary Legislative Procedure. At the time of writing (December 2022), the dialogue between the Council and the European Parliament has started, yet discussions promise to remain difficult. On the one hand, some member states believe the instrument's scope and the Commission's discretion is going too far and therefore demand more say over the use of the new instrument. On the other hand, MEPs would like to see the scope broadened even further, giving the Commission a strong mandate for its implementation (Allenbach-Ammann 2022; Moens 2022; Moens and Hanke Vela 2021). Furthermore, legal questions remain on the compatibility of the ACI with international law (Deepak 2022), including WTO rules (Baetens and Bronckers 2022). Although the proposal will likely provoke more inter-institutional discussions between the Council, the European Parliament and the Commission, it is without a doubt that once adopted this new instrument to tackle economic blackmailing will give the EU more leverage to back up its geopolitical ambitions. While the instrument is not finalized or agreed upon at the time of writing, it is intriguing to analyse the EU's justification of the ACI to improve our understanding of what the geopoliticization of trade entails and how the EU adjusts to this new phenomenon.

3. Theory

Recently, we increasingly witness that the EU's discourse and pundits' analyses have shifted from a long-time recognition of a 'Normative Power Europe' to a 'geopolitical power Europe'. Although discussion may exist on whether 'geopolitical power Europe' fully excludes 'Normative Power Europe' (Orbie 2021), a shift has been observed where the latter has become subordinate to the former. This remarkable shift becomes even more surprising when taking into account Diez' (2004, 2005) critical assessment of Manners' (2003) 'Normative Power Europe' concept, which has been central to the debates and understandings of Normative Power Europe over the past two decades. Indeed, by building on discourse theory, Diez (2004, 2005) noted that the 'Normative Power Europe' discourse in essence entails a strategy of discursive othering. By adopting this othering strategy, the EU generates a difference between the Self and the Other through which an international European identity is constructed and certain policy actions are legitimized. Building on this, and acknowledged by Manners himself (2005), Diez (2004, 2005) criticized the fact that the EU's othering strategy had increasingly shifted from a self-reflexive *temporal othering* since the start of European integration toward *geopolitical othering* since the Maastricht Treaty and the end of the Cold War. While temporal othering saw the Other as the EU's own dark past, legitimizing EU decision-making towards more European integration, Diez notes that since the 1990's the EU has increasingly legitimized its own unique standing and decisions by morally referring to a 'geopolitical other'. This practice of othering, which constructed an international identity for the EU through the logic of difference between the superior Self and the geopolitical Other was further emphasized by discursively presenting the Other as an existential threat; inferior; a violator of universal principles; or different (Diez 2005). Manners (2005) acknowledged Diez's assessment, but also noted that practices of othering are unavoidable in human social existence. Consequently, Manners made the case for more self-reflexive and positive othering strategies. Both authors agreed on the need to pay more attention to the power behind the EU's normative power representations. They specifically argued for more humble discursive power representations that construct non-hierarchical relationships by adopting 'temporal othering' and even 'abject othering'. With temporal othering, the EU would recognize its own past as the Other to position the current Self and legitimize present policy decisions. With abject othering, the EU would present the Other as being part of the Self, recognizing the similarities the Other and the Self actually share (Diez and Manners 2007). Nonetheless, despite their efforts toward these more positive othering strategies, the EU for almost two decades maintained its discursive approach of positioning the EU normative Self in opposition to the geopolitical Other.

Applied to EU trade policy, Diez' observation concretely entailed that since the 2000s, the EU's trade discourses had consistently portrayed the EU Self as transcending geopolitics — a 'normative' power — pursuing free trade and multilateralism, while other major powers were viewed as essentially geopolitical — self-interested, protectionist and regionalist. However, when taking into account the new reality of a geopolitical turn in EU external relations, which according to many authors is also materializing itself in EU trade, the long-time predominant idea of a 'normative' EU *vs.* a 'geopolitical' Other becomes increasingly fluid. Indeed, the growing acceptance of the geopoliticization of EU trade policy, both in academic and policy circles, raises questions when mirrored against the background of EU trade discourses since the 2000s (Diez 2004, 2005). Now that the EU profiles itself as a geopolitical actor in trade, apparently aligning itself with the formerly despised other, the question raises what this means for the discursive representation vis-à-vis the (former) self and others. In the empirical part of the paper, we will analyse this by pragmatically using the distinction between temporal and geopolitical othering.

4. Methodology and data

We study the rather sudden turn in EU trade policy from a normative and geopolitics-averse to a more proactively geopolitical stance by looking at the prevalence of othering strategies in the rhetoric of EU actors. It is important to note that this perspective has rarely been applied to the study of EU trade policy. Material and economic issues (like trade) have long been reified in political science as hard subject matters that require positivist or quantitative analysis and thus lie beyond the scope of the linguistic, discursive, or post-positivist approaches. By studying the presence of othering strategies in the EU's discourse on international trade, we hope to contribute to the growing ideational literature on EU trade policy (*cf.* Jacobs and Orbie 2020).

As a discursive mechanism, 'othering' has its antecedents in poststructuralist theory. It is seen as a fundamental force that plays a central role in constructing the divides and fault lines that constitute the political landscape and the public debate (Laclau and Mouffe 2014). To theorize the discursive mechanism of 'othering', poststructuralist discourse analysts take recourse to the philosophy of Hegel, who first posited the idea that one's self-defined identity can be constructed through and predicated on an imagined and constitutive Other. Othering is then deployed by the dominant social group as a way to legitimize its hegemony. In this case, othering involves the identification of some mythical Other, to whom various traits and characteristics are ascribed. These traits are the reverse mirror image of the way the dominant group perceives itself. This way, othering delineates who does and does not belong to the dominant group, while also reaffirming the alleged superiority of the dominant group (Jensen 2011).

Practically, discursive analyses of othering collect and analyse data about the presence of references, predications, arguments, perspectives, metaphors, *topoi*, and labels that betray the identification and differentiation of a superior in-group and an inferior out-group (Jiwani and Richardson 2011). These rhetorical devices can result in a variety of othering mechanisms, including temporal othering (the Other is backwards or belongs to the past); geographical othering (the Other is elsewhere or far away); abject othering (the Other is part of the in-group but is repressed and excluded from it) or liminal othering (the Other is close to the in-group but can never join it). In the context of this chapter, we analyse the presence of these rhetorical devices in the EU's official discourse on the Anti-Coercion Instrument, so as to detect and identify how othering mechanisms are at work in this discourse.

In doing so, we contribute to a rich tradition in EU foreign policy analysis that uses othering as an analytic perspective to make sense of how the EU perceives both itself and the surrounding world (Hornat 2019; Derous 2018; Pace 2005; Tekin 2010). Othering analyses have played a particularly important role in the academic debate surrounding the EU's status as a Normative Power. Tomas Diez (2004, 2005; Manners, and Diez 2007) for instance argued that the two dominant othering mechanisms through which the EU constitutes itself are its own violent, war-torn past (a form of temporal othering) and the combination of different identities, cultures, political systems and geographies by which it is surrounded (which Diez often referred to as 'geopolitical' othering). According to Diez, the first othering mechanism declined in favour of the second. Yet, as mentioned, our analysis will assess how this plays out in the present context, by looking at which othering mechanisms are predominant in the EU's official discourse on the Anti-Coercion Instrument.

In terms of data collection, we will study a corpus of six documents (132 pages, available upon request). This corpus comprises two press releases from the European Commission; a Communication from the Commission to the Council and the European Parliament; a Joint declaration by the Commission, the Council, and the European Parliament; the Commission's proposal for a regulation to create the Anti-Coercion Instrument; and the Commission's Impact Assessment Report linked to the proposal. We have compiled this corpus to cover what we believe to be a representative and comprehensive sample of documents — documents for internal as well as external use, for political as well as policy-making purposes, and of a fundamental as well as a technical nature are all present in this mix. Additionally, we integrated several EU official statements on the ACI in relevant media outlets into our analysis. In our analysis, we have coded how EU actors justify the introduction of the ACI, particularly in reference to the EU's previous trade policy stance (temporal othering) and the trade policies of third countries (geographical othering).

5. The Anti-Coercion Instrument: A two-fold othering strategy

Below, we give a detailed analysis of how the EU uses othering mechanisms through its official discourse on the Anti-Coercion Instrument. Building on previous findings by Diez (2004, 2005; Manners and Diez 2007), we observe a two-fold othering strategy within the EU's discourse. On the one hand, the EU adopts a 'temporal othering', opposing the assertive (current) Self to the naïve former Self, who is cast as the Other. On the other hand, it adopts a 'geopolitical othering', opposing the good geopolitical Self to the bad geopolitical Other. Consequently, we will structure our analysis based on this two-fold othering strategy within the EU's discourse.

5.1 Temporal othering: Assertive current EU versus Naïve former EU

The EU discourse in several documents contrasts the EU's current more assertive trade rationale — the Self — versus the previously more naïve free-trade and normative trade stance — the Other. Indeed, in a Press Release from the Commission, current Trade Commissioner Dombrovskis underscored the need to strengthen the "EU's resilience" and noted that: "As part of our new EU trade policy approach, we have committed to being more assertive in defending our interests" (European Commission 2021c). The reference to being 'more assertive in defending interests' recognizes that the EU's previous trade policy course was not assertive enough. This narrative underlining the need for a more assertive focus was echoed in the impact assessment report on the Commission's proposal for the ACI regulation, which noted that the possible countermeasures under the instrument, "as a last resort, allow the EU to be assertive where needed and the response to be appropriately calibrated." (European Commission 2021d). Within the discourse of the EU, we also clearly observe that the ACI is framed within a broader signal to other actors that the EU is moving away from its previously 'naïve' trade policy. The resolution to be "no longer naïve" has become one of the most used speaking points in EU trade policy in recent years. The ACI is presented as a "signal to international partners that the Union is not willing to accept economic coercion. It highlights the assertiveness and the resilience of the Union, and supports the efforts to ensure open strategic autonomy" (European Commission 2021b).

Additionally, when looking at EU official comments in media outlets, this credo is regularly echoed. Indeed, when commenting on the proposal for an Anti-Coercion Instrument, an EU trade diplomat noted that "the EU should not be naïve in its trade and foreign policy" (Moens and Hanke Vela 2021). When discussing the EU's new trade approach, including the ACI, the Director-General of DG Trade Sabine Weyand further argued that the EU also needs "autonomous instruments that protect us from those who take advantage of our openness" and stated "I believe that we must accept this duality, whereby we continue to defend a multilateral order based on rules, but also accept that it is essential to do so from a stronger position, equipping ourselves with all necessary instruments" (Weyand 2022). Former EU Trade Commissioner Hogan additionally stated that the EU's belief in openness "does not mean that we are woolly-headed idealists" (European Commission 2020). In these statements, Commission representatives make clear that their trade rationale has significantly evolved, whereby they are moving towards a less naïve and more assertive stance in trade, equipping themselves with the necessary new tools to achieve this.

However, when taking a reflexive perspective, this recurring 'temporal othering' between a currently assertive EU trade Self versus a previously naïve EU trade Self can be critically interrogated. Specifically, we could question if the EU really refrained completely from the use of assertive (or geopolitical) use of trade instruments in the past. The contrast between the 'assertive' current Self and the 'naïve' former Self might be less distinct than the Commission likes to portray today. Scholars have already pointed to the fact that when it comes to developing countries, with which the EU has an asymmetrical relationship, the EU previously already used trade in a geopolitical way with a pure focus on attaining foreign policy objectives (*e.g.* Young and Peterson 2014, p. 184). Building on this, various previous EU trade policies such as the European Partnership Agreements, certain Free Trade Agreements (*e.g.* with Korea or Vietnam), TTIP as an economic NATO, GSP+ conditionalities and so forth could provide interesting case studies to contest the assumption that we are now suddenly witnessing an awakening of a geopolitical EU trade policy, and may rather confirm that the EU has always adopted geopolitical trade policies, but maybe in a less overt way. In line with Diez and Manners (2007), this temporal othering could be seen as a relatively innocent and harmless strategy to justify the EU's introduction of new, geopolitically-motivated trade instruments. But as we discuss in the next section, temporal othering is not the only othering mechanism that is used to justify the EU's trade policy turn.

5.2 Geopolitical othering: the good geopolitical EU versus the bad geopolitical other

The second discursive othering strategy we observed is a distinction between what we call a 'negative' 'offensive' geopoliticization of trade policy of the Other versus a 'good' 'defensive' geopoliticization of trade policy of the Self.

In the Commission's Press Release on 8 December 2021, Executive Vice--President and Commissioner for Trade Dombrovskis noted the following:

> *At a time of rising geopolitical tensions, trade is increasingly being weaponised and the EU and its Member States becoming targets of economic intimidation. We need the proper tools to respond. With this proposal we are sending a clear message that the EU will stand firm in* defending *its interests. The main aim of the anti-coercion tool is to act as a deterrent* (European Commission 2021e, emphasis added).

Within this statement, as well as in all the other EU official documents we can see that the EU's discourse regularly refers to a so-called "weaponization of trade" and "economic intimidation", which the EU and its member states are a victim of and which create "geopolitical challenges". As opposed to this "weaponization of trade", the EU positions itself on the defensive side focusing on "deterrence" and the need to "defend its interests". Indeed, by creating this distinction between the EU as the victim and the Other as the aggressor, there is othering taking place in which the EU is only focusing on geopolitically using trade in a defensive and deterrent way instead of using the Other's offensive 'weaponization' of trade. In another Press Release in which the Commission answers questions concerning the ACI, this message is again echoed by the Commission when it refers to "deterrence being the primary function" of the ACI and noting that trade countermeasures against economic coercion are only "a last resort" (European Commission 2021f). By highlighting that the use of EU trade policy as a response to economic coercion is only 'a last resort' for the EU, it again underscores its more defensive vision on using trade as a geopolitical tool. Additionally, we find several other references in which the EU presents itself as reactive to geopolitical first moves of others, like "the need to navigate rising global tensions with trade being increasingly weaponized in a geo-economic context" (European Commission 2021b). The EU's more defensive reading of its own geopoliticization of trade was also particularly apparent in its rhetoric where it framed the ACI as a way "to preserve the Union and Member States autonomy in policy-making and shield trade and investment from weaponization" (European Commission 2021b).

Furthermore, the Commission not only presents the ACI as a response to aggressive geopolitics by others, but also emphasizes that it will use the sanctions that are made possible by the instrument only when all other options are exhausted. The instrument is framed as an "instrument explicitly prioritizing a non-interventionist approach" with "countermeasures only as a last resort" (European Commission 2021b). By regularly referring to the EU's 'non-interventionist approach', the EU creates an image of the Other which does use trade as a way to influence the legitimate policy options of third countries. The EU's more defensive approach of 'geopoliticization of trade' is also apparent in its rhetoric stressing the need to react to third countries that use trade as a weapon by first opting for means such as diplomacy and negotiation. Concretely, the ACI proposal mentions "to encourage third countries to stop the economic coercion through non--interventionist measures (such as diplomacy), and predominantly regard the use of countermeasures as a last resort whose collateral damage must be weighed before action" (European Commission 2021b; European Commission 2021g). We can thus clearly observe that the EU is positioning itself as the 'good' geopolitical trade actor prioritizing non-interventionism and less confrontational measures such as diplomacy, while the other 'bad actor' is clearly linked to a more interventionist approach that immediately weaponizes trade policy to impose its objectives.

In line with our critical reflection on the EU's temporal othering and the question to what extent the EU has refrained from using geopolitical instruments in trade in the past, we could question the Union's framing about the "interventionist" trade policies of others. The Commission seems aware of this potential contradiction, and tries to pre-empt it by differentiating between "unduly" and appropriate interference in third countries' policies: "[t]he proposed instrument is a response to the rising problem of economic coercion and aims to protect the Union's and Member States' interests and sovereign choices. It will empower the Commission to apply trade, investment or other restrictions towards any non-EU country unduly interfering in the policy choices of the EU or its Member States" (European Commission 2021f; European Commission 2021c). This differentiation is regularly repeated in other statements: "[t]he objective of influencing partner countries is not illegitimate in itself, and, certainly, there are legitimate means by which to see to do so. However, the (mis)use of trade or investment restrictions with the objective of attaining a specific outcome lying within the legitimate policymaking space of the EU or Member State goes beyond and should be differentiated from the ordinary use of soft powers to influence partner countries" (European Commission 2021g). With this statement from the impact assessment to the proposal for an ACI regulation, the Commission clearly voices the distinction between what it sees as the legitimate use of trade to influence the other versus the illegitimate "(mis)use of trade". By doing this, the EU again separates itself from other actors' 'illegitimate' geopoliticized trade policies. In another statement a similar message was repeated: "[t]hose countries may try to obtain a certain policy direction by restricting trade or investment — or threatening to do so — to the detriment of EU businesses including those operating in these third countries. Such practices unduly interfere with the legitimate policymaking space of the EU and its Member States and undermine the EU's open strategic autonomy" (European Commission 2021c). By repeatedly referring to "those countries" and "unduly interference" which undermined the EU's "open strategic autonomy", the EU again not only opposes the Self versus the Other, which threatens the EU with a more offensive 'geopoliticization of trade', but also creates a justification for its own more 'defensive' form of geopolitical trade.

Lastly, to legitimize its 'good' geopolitical turn in trade, the EU also regularly refers to international law in its othering discourse. In the Commission proposal for a regulation for an Anti-Coercion instrument, the text defines coercion as "an action prohibited by international law when a country deploys measures such as trade or investment restrictions in order to obtain from another country an action or inaction which that country is not internationally obliged to perform and which falls within its sovereignty" (European Commission 2021b). By doing this, the EU positions itself against the illegal behaviour of the Other, again making the case for a 'justified' and 'legal' reaction with its own trade measures. This message is often reflected in EU statements in media outlets. When answering questions regarding the Anti--Coercion Instrument, Director-General of DG Trade Sabine Weyand promoted the Commission proposal by noting that "[w]hat is important in this respect is to clearly understand that we are developing an instrument to protect our interests in case a third-party country withdraws from international law. However, any European response to such a violation will always be in keeping with international law" (Weyand 2022). With this discourse on the ACI, the EU clearly distinguishes third countries that are 'withdrawing from international law' through their harmful trade measures from the EU itself that will 'always be in keeping with international law'. This distinction between the EU's good legal behaviour and the Others' illegal actions was again put forward more elaborately by Weyand in another statement discussing the EU's response against economic coercion: "As we are an actor based on law, our response has always been structured around the legal opportunities that would allow us to assert our interests and values in international forums, particularly the WTO. However, it is clear that we now live in a world in which we do not have the means to firmly respond if another country withdraws from international law and exerts pressure to prevent us from defining our policies" (Weyand 2022). These references to international law and the legality within which the EU behaves, versus the illegality of the other's actions, again underscore the distinction the EU makes between its 'good' and 'defensive' versus other's 'bad' and 'offensive' geopoliticization of trade.

Like the temporal othering, also the geopolitical othering strategy of the Commission to justify the ACI can be nuanced and criticized. For example, the fact that the EU refers to international law to legitimize its own 'defensive' geopolitical trade could already be contested from a WTO law perspective and is certainly not agreed upon with consensus by legal experts (Baetens and Bronckers 2022; Kommerskollegium 2022). Furthermore, as mentioned above, the Commission's claims about the lack of interventionist approaches within the EU's trade policy could easily be nuanced when taking into account criticisms of the EU's own interventionist trade policies such as its TSD chapters, GSP+ schemes or other new proposals like the carbon border adjustment mechanism. Lastly, the fact that the EU positions its new geopolitical trade tool on the defensive side might be understood as an attempt to legitimize its geopolitical turn in trade internally and externally, but this doesn't mean that third actors also perceive the ACI as a 'defensive' instrument and consequently react in the desired way. Indeed, the ACI and the EU's discourse could (and probably will) be interpreted offensively by third countries and may therefore lead to possible escalation or more trade disputes. China's 'Global Times', for example, has referred to the ACI as a "bullet launcher on the grounds of vaguely defined 'coercive' practices by non-EU economies" (Global Times 2022). Furthermore, US analysts have also criticized the ACI, questioning whether "Europe is on the defense or the offense?" (Busch 2022).

When considering Diez' (2004, 2005; Manners and Diez 2007) earlier critiques of the EU's geopolitical othering practices since the 2000s, contrasting normative EU trade policy versus other geopolitical trade actors, our analysis has revealed a remarkable evolution. While the EU uses the more self-reflexive temporal othering, referring to its previously naïve stance, to justify its assertive turn in trade, it still adopts a hierarchical form of geopolitical othering, but now contrasts its own 'good' geopolitical trade policy with others' 'bad' geopolitical trade policies. Considering Diez and Manners' earlier critiques of the EU's geopolitical othering practices of the early 2000s, the EU's trade policy othering strategy 2.0 still has room for progress when it comes to using less hierarchical discursive strategies. Although the way in which the EU uses geopolitical othering has changed, Diez' (2004, 2005; Manners and Diez 2007) critiques of the EU's othering practices still have value in the present context.

6. Conclusion

This chapter observed a double othering strategy in the EU's justification of the Anti-Coercion Instrument. On the one hand, the Union contrasts its current assertive turn in trade against its previous 'naïve' normative and free trade-oriented policy. On the other hand, we observed a juxtaposition between a 'bad' 'offensive' geopoliticization of trade policy versus a 'good' 'defensive' geopoliticization of trade. The rhetoric within the various official documents and media statements which were analysed suggests that the EU makes this distinction by adopting a strategy of othering in which it situates its own geopolitical trade policy on the good defensive side, while linking the bad offensive geopoliticization of trade to other actors such as China, Russia or the US. The EU's new geopolitical trade policy is hence framed as a 'provoked' turn in response to the offensive geopoliticization of trade policy of other international actors. Therefore, this othering strategy allows the EU to justify its geopolitical turn in trade as a necessary exit from its previous naïve trade stance in previous decades, while, at the same time, distancing itself from offensive geopolitical trade by other international actors. In doing so, the EU maintains its 'unique standing' in trade while also adapting to a new geopolitical context. The continued, yet updated, version of its othering discourse allows the EU to adapt itself to an increasingly growing context of geoeconomic competition in trade, without losing face and creating policy incoherence with its more normative trade objectives.

When assessing these findings in the context of earlier calls for more positive and self-reflexive 'othering strategies' (Diez 2004, 2005; Manners and Diez 2007), this 2.0 version of the EU's discursive othering in trade remains an easy target for critique. First, the EU's presentation of its former self as doing 'naïve' trade policy effectively obfuscates the longstanding geopolitical and colonial dimensions of its trade relations with neighbouring and so-called developing countries (cf. Orbie 2021). From a critical perspective, it would be hard to maintain that EU trade policy has ever been a naïve undertaking that failed to take political, economic, historical and ideological agendas into account (*e.g.* Heron and Siles-Brügge 2012; Langan and Price 2021). While temporal othering originally referred to a recognition of the dark pasts of European history, which inevitably entails a self-reflexive and less worrying type of othering, the current temporal othering strategy seems to paint an uncritical and unreflexive picture of the former self in a way that legitimizes the current geopolitical shift.

Second, it is difficult to indisputably claim that the EU is not engaging in offensive geopoliticization of trade. Long-time trade policy measures such as GSP+, more assertive and enforceable sustainability chapters in trade agreements, specific trade conditionalities within the EU's neighbourhood and enlargement policies, and newer trade policy initiatives such as the EU-US Trade and Technology Council could prove some examples in case. Although the EU may thus rightfully position itself on the defensive side of the new geopolitical trade spectrum, it would be more honest, and in line with the EU's self-proclaimed geopolitical ambitions, to also recognize its involvement in 'offensive' geopoliticization of trade. Furthermore, notwithstanding the fact that the EU might believe that it is taking a more 'defensive' or 'good' geopolitical turn in trade compared to more 'offensive' or 'bad' actors, this self-perception might not be shared by third actors, who might perceive the EU's new Anti-Coercion Instrument as offensive (cf. Global Times 2022; Busch 2022). There is, thus, still room for a more positive and less hierarchical strategy such as abject othering, whereby the EU acknowledges the Other is not necessarily that different from the Self. Such a position would not only be more reflexive but also help to avoid possible escalations or trade wars in the future.

REFERENCES

Adriaensen, Johan, and Evgeny Postnikov (2022), *A Geo-Economic Turn in Trade Policy?*. New York: Palgrave Macmillian.

Ahrens, Bettina (2018), "Normative power Europe in crisis? Understanding the productive role of ambiguity for the EU's transformative agenda." *Asia Eur J* 16, pp. 199–212.

Allenbach-Ammann (2022), "Bringing a gun to trade negotiations.", *Janos.* 2022. Available athttps://www.euractiv.com/section/economy-jobs/news/bringing-agun-to-trade--negotiations/ (Accessed 27 October)

Allenbach-Ammann (2022), "EU member states clip Commission wings in anti-coercion tool discussions", *Janos,* available at: https://www.euractiv.com/section/economy-jobs/news/eu-member-states-clip-commission-wings-in-anticoercion-tool-discussions/ (Accessed 6 December, 2022).

Baetens, Freya, and Marco Bronckers (2022), "The EU's Anti-Coercion Instrument: A Big Stick for Big targets", *EJIL: Talk!,* available at: https://www.ejiltalk.org/the-eus-anti-coercion-instrument-a-big-stick-for-big-targets/ (Accessed 27 October, 2022.)

Beattie, Alan (2019), "Brussels reheats an old tool for a new trade war", *Finantial,* available at: https://www.ft.com/content/828f35b6-49e6-11e9-8b7f-d49067e0f50d (Accessed 27 October, 2022).

Beattie, Alan (2020), "Trade Secrets newsletter", *FT Channels,* available at: https://channels.ft.com/en/tradesecrets/air-miles/ (Accessed 27 October, 2022).

Biscop, Sven (2018), *European Strategy in the 21st Century,* New York: Routledge.

Biscop, Sven, Tobias Gehrke, and Bernard Siman (2022), *Tanks versus Banks: Russian Military versus EU Geoeconomic Power* [pdf], available at: https://www.egmontinstitute.be/app/uploads/2022/04/Biscop-Gehrke-Siman_PolicyBrief276.pdf?type=pdf.

Bossuyt, Fabienne, Jan Orbie, and Lotte Drieghe (2020), "EU external policy coherence in the trade-foreign policy nexus: foreign policy through trade or strictly business?", *Journal of Iinternational Relations and Development* 23, pp. 45-66.

Busch, Marc (2022), "Europe's anti-coercion instrument is a wake-up call for the global economy", *The Hill,* available at: https://thehill.com/opinion/international/3257222-europes-anti-coercion-instrument-is-a-wake-up-call-for-the-globaleconomy/ (Accessed 12 December, 2022).

Carmen, Gebhard and Norheim-Martinsen, Per Martin (2011), "Making sense of EU comprehensive security towards conceptual and analytical clarity", *European Security,* 20(2), pp. 221-241, doi: 10.1080/09662839.2011.564613.

Cooper, Robert (2000), *The Post-Modern State and the World Order,* London: Demos.

Damro, Chad (2012), "Market power Europe", *Journal of European Public Policy,* 19(5), pp. 682-699.

Derous, Marjolein (2018), "Problematizations in the EU's external policies: the case of Singapore as the other", *Asia Eur J* 16, pp. 423–437.

Diez, Thomas (2004), "Europe's others and the return of geopolitics". *Cambridge Review of International Affairs,* 17(2), pp. 319-335.

Diez, Thomas (2005), "Constructing the Self and Changing Others: Reconsidering Normative Power Europe", *Millennium,* 33(3), pp. 613–636.

Diez, Thomas, and Ian Manners (2007), "Reflecting on normative-power Europe", in Berenskoetter, Felix and Williams, Michael J., *Power in world politics,* New York: Routledge, pp. 173-188.

Duchene, Francois (1972), "Europe's Role in World Peace", in: Mayne, Richard (ed.) *Europe Tomorrow: Sixteen Europeans Look Ahead*, London: Fontana.

Deepak, Raju (2022), "Proposed EU Regulation to Address Third Country Coercion – What is Coercion?", *EJIL: Talk!*, available at: https://www.ejiltalk.org/proposedeu-regulation-to-address-third-country-coercion-what-is-coercion/ (Accessed 27 October 2022).

De Ville, Ferdi, and Gabriel Siles-Brugge (2018), "The Role of Ideas in Legitimating EU Trade Policy", in Khorana, Sangeeta and García, María, *Handbook on the EU and International Trade*, Northampton: Edward Elgar.

De Ville, Ferdi (2019), "Naive no longer? The hardening of EU trade policy discourse and practice towards China and its limits", Paper Presented at the 2019 Conference: *Politicologenetmaal*, Antwerp University.

De Ville, Ferdi (2022), "The European Union's unilateral turn in trade policy", Paper presented at the 2022 ECPR Joint sessions, Antwerp University.

European Commission (2021), "Strengthening the EU's autonomy — Commission seeks input on a new anti-coercion instrument", *News Archive*, Brussels, 23 March 2021.

European Commission (2021), "Commission Staff Working Document Impact Assessment Report, accompanying the document 'Proposal for a Regulation of the European Parliament and of the Council on the protection of the Union and its Member States from economic coercion by third countries", SWD (2021)371, Brussels, 8 December 2021.

European Commission (2021), "Commission Staff Working Document, Executive Summary of the Impact Assessment Report, accompanying the document 'Proposal for a Regulation of the European Parliament and of the Council on the protection of the Union and its Member States from economic coercion by third countries", SWD (2021) 372, Brussels, 8 December 2021.

European Commission (2021), "EU strengthens protection against economic coercion", *News Archive*, Brussels, 8 December 2021.

European Commission (2021), "Questions and Answers: Commission proposal for an Anti-Coercion Instrument", *Press Release* 2021/6643, Brussels, 8 December 2021.

European Commission (2021), "Regulation of the European Parliament and the Council", Regulation COM2021/0406, Brussels, 8 December 2021.

European Commission (2021), "Trade Policy Review — An Open, Sustainable and Assertive Trade Policy", COM2021/66 final, Brussels, 18 February 2021.

EU Parliament (2019), "Free trade or geo-economics? Trends in world trade", available at: https://www.europarl.europa.eu/thinktank/en/document/EXPO_IDA(2019)639306 (Accessed 27 October 2022).

EU Parliament (2020), "The Von der Leyen Commission's priorities for 2019-2024", available at: https://www.europarl.europa.eu/thinktank/en/document/EPRS_BRI (2020)646148 (Accessed 27 October 2022).

Felbermayr, Gabriel (2018), "Trumpian Turn in EU Trade Politics and the Silence of Germany", *EconPol* Opinion 6.

Global Times (2021), "EU flexes muscle with 'anti-coercion' bill, risks being hijacked by Lithuania", available at: https://www.globaltimes.cn/page/202112/1241041.shtml (Accessed 12 December 2022).

Hackenbroich, Jonathan (2022), "The EU's geo-economic revolution", available at: 2022. https://ecfr.eu/article/the-eus-geo-economic-revolution/ (Accessed 27 October).

Helwig, Niklas, and Mikael Wigell (2022), "The EU's quest for geoeconomic power", *FIIA Briefing Paper*, March 2022/334.

Heron, Tony, and Gabriel Siles-Brugge (2012), "Competitive liberalization and the 'Global Europe' services and investment agenda: Locating the commercial drivers of the EU–ACP economic partnership agreements", *JCMS: Journal of Common Market Studies, 50*(2), pp. 250-266.

Hoekman, Bernard, and Michel Kostecki (2001), *The political economy of the world trade system: The WTO and beyond,* New York: Oxford University Press.

Hogan, Phill (2020), "Speech by Commissioner Phil Hogan at Launch of Public Consultation for EU Trade Policy Review — Hosted by EUI Florence", Speech by Commissioner Phil Hogan at the European Comission, 16 june 2020.

Hornát, Jan (2019), "Transatlantic 'Othering': European External Action Identity and the Trump Administration", *Studia Europejskie-Studies in European Affairs, 1,* pp. 27-42.

Jacobs, Thomas, and Jan Orbie (2020), "Discourse theory as a novel approach for research on EU trade policy", in: Bigo, Didier, Thomas Diez, Evangelos Fanoulis, Ben Rosamond, and Yannis A. Stivachtis. *The Routledge Handbook of Critical European Studies*, London: Routledge, pp. 254-266.

Jacobs, Thomas, Niels Gheyle, Ferdi De Ville, and Jan Orbie (2022), "The Hegemonic Politics of 'Strategic Autonomy' and 'Resilience': Covid-19 and the Dislocation of EU Trade Policy", *JCMS: Journal of Common Market Studies* 61 (1), pp. 3-19.

Jensen, Sune Qvotrup (2011), "Othering, identity formation and agency", *Qualitative studies, 2*(2), pp. 63-78.

Jiwani, Yasmin, and Richardson John E (2011), "Discourse, ethnicity and racism", in Van Dijk, Teun. *Discourse studies: A multidisciplinary introduction*, London: Sage, pp. 241-262.

Keukeleire, Stephan (2002), Au-delà de la PESC, La politique étrangère structurelle de l'Union européenne [pdf], available at: https://www.afri-ct.org/wp-content/uploads/2006/03/keuk2001.pdf.

Keukeleire, Stephan (2003), "The European Union as a diplomatic actor: internal, traditional, and structural diplomacy", *Diplomacy and Statecraft, 14*(3), pp. 31-56.

Keukeleire, Stephan, Kronenberger, Vincent, and Wouters, Jan (eds.) (2004), *EU Structural Foreign Policy and Structural Conflict Prevention, The European Union and Conflict Prevention : Policy and Legal Aspects*, Den Haag: TMC Asser institute.

Kommerskollegium, National Board of Trade Sweden (2022), "Analysis: the EU Proposal for an Anti-Coercion Instrument", available at: https://www.kommers kollegium.se/en/publications/reports/2022/the-eu-proposal-for-an-anti-coercioninstrument/ (Accessed 27 October 2022).

Laclau, Ernesto, and Chantal Mouffe (2014), *Hegemony and Socialist Strategy*, London: Verso Books.

Langan, Mark, and Sophia Price (2021), "Migration, development and EU free trade deals: The paradox of Economic Partnership Agreements as a push factor for migration", *Global Affairs*, *7*(4), pp. 505-521.

Lau, Stuart, and Moens, Barbara (2022), "China's trade attack on Lithuania exposes EU's powerlessness", *Politico* 16 December 2021, available at: https://www.politico.eu/article/chinatrade-attack-on-lithuania-exposes-eu-powerlessness/ (Accessed 27 October 2022).

Manners, Ian (2002), "Normative power Europe: a contradiction in terms?", *JCMS: Journal of common market studies, 40*(2), pp. 235-258.

Manners, Ian (2009), "The Social Dimension of EU Trade Policies: Reflections from a Normative Power Perspective", *European Foreign Affairs Review*, Issue 5, pp. 785-803.

Meunier, Stephanie, and Nicolaidis, Kalypso (2019), "The Geopoliticization of European Trade and Investment Policy", *JCMS 57* (1) pp. 103-113.

Moens, Barbara, and Vela, Jakob Hanke (2021), "EU flexes geopolitical muscle with new trade weapon", *Politico* 6 December 2021, available at: https://www.politico.eu/article/eus-newesttrade-tool-allows-brussels-to-hit-back-hard-against-economic-blackmail/ (Accessed 27 October 2022).

Moens, Barbara (2022), "Free traders fear EU risks going over to the dark side with new superpower", *Politico*, 9 February 2022, available at: https://www.politico.eu/article/free-tradersfear-eu-dark-side-new-superpower/ (Accessed 27 October 2022).

Moens, Barbara, and Burchard, Hans von der (2022), "Europe First: Brussels gets ready to dump its free trade ideals", *Politico*, 5 December 2022, available at: https://www.politico.eu/article/ursula-von-der-leyen-joe-biden-trade-europe-first-brussels-gets-ready-to-dump-its-free-trade-ideals/ (Accessed 7 December 2022).

Newman, Edward, and Stefan, Cristina G. (2020), "Normative Power Europe? The EU's Embrace of the Responsibility to Protect in a Transitional International Order", *JCMS*, 58, pp. 472– 490.

Nicosia Luca (2019), "In Search of a European Strategy? From a Normative to a Pragmatic Approach." *E-IR*, available at: https://www.e-ir.info/2019/12/03/in-search-of-a-european-strategy-from-a-normative-to-a-pragmatic-approach/.

Orbie, Jan, and De Ville, Ferdi (2020), Impact of the Corona Crisis on EU Trade Policy: Our Five Cents to the Debate", *United Nation University UNU-CRIS Policy Brief*, available at: https://cris.unu.edu/sites/cris.unu.edu/files/PB-20.2%20-%20Jan%20 Orbie%20and%20Ferdi%20De%20Ville.pdf.

Orbie, Jan (2021), "EU trade policy meets geopolitics: what about trade justice?", *European Foreign Affairs Review*, 26(2), pp. 197-202.

Pace, Michelle (2005), *The politics of regional identity: meddling with the Mediterranean*, New York: Routledge.

Peterson, John (2007), *EU Trade Policy as Foreign Policy: Does Strategy plus Activity=Strategic Action?* [pdf], available at: http://aei.pitt.edu/7998/1/peterson-j-10g.pdf.

Pilegaard, Jess (2009), "...and Never the Twain Shall Meet? An Institutionalist Perspective of EU Trade and Development Policies in the context of the EPA negotiations", in Faber, Gerrit and, Orbie, Jan (eds.) *Beyond Market Access for Economic Development*, New York: Routledge.

Poletti, Arlo, and Sicurelli, Daniela (2018), *The political economy of normative trade power Europe*, New York: Springer.

Rabinovych, Maryna, and Novakova, Zuzana (2019), "Paradigmatic change with much continuity?", *Global Affairs* 5(1), pp. 73-79.

Schmitz, Luuk, and Timo Seidl (2022), "As Open as Possible, as Autonomous as Necessary: Understanding the Rise of Open Strategic Autonomy in EU Trade Policy", *JCMS: Journal of Common Market Studies*.

Storey, Andy (2006), "Normative Power Europe? Economic Partnership Agreements and Africa", *Journal of Contemporary African Studies*, 24. pp. 331-346.

Tekin, Beyza Ç. (2010), *Representations and Othering in Discourse: The construction of Turkey in the EU context* (Vol. 39), Amsterdam: John Benjamins Publishing.

Wagnsson, Charlotte, and Hellman, Maria (2018), "Normative Power Europe Caving In? EU under Pressure of Russian Information Warfare", *JCMS*, 56. pp. 1161– 1177.

Weiler, Joseph (2020), "Europe Must Learn Quickly to Speak the Language of Power: Part I", *EJIL: Talk!*, available at: https://www.ejiltalk.org/europe-must-learn-quicklyto-speak-the-language-of-power-part-i/ (Accessed 27 October 2022).

Weyand, Sabine (2022), "The Double Integration Doctrine, a Conversation With Sabine Weyand", *Groupe d'études géopolitiques*, available at: https://geopolitique.eu/en/2022/01/31/thedouble-integration-doctrine-sabineweyand/ (Accessed 27 October 2022).

Young, A. (2019), "Two wrongs make a right? The politicization of trade policy and European trade strategy", *Journal of European Public Policy*, 26(12), pp. 1883-1899, doi: 10.1080/13501763.2019.1678055.

Young, Alasdair, R., and Peterson, John (2014), "Trade Policy as Foreign Policy", in Young, Alasdair, R., and Peterson, John, *Parochial Global Europe: 21st Century Trade Politics*, Oxford: Oxford Academic, pp. 183-214.

CHAPTER 9
GREEN HORIZONS — TOWARDS A MORE SUSTAINABLE TRADE AFTER THE TSD REVIEW[148]

Eline Blot

Abstract: All eyes are on the European Commission following the communication on a new approach to Trade and Sustainable Development (TSD) Chapters in EU Free Trade Agreements (FTAs). The focal point of EU trade policy recently shifted back towards bilateral trade agreements with a greater scrutiny on the sustainability objectives embedded in the TSD Chapters such as tackling global emergencies including the climate crisis, deforestation, and biodiversity loss. But what does this new approach entail, and how effective will it be at improving the monitoring and enforceability of the TSD Chapters? This chapter reviews the new TSD Chapter approach and assesses its overall objective to address sustainability concerns linked to international trade. The chapter discusses missed opportunities for enhancing sustainability in EU trade agreements and reflects what the new TSD approach could mean for newly concluded and ongoing trade agreements.

Keywords: EU trade agreements; sustainable development; enforceability; monitoring mechanisms, civil society

1. Introduction — The trade and climate nexus

Progress towards achieving the Sustainable Development Goals (SDGs) is not yet occurring at the pace and extent required to deliver the SDGs by 2030. This final decade began with an unprecedented modern-day pandemic,

[148] I would like to thank Antoine Oger for his insightful contribution to this chapter and support, as well as Marianne Kettunen who helped launch my work on the Trade and Sustainable Development Chapters. Finally, I would like the thank the editors for inviting me to contribute to the Special Issue and for their comments, along with the reviewers.

pushing the world's most vulnerable into an even more precarious situation (United Nations, 2022). The sudden and steep reduction of greenhouse gas emissions worldwide brought on by the pandemic and subsequent lockdown policies, have been more than compensated for in 2021, as the return to "business as usual" saw energy-related CO2 emissions break new records (United Nations, 2022). Furthermore, and amid the aftermath of the worst effects of the pandemic, Russia's war in Ukraine triggered an energy crisis, which was felt mostly in Europe but also exacerbated a global food crisis.

In such a tense geopolitical environment, trade is often presented as a solution to foster cooperation and sustainability worldwide. Although Europe is a frontrunner regarding progress towards the SDGs, it still faces internal challenges in the areas of sustainable dietary habits, agriculture, climate and biodiversity. Europe's lacking performance in these areas is partly due to the international spillovers generated by its trade patterns (Lafortune *et al.*, 2021).

Indeed, the European Union's (EU) trade policy has been familiar to controversies, recalling civil society organisations and at times, Member States' protest against the negotiation and ratification of free trade agreements (FTAs). Examples include the trade deals with Canada and the Mercosur region, which were unpopular among civil society due to a lack of safeguards for environmental action, human and labour rights embedded into the agreements (Nienaber, 2016; Toni & Tubiana, 2021).

In an effort to rebuild the climate credibility of its trade policy, the EU announced it would review its approach to the Trade and Sustainable Development (TSD) Chapters, after already having published a non-communication on TSD Chapters in 2018 (European Commission Services, 2018). Acknowledging its contribution to the global environmental degradation embodied in trade, the European Commission published the new TSD Action Plan in June 2022, detailing twenty action points to be undertaken to ensure that EU FTAs deliver for the environment and sustainable development (European Commission, 2022d).

Box 9.1. What is the TSD Chapter and why is it relevant?

The TSD Chapter has been a common feature of EU FTAs since 2011, with the signature of the first "new generation" trade deal between the EU and the Republic of Korea. It houses commitments made by the trade partners to tackle social and environmental concerns linked to trade such as labour conditions and human rights; gender equality; climate change; or illegal, unreported and unregulated fishing activities. These provisions aim to prevent unwanted social and environmental consequences from trade liberalisation and leverage trade agreements to support sustainable development.

Still, the effectiveness of the TSD Chapters to enforce the commitments made by the trade partners has been called into question (Harrison & Paulini, 2020). Issues include the TSD enforcement mechanism, or dispute settlement mechanism, which has been criticised as "toothless" compared to its counterpart, the general FTA dispute settlement mechanism. However, recently a precedent has been set that the TSD Chapter commitments are legally binding. This follows a TSD expert panel ruling on the EU-Korea dispute regarding Korea's failure to make sufficient progress towards ratifying the International Labour Organisation (ILO) conventions once the FTA was in force (Blot, Oger, & Harrison, 2022).

In recent years the European Commission has make efforts to improve the enforceability of the TSD Chapter such as the appointment of the Chief Trade Enforcement Officer to follow up on the implementation and enforcement of the TSD Chapter commitments. Also, the launch of the online platform known as the 'Single Entry Point' (SEP) provides stakeholders with the opportunity to bring potential violations of the TSD Chapters to the attention of the European Commission.

This chapter reviews the EU's new approach to TSD Chapters and aims to assess whether the new approach is sufficient to deliver sustainable trade in the future, building on work by the Institute for European Environmental Policy and existing literature. In section 2, the author classifies the content of the new TSD approach into five categories, which are then assessed in more detail. Following this assessment, section 3 discusses what additional measures could have strengthened the new TSD approach. Section 4 reflects on what the new TSD approach means for recently concluded trade agreements, as well as those still under negotiation. Section 5 concludes this chapter, summarising the main findings and reflections on the new TSD approach.

2. Assessment — What is in the new approach to TSD Chapters

The following sub-sections review the action points of the new TSD Chapter approach. Table 1 presents an overview of the twenty action points, as well as their correspondences into each of the following five categories:

i. Leveraging FTAs for sustainability;
ii. Enhancing the environmental credentials of FTAs;
iii. Empowering broader civil society;
iv. Targeted actions for the Domestic Advisory Groups (DAGs);
v. Strengthening enforceability of environmental and social commitments.

Table 9.1. The TSD Chapter Action Points and their categorization

Categorisation	TSD Chapter Action Points
Leveraging FTAs for sustainability	(1) Step up cooperation with trade partners on compliance with international labour and environmental standards.
	(2) Support and incentivise reform processes and capacity building in trade partner countries through technical and financial assistance, when needed.
	(3) Use trade agreements to facilitate dialogue with partner countries.
Enhancing the environmental credentials of FTAs	(4) Tailored approach to TSD Chapters, identifying country-specific sustainability priorities, and early and better targeted impact assessments.
	(5) Negotiate detailed and time-bound roadmaps with milestones, where appropriate, with a clear role for civil society for the monitoring and implementation.
	(6) Prioritise market access for environmental goods and services.
	(7) Ensure (sustainability) impact assessments analyse all relevant FTA chapters, and identify which provisions and commitments are most likely to have an impact on sustainability issues.
Empowering broader civil society	(8) Develop a comprehensive EU approach across services, using all available instruments to monitor the implementation of the TSD commitments.
	(9) Work with EU Delegations in their support and definition of best practices, as trade partners work with their local Domestic Advisory Groups (DAGs).

	(10) Support continuous involvement of the European Parliament in the implementation of TSD Chapters and assist it in its effort for regular country-specific discussions on trade and sustainable development.
	(11) Revise the Operating Guidelines for the Single Entry Point to increase transparency and predictability for stakeholders.
	(12) Ensure an inclusive consultation process with civil society through all stages of the lifecycle of FTAs.
Targeted actions for the DAGs	(13) Further strengthen the role of EU DAGs by providing resources for their logistical support, capacity building and functioning.
	(14) Increase involvement of EU DAG representatives in TSD Member States' Expert Groups and TSD Committee meetings.
	(15) Promote and facilitate interaction between EU and partner countries' DAGs.
	(16) Foster transparency on the composition of DAGs.
	(17) Exchange views with EU DAGs on EU TSD-related technical assistance projects.
	(18) Ensure that the remit of the DAGs extends beyond TSD in order to cover the entirety of the FTA.
Strengthening enforceability of environmental and social commitments	(19) Further strengthen enforcement of TSD commitments in future agreements:
	(a) Extend the general state-to-state dispute settlement (SSDS) compliance stage to the TSD Chapter.
	(b) Involve DAGs in monitoring the compliance stage.
	(c) Extend the possibility to apply trade sanctions in cases of failure to comply with obligations that materially defeat the object and purpose of the Paris Agreement or in serious instances of non-compliance with the ILO fundamental principles.
	(20) Prioritise the enforcement of TSD cases based on the importance of the nature of the commitments at issues, the seriousness of the violation and the impact on the environment or workers.

2.1 Leveraging FTAs for sustainability

The first three action points aim to leverage the cooperative framework of FTAs to encourage sustainability reform by increasing cooperation, dialogue, and assistance with the trade partner country. Trade deals typically encapsulate both a "trade and investment agreement" in addition to a "political and cooperation agreement" which makes them ideal avenues to pursue cooperation on global challenges such as climate change and environmental degradation (Arróniz Velasco & Peters, 2022).

A platform for continuous dialogue between trade partners is necessary to discuss evolving sustainability and trade issues, as well as follow up on the implementation of, and compliance with bilateral commitments under the FTA.

For less developed countries, the EU aims to provide targeted technical and financial assistance to support the elevation their domestic standards to meet the EU requirements and standards. Such support is essential to ensure no country is excluded from international trade, while elevating sustainability standards worldwide (Kettunen, Gionfra, & Monteville, 2019).

This is relevant in the context of both the EU's autonomous trade policy measures and domestic environmental policies which will set new requirements and standards for goods and services sold on the EU market. Cooperation and dialogue aim to ensure partner countries' understanding of, and compliance with these upcoming sustainability initiatives. Examples of such initiatives include the carbon border adjustment mechanism, the deforestation-free supply chains Regulation, and the Ecodesign for sustainable products Regulation (Halleux, 2022; Šajn, 2022; Titievs.kaia, Morgado Simões, & Dobreva, 2022).

2.2 Enhancing the environmental credentials of FTAs

Action points four through eight propose approaches to bolster the environmental credentials of EU FTAs, both within and outside the TSD Chapter. Firstly, to put an end to the one-size-fits-all approach to TSD Chapters (i.e., a default set of provisions across TSD Chapters in various FTAs), the European Commission proposes to introduce a tailored approach. This new approach would entail the identification of country-specific environmental and social priorities based on a more comprehensive impact assessment, supported by civil society inputs. The findings of these assessments and consultations would be taken up into the TSD Chapter with provisions to address these country-specific issues.

Building on the country-specific assessment, action point five would see the European Commission negotiate, where deemed appropriate, so-called "implementation roadmaps" with timelines and milestones for the delivery of TSD commitments. These roadmaps have the potential to accelerate progress towards achieving the SDGs when linked to international environmental frameworks (Blot & Kettunen, 2021). However, the non-committal phrasing of this action point indicates that the European Commission may be apprehensive to negotiating these roadmaps for every future FTAs.

At a global level, the prioritisation of market access for environmental goods and services launched the start of negotiations of the Environmental Goods Agreement at the World Trade Organisation in 2014. However, after two years, negotiations ceased with the conclusion that tariff liberalisation for environmental goods would not be sufficient. Additional efforts must be undertaken to address the non-tariff barriers that environmental goods face to market access (de Melo & Solleder, 2020). Therefore, action point six is a positive step to address the trade barriers environmentally-friendly goods and services face compared to environmentally polluting goods and services (Shapiro, 2021).

Action point seven focuses on the targeted use of impact assessments as tools to improve the environmental credentials of FTAs. The early-stage impact assessment, conducted in close collaboration with the partner country and civil society, would serve as the basis for scoping country-specific environmental and social priorities to be addressed with tailored TSD Chapter provisions. At a later stage, these country-specific priorities would be further assessed in the Sustainability Impact Assessments and monitored with the ex-post impact assessments. These assessments would be supported by continuous involvement of civil society, and more refined methodologies such as the new guidance for assessing EU trade agreements impact on biodiversity (IEEP, Trinomics, IVM, & UNEP-WCMC, 2021). The knowledge obtained from better and more granular environmental impact assessments, as well as stakeholder consultation, should steer the uptake of country-specific environmental provisions in the TSD Chapter, as well as in sector-specific chapters, where relevant.

These action points could significantly improve the environmental credentials of FTAs, however, the devil is in the details. For example, if the country-specific TSD provisions do not use stronger language than past TSD Chapters, enforceability may remain an issue. Furthermore, the enforceability of the implementation roadmaps is also unclear because the roadmaps would be negotiated in parallel with the TSD Chapter, thereby not falling explicitly under any enforcement mechanism. Going forward, the European Commission should also provide more transparency on how the findings of the impact assessments are taken up into the final text of the agreement, and communicate how the TSD commitments aim to address specific findings related to labour and environmental issues concluded by the impact assessment (Blot & Kettunen, 2021).

2.3 Empowering broader civil society

This sub-section elaborates on the role of broader civil society, while the following sub-section discusses the role of the FTAs designated stakeholder monitoring mechanism, the Domestic Advisory Groups (DAGs). The new approach to TSD Chapters aims to more closely integrate the role of civil society throughout the FTA and states that civil society consultations will form an integral part of the FTA life cycle, from early gap-analysis to the monitoring of TSD implementation once the agreement is in force.

The first action point of this category aims to develop a comprehensive approach to better utilise and coordinate between existing instruments for the monitoring of TSD Chapter implementation. Greater coordination regarding monitoring efforts is essential for current FTAs, but especially in the context of the new TSD approach which will require more targeted monitoring of country-specific priorities. Current monitoring efforts are undertaken by both EU Institutions and civil society at varying levels.

On one hand, the role of the civil society and the European Parliament in the monitoring of the TSD Chapters is explicitly stated and valued. The European Commission intends to utilise all existing expertise, and available instruments and programmes to facilitate the monitoring of TSD Chapter implementation, while expanding on the number of stakeholders to be involved in the process. This encompasses EU Delegations, Member States, and a stronger role of the European Parliament notably through its Committee on International Trade.

On the other hand, the European Commission has proposed to "split up" politically contentious agreements, such as those with Mercosur and Mexico, to simplify the ratification process (Moens & Hanke Vela, 2022). The splitting of a trade agreement involves negotiating two separate agreements: one on trade and investment and a political and cooperation agreement. With the recent conclusion of the EU-Chile trade deal, which was also split (European Commission, 2022a), the European Commission indicates its intention to circumvent the role of Member State governments in ratifying the trade section of the agreement.

If this approach to ratifying trade agreements becomes the new norm, the role of the European Parliament as representatives of EU citizens must be reinforced and informed on the negotiations where appropriate. In this manner, the European Parliament could provide checks as to the level of sustainability negotiated in the text and minimise the political blowback once the agreement text is concluded.

2.3.1 Operating guidelines of the Single Entry Point

Civil society actors have access to a wealth of knowledge to feed into the FTA process. These insights are especially critical for the development of (ex-post) impact assessments, for which environmental data is often lagged (IEEP *et al.*, 2021). Furthermore, civil society organisations in trade partner countries typically have a better understanding of specific environmental and social concerns on the ground before these issues are documented in databases (Blot & Kettunen, 2021).

The understanding of country-specific issues is not only integral for the impact assessments and the monitoring of TSD Chapter implementation once the agreement is in force but also for flagging potential violations of TSD commitments to the European Commission. Therefore, to empower stakeholders in the monitoring of TSD commitment implementation, action point eleven proposes to revise the Operating Guidelines of the Single Entry Point (SEP) to improve the platform's accessibility (European Commission, 2022c).

Launched in 2020, the SEP is a contact point for EU stakeholders to file complaints regarding a trade partner's non-compliance with TSD Chapter commitments, as well as market access issues. Although it is an EU-based platform, it is possible for an EU organisation or citizen to file a complaint representing the interests of those outside the EU, on the condition that this is clearly stated. However, with its introduction, the initial functioning of the SEP was drawn into question concerning its transparency, and accessibility regarding the burden of evidence required by complainants to file (Henriot & Van den Berghe, 2021).

Regarding transparency, the SEP revised guidelines explain the steps taken from the initial receipt of a complaint[149], the complaint assessment, and the weighing of countermeasures dependent on the gravity of non-compliance. The complainant is assigned a contact person who is

[149] With confirmation of receipt within 10 working days.

required to keep track of progress on the complaint[150]. Moreover, a deadline for the delivery of the preliminary assessment of the complaint is set[151], making the process time bound. However, this could be considered a soft deadline, because the European Commission reserves the right to suspend the deadline if more time is required for the assessment.

On accessibility of the platform, the European Commission acknowledges stakeholders' concerns surrounding the burden of evidence placed on the complainant in cases related to TSD non-compliance. With the review of the guidelines, the European Commission clarifies that there is no expectation for the complainant to provide full information regarding the TSD commitment violation. One solution provided to facilitate complaint submissions is for stakeholders to engage in "pre-notification". This allows stakeholders to consult with SEP contacts to discuss issues such as the legal basis of the complaint and the available information, prior to filing the complaint.

Since its inception, the SEP has received one complaint pertaining to non-compliance of TSD commitments. The complaint was filed on 17 May 2022 by CNV International on behalf of trade union organisations in Peru and Colombia regarding the violation of the right to trade union freedom, collective bargaining and the right to equality (Van Beers, 2022). So far it has been reported that the European Commission has suspended the deadline for the preliminary assessment (POLITICO Pro, 2022).

Regarding the scope of TSD violations, the European Commission clarifies in the revised guidelines that the nature of the TSD violation to which a complainant has filed, must be systemic in nature, meaning it should not be an isolated case of non-compliance. At first glance this could limit the scope of violations that could result in a suspension of trade arrangements. However, systemic failures to apply laws or regulations aligned with TSD commitments would also constitute a violation.

2.4 Targeted actions for the Domestic Advisory Groups (DAGs)

This sub-section assesses action points thirteen through eighteen, which list specific actions to enhance the role and functioning of the DAGs. Each FTA since the EU-Korea FTA is required to set up a DAG, which is a small group

[150] For example, a first update on progress is expected within 20 working days from the receipt of the complaint.

[151] The deadline to deliver the preliminary assessment is set at 120 working days following the receipt of complaint.

of business, labour, and environmental stakeholders tasked with monitoring TSD Chapter implementation (Mazzola, 2018).

These action points aim to reinforce the capacity, legitimacy, efficacy, and transparency of the DAGs, as well as mainstream DAG involvement to cover sustainability in sector-specific chapters. Previous assessments concluded that the EU DAGs face several issues such as an underrepresentation of environmental stakeholders and insufficient resources to further investigate environmental and social concerns (Blot & Kettunen, 2021; Blot *et al.*, 2022). Therefore, it is essential that DAGs receive adequate resources for their logistical support, capacity building and functioning, which in turn can incentivise environmental stakeholders to join the DAGs.

Box 2 provides an example of how EU and partner country DAGs can come together to discuss sustainability priorities and develop concrete recommendations on how to further cooperate on environmental and social issues.

Box 9.2. Outcomes from the EU-Vietnam DAGs

On 18 October 2022, the EU and Vietnam DAGs met in Hanoi for the second time, along with the EU-Vietnam TSD Committee. This DAG session aimed to foster a collaborative approach to support stakeholders involved in value chains linked to deforestation patterns, in light of the upcoming EU Regulation tackling global deforestation (European Economic and Social Committee, 2022). This is aligned with the TSD approach to address sustainability concerns through collaborations and partnerships rather than legal obligations and sanctions.

This DAG-to-DAG meeting yielded some concrete results on sustainability aspects such as:

- An agreement to create a common working group aimed at in-depth joint discussion on EU-Vietnam supply chains in the context of due diligence. The working group will meet online and report to the next DAG-to-DAG meeting.
- The suggestion that a roadmap on climate and environmental protection should be developed by the Parties.
- Both DAGs reminded the Parties of their commitments to ratify and implement all the ILO fundamental conventions, which, as a result of the International Labour Conference (ILO, 2022), should include ILO conventions 155 and 187 on occupational safety and health.

This DAG-to-DAG meeting illustrates how civil society involvement in FTA implementation in the DAG framework can initiate recommendations that may have strong resonance on sustainability aspects for both Parties. Yet, the phrasings used by the DAGs emphasise that these civil society considerations are collaborative in nature (*e.g.*, partnerships, common working groups) or limited to suggestions and recommendations. The continuous monitoring of the implementation of the EU-Vietnam agreement will demonstrate whether these recommendations are taken on by the Parties as new legal obligations.

Yet, concerning their monitoring capabilities, DAG members felt no accountability from the European Commission to respond to their concerns raised on TSD implementation by partner countries. In the case of the EU-Korea dispute on labour rights provisions, DAG members had notified the European Commission about Korea's inaction to ratify the core ILO conventions in 2013. However, it wasn't until 2018, after the European Parliament issued a resolution on the matter, that the European Commission formally acknowledged the concerns and sought out bilateral consultations with Korea (Blot *et al.*, 2022).

To address such issues going forward, the European Commission has clarified that EU DAGs are permitted to file complaints on TSD violations to the SEP. However, the workings of the DAGs benefit from having a direct line of contact with the European Commission. The possibility for EU DAGs to submit any concerns on TSD violations via the SEP along with other stakeholders risks delegitimising the DAGs as the monitoring mechanism of TSD implementation. It could be more beneficial for the European Commission to introduce a rapid response mechanism which would require the Commission to acknowledge and respond to concerns brought up by the DAGs within a predetermined timeframe (Blot & Kettunen, 2021; Blot *et al.*, 2022).

2.5 Strengthening the enforceability of environmental and social commitments

Finally, one of the main criticisms of the TSD Chapters was the toothlessness of the dispute settlement mechanism and the lack of outcome-oriented resolutions. Assessments of the TSD dispute settlement mechanism conclude that while the TSD provisions are legally binding, there is no mechanism in place to ensure the disputed trade partner effectively addresses the TSD violation within a specified timeframe (Blot & Kettunen, 2021; Blot *et al.*, 2022).

To prove its commitment to trade and sustainability, action point nineteen strengthens TSD enforceability by extending the FTA's general state-to-state dispute settlement (SSDS) compliance stage to the TSD Chapter. This requires the Party in violation to inform how it plans to implement the expert panel's decision within a predetermined timeframe. Going further, the European Commission proposes the possibility of trade sanctions as a last resort for violations of the ILO fundamental principles and the Paris Agreement. These sanctions will most likely take the form of suspension of trade concessions, as quantifying failures to protect the environment in monetary terms remains an issue.

A sanctions-based outcome of TSD violations can only be triggered by the SSDS, meaning no private or non-governmental organisation can file a complaint resulting in the suspension of trade concessions. Rather, these actors can file grievances regarding a TSD violation or a market access barrier through the SEP system. The implementation of sanctions would follow an expert panel's decision as well as further failure from the violating party to bring itself into compliance.

The European Commission's more assertive stance on handling trade and sustainability disputes is promising. Yet, the extent to which this new approach will foster sustainability in trade partner countries remains to be seen. For example, a breach in the implementation of the Paris Agreement is worded as "any action or omission which materially defeats the object and purpose of the Paris Agreement." Without a set precedent of what action or inaction could be considered a breach, it is unclear how this new stance will be enforced. Moreover, regarding the composition of expert panels, there should be transparency as to the relevant expertise of the panellists handing TSD disputes (Henriot & Van den Berghe, 2021).

3. Discussion — What could have strengthened the review of the TSD Chapters?

The European Commission's review of the TSD Chapter approach cements the EU's position as a global leader regarding the integration of sustainability in trade policy. Yet, there are missed opportunities that could have further enhanced the sustainability of the EU's FTAs.

The left column of Table 9.2, shown below, summarises some of the most noteworthy explicit commitments made by the European Commission to foster sustainable trade. The right column provides a few missed opportunities that could have been integrated in the review of the TSD approach. The omission of these measures could potentially challenge progress towards more sustainable trade in the future. The final rows of the table highlight the non-committal phrasings used in the TSD review and uncertainty surrounding the implementation of the new TSD approach.

Table 9.2. Explicit commitments and non-committal phrasings in the TSD review that could foster or challenge sustainable trade

Fosters sustainable trade	Challenges sustainable trade
Tailored TSD provisions to address country-specific sustainability priorities.	No formal consideration on how to achieve pre-agreement commitments.
Paris Agreement and ILO conventions as essential elements, with sanctions for non-compliance as a last resort.	No consideration of compliance with other multilateral environmental agreements as an essential element.
More actionable and outcome-oriented dispute settlement mechanism.	Limited applicability to existing FTAs, with questionable enforceability if introduced as an accompanying document after the FTA has been ratified.
Better involvement of, and support to civil society including in partner countries, to improve monitoring efforts.	No "ratchet-up" mechanism to revise TSD provision after the agreement is in force.
Financial and technical support for reform processes and capacity building in partner countries.	
Non-committal phrasings in the TSD review	
The introduction of implementation roadmaps could foster greater sustainability commitments than those in the TSD Chapter, as well as more civil society involvement.	The applicability of implementation roadmaps is unclear, i.e., the decision is left to the will of the Parties. It is also unclear the extent to which the implementation roadmaps will be enforceable.
The possibility to use FTAs as a channel to align bilateral trade rules with EU legislation that can be more ambitious on certain sustainability aspects (*e.g.*, deforestation-free supply chains Regulation).	Risk of non-ambitious implementation or backsliding of new TSD approach in upcoming FTAs.

First, the European Commission aims to step up engagement with trade partners regarding sustainability. Yet, one key missed opportunity is the absence of pre-agreement efforts in the scoping phase of trade negotiations. Pre-agreement cooperation would commit parties to implement certain national policy frameworks pertaining to sustainability. Whether or not trade negotiations are successful, the pre-agreement efforts signal to EU trade partners that tangible efforts on sustainability are central to EU trade (Blot *et al.*, 2022).

Second, there is no further consideration of compliance with other multilateral environmental agreements beyond the Paris Agreement. While the integration of the Paris Agreement as an essential element of future trade agreements is positive, the reality is that the scope is limited to the climate crisis. The EU should seek concrete commitments from its trade partners to tackle other environmental priorities linked to the SDGs such as protected areas and biodiversity conservation (Kettunen *et al.*, 2021), sustainable forest management and restoration, and sustainable production and consumption through circular economy principles.

Third, some of the most ambitious points of this communication such as the mainstreaming of sustainability provisions, the tailored approach to the TSD Chapter provisions, and the outcome-oriented dispute settlement aligned with the SSDS compliance stage, will not be back-cast onto existing agreements. While this is less problematic for agreements with developed countries that often have similar levels of environmental regulation as the EU, the same is not true for some trade partners with specific environmental and social concerns.

Lastly, the new approach does not include a "ratchet-up" mechanism to take into account the ever-changing environmental reality, which would allow trade partners to revise and strengthen environmental commitments over time. The triggering of such a mechanism could be at the discretion of both trade partners, or linked to the progression of the "implementation roadmaps" (Blot *et al.*, 2022).

4. Reflection — What does the new approach mean for future trade agreements?

Supply chain disruptions and materials scarcity triggered by the pandemic and continued by the war in Ukraine has seen the EU reaffirm its pro-trade stance. The European Commission and the Council are keen to conclude ongoing negotiations such as those with Australia, Indonesia, India, Mexico, and Mercosur. By concluding these trade agreements, the EU hopes to secure a more reliable stream of raw materials to meet the expected increase in demand brought on by the green and digital transitions.

Since the communication on the new approach to TSD Chapters, two trade agreement have been concluded, specifically the bilateral agreements with New Zealand and Chile. This section briefly discusses the implementation of the new TSD approach in the EU-New Zealand and the EU-Chile agreements and reflects on the importance of an ambitious implementation of the new TSD approach into upcoming FTAs.

4.1 The EU-New Zealand Trade Agreement

Despite the novelty of the TSD Chapter review, the new approach is clearly on display in the EU-New Zealand FTA (European Commission, 2022b). The agreement's ambitious outcomes regarding trade and sustainability are due to the willingness and cooperation between both Parties. Some novelties in this trade agreement include two new Chapters dedicated to Māori trade and Sustainable Food Systems, as well as two new articles in the TSD Chapter on Trade and Fossil Fuel Subsidy Reform and Trade and Gender Equality. Finally, the TSD Chapter contains an annex with a non-exhaustive list of specific environmental goods and services of which the trade is to be liberalised, including circular economy-related services.

The EU-New Zealand trade agreement is the first of the EU's FTAs to remove the dispute settlement mechanism from the TSD Chapter. In this agreement, TSD disputes will be handled under the general dispute settlement Chapter, which introduces the possibility of sanctions for actions or omissions which materially defeat the object and purpose of the Paris Agreement.

Considering New Zealand's green ambitions regarding trade and sustainability, it is unlikely that their government would take actions that would materially defeat the objective of the Paris Agreement. However, it remains uncertain what actions or omissions are at odds with the Paris Agreement, as well as who would determine potential infringements. For example, the Nationally Determined Contribution of New Zealand and the EU are considered to be, respectively, "highly insufficient" and "insufficient". In this case, how could the Parties' submission of their Nationally Determined Contributions, deemed "insufficient", not be considered defeating the objectives of the Paris Agreement?

4.2 The EU-Chile Advanced Framework Agreement

Compared to the EU-New Zealand FTA, the EU-Chile agreement does not appear to hold the same level of bilateral commitment to the implementation of the Paris Agreement, as it does not specify the "obligation to refrain from any action or omission which materially defeats the object and purpose of the Paris Agreement." Moreover, the general dispute settlement Chapter does not reference the ILO conventions, the Paris Agreement, or the TSD Chapter, as is the case in the EU-New Zealand agreement. Instead, the EU-Chile agreement has limited the enforceability of the TSD provisions back within the confines of the TSD Chapter.

While this may appear as backsliding on the part of the European Commission to fully implement the new TSD approach, taking a closer look at the EU-Chile TSD dispute settlement articles indicates a new outcome-oriented approach to dispute resolution. For TSD dispute settlement under the EU-Chile agreement, once a panel of experts has been convened and they have issued their resolution on the matter, the Parties are expected to discuss actions or measures to be undertaken considering the expert panel's recommendations. Furthermore, these actions or measures are expected to be implemented no later than three months after the expert panel's resolution is made public (European Commission, 2022a). This precise wording aims to ensure that the TSD dispute settlement resolution is taken beyond the expert panel's decision and delivers outcomes to be implemented, and no longer relying on the will of the Parties to take action (Blot & Kettunen, 2021; Blot *et al.*, 2022).

A final and most notable addition to the TSD Chapter is Article 26.23 "Review" which obligates the TSD sub committee to discuss the effective implementation of the TSD provisions, considering major policy developments and developments in international agreements. Following the outcomes of these discussions, either Party may request the review of the TSD provisions at any time after the entry into force of the agreement.

This is a significant addition to the TSD Chapter, as it opens the door for amenable TSD provisions to better reflect the evolving nature of environmental and labour standards in FTAs (Blot & Kettunen, 2021; Blot *et al.*, 2022). Yet, the inclusion of a Review Article in new FTAs is not reflected in the new TSD approach, therefore, it is uncertain whether similar articles will be introduced in all FTAs going forward.

4.3 Upcoming trade agreements

With several other agreements in, or nearing, the final rounds of negotiations, the European Commission should seek to fully implement the new TSD. 9.. lists bilateral trade agreements currently being pursued by the EU as well as country-specific environmental considerations that should be addressed with the new TSD approach.

Table 9.3. List of upcoming bilateral trade agreements and environmental considerations

Bilateral agreement	Country-specific environmental considerations
EU-Australia	With its abundance of natural resources paired with the current political climate, Australia's leverage in negotiations has strengthened as the EU seeks to decrease its dependency on Russia. However, Australia's relatively less ambitious climate and environmental agenda compared to that of the EU and New Zealand could potentially undermine the environmental contents of the FTA.
EU-Mexico	Both Parties have come to an agreement in principle on the contents of the deal, however, the agreement has not officially concluded. In a joint statement, members of civil society have urged policymakers to not ratify the agreement in its current state (Transnational Institute, 2022). Yet, the European Commission has proposed to "split up" to simplify the ratification process within the EU (Moens & Hanke Vela, 2022).
EU-Mercosur	Civil society and some Member States oppose the ratification of the deal as it currently stands. In response, to save the deal, the European Commission and European External Action Service have been working on an accompanying instrument to address the environmental and human rights concerns of stakeholders. However, the content and degree of enforceability of this accompanying instrument remains unclear (Voituriez, Cremers, Guimarães, Moutinho, & Zerbini Benin, 2022).
EU-Indonesia	The liberalisation of palm oil trade under the FTA without adequate safeguards in place for deforestation could create additional economic incentives to accelerate forest conversion into palm oil plantations (Wittkopp, Ghislain, Fournier, & Ulmer, 2018). The TSD Chapter should take careful consideration of the wording on deforestation provisions, as well as in any other sector-specific chapter in the FTA that risks contributing to deforestation. The negotiations have been postponed by Indonesia's request, yet the EU Trade Commissioner Dombrovs.kis is keen to push bilateral negotiation efforts up the political agenda.

EU-India	The EU is keen to secure a deal with India for both economic and political reasons, and both sides hope to conclude negotiations before the end of 2023. However, the rushed relaunch of trade talks begs the question how closely the European Commission plans to adhere the new TSD approach. For example, the commitment to scope out country-specific environmental and social priorities early in the negotiation process is unlikely to be fulfilled, since negotiations have already started. This is particularly worrying as this FTA could be key in ensuring the ratification of core human rights and labour conventions in India.

5. Conclusion

The new TSD Chapter approach is ambitious and introduces for the first time concrete enforcement mechanisms for EU FTAs to foster sustainability in trade partner countries. The approach sets a course for embedding sustainability in FTAs by introducing new measures and mechanisms to ensure trade delivers for sustainable development.

The review overhauls the "one-size-fits-all" approach to TSD Chapter provisions in favour of a more tailored approach. It addresses the toothlessness of the TSD dispute settlement by adjusting the process to be both actionable and outcome-oriented. Furthermore, the European Commission commits to embed both the Paris Agreement and core ILO conventions as essential elements into future FTAs. The new approach to the TSD Chapter also aims at reinforcing the role of civil society, both in the EU and in the trade partner country, in the monitoring of FTAs. Lastly, the EU intends to provide financial and technical assistance for reform processes and capacity building in partner countries, as well as increased dialogues, which aims to support the implementation of new sustainability standards and frameworks.

Yet, concerns remain related to the implementation and applicability of the new TSD approach due to some non-committal phrasings used in the review. In this regard, it is unclear what criteria the European Commission will use when deciding which trade partner to negotiate an "implementation roadmap" with. Moreover, some of the most ambitious sections of the TSD review will not apply to existing agreements, and the extent to which it is ambitiously implemented in already negotiated, but not yet concluded trade agreements, remains questionable.

Although the new TSD approach does not specify the introduction of a "review clause" or a "ratchet-up" mechanism, the EU-Chile agreement does include an article allowing the trade partners to renegotiate the contents of the TSD Chapter if deemed appropriate. The implementation of similar articles into future trade agreements is recommended, thereby ensuring that the contents of FTAs can better reflect the ever-evolving nature of sustainability issues.

Looking ahead, 2023 could yield several new trade agreements. Therefore, it is essential that the EU follows through with the implementation of the new TSD approach and tackles its contribution to global environmental degradation through trade.

REFERENCES

Arroniz Velasco, I., & Peters, J. (2022), "How EU trade deals can increase climate action", *E3G*, retrieved from: https://www.e3g.org/publications/how-eu-trade-deals-can-increase-climateaction/.

Blot, E., & Kettunen, M. (2021), "Environmental credentials of EU trade policy: A comparative analysis of EU free trade agreements", *IEEP*, retrieved from: Brussels and London: https://ieep.eu/uploads/articles/attachments/fa0af713-08e5-4800-b263-439138f627c4/Environmental%20credentials%20of%20EU%20trade%20policy%20(IEEP%202021).pdf?v=63785611056.

Blot, E., Oger, A., & Harrison, J. (2022), "Enhancing sustainability in EU Free Trade Agreements: The case for a holistic approach", *IEEP*, available at: https://ieep.eu/publications/global-challenges-and-sdgs/enhancing-sustainability-in-eu-free-trade-agreementsthe-case-for-a-holistic-approach.

de Melo, J., & Solleder, J.-M. (2020), "The EGA Negotiations: Why They Are Important, Why They Are Stalled, and Challenges Ahead", *Journal of World Trade*, 54(3), pp. 333-347, available at: https://kluwerlawonline.com/journalarticle/Journal+of+World+Trade/54.3/TRAD2020015.

European Commission (2022), "EU-Chile: Text of the agreement", retrieved from https://policy.trade.ec.europa.eu/eu-trade-relationships-country-and-region/countries-andregions/chile/eu-chile-agreement/text-agreement_en.

European Commission (2022), "EU-New Zealand: Text of the agreement", available at: https://policy.trade.ec.europa.eu/eu-trade-relationships-country-and-region/countries-and-regions/new-zealand/eu-new-zealand-agreement/text-agreement_en.

European Commission (2022), *Operating guidelines for the Single Entry Point and complaints mechanism for the enforcement of EU trade agreements and arrangements* [pdf], available at: https://trade.ec.europa.eu/access-to-markets/en/form-assets/operational_guidelines.pdf.

European Commission (2022), "The power of trade partnerships: together for green and just economic growth", *Press Release*, Brussels: European Commission, available at: https://ec.europa.eu/commission/presscorner/detail/en/ip_22_3921.

European Commission Services (2018), "Feedback and way forward on improving the implementation and enforcement of Trade and Sustainable Development chapters in EU Free Trade Agreements", *Press release*, Brussels: European Commission, available at: https://trade.ec.europa.eu/doclib/docs/2018/february/tradoc_156618.pdf.

European Economic and Social Committee (2022), "2nd DAG-to-DAG meeting under the EU-Vietnam FTA", retrieved from: https://www.eesc.europa.eu/en/agenda/our-events/events/2nd-dag-dag-meeting-under-eu-vietnam-fta.

Halleux, V. (2022), "Towards deforestation-free commodities and products in the EU", European Parliamentary Research Services, available at: https://epthinktank.eu/2022/02/15/towards-deforestation-freecommodities-and-products-in-the-eu-eu-legislation-in-progress/.

Harrison, J., & Paulini, S. (2020), *The Trade and Sustainable Development Chapter in the EU-Mercosur Association Agreement* [pdf], available at: https://www.clientearth.org/media/rs5enobx/the-trade-and-sustainable-development-chapter-in-the-eu-mercosurassociation-agreement-ext-en.pdf.

Henriot, C., & Van den Berghe, A. (2021), *A new blueprint for environmental provisions in EU trade agreements* [pdf], available at: https://www.clientearth.org/latest/documents/a-new-blueprint-for-environmental-provisions-in-eu-tradeagreements/.

IEEP, Trinomics, IVM, & UNEP-WCMC (2021), *Methodology for assessing the impacts of trade agreements on biodiversity and ecosystems*, Luxembourg: Publications Office of the European Union, available at: https://ec.europa.eu/environment/news/trade-and-biodiversity-new-methodology-betterassess-impacts-2021-05-19_en.

ILO. (2022), *International Labour Conference adds safety and health to Fundamental Principles and Rights at Work*, available at: https://www.ilo.org/global/about-theilo/newsroom/news/WCMS_848132/lang--en/index.htm.

Kettunen, M., Dudley, N., Gorricho, J., Hickey, V., Krueger, L., MacKinnon, K., Sekhran, N. (2021), *Building on Nature: Area-based conservation as a key tool for delivering SDGs*, available at: https://ieep.eu/uploads/articles/attachments/623b509b-76d8-4a31-b7a8-d456e277d475/BUILDING%20ON%20NATURE%20-%20FINAL%20(full%20document).pdf?v=63789247230.

Kettunen, M., Gionfra, S., & Monteville, M. (2019), *EU Circular Economy and Trade Report*, available at: https://ieep.eu/publications/global-challenges-and-sdgs/eu-circular-economy-and-trade-report.

Lafortune, G., Cortés-Puch, M., Mosnier, A., Fuller, G., Diaz, M., Riccaboni, A., Oger, A. (2021), *Europe Sustainable Development Report 2021: Transforming the European Union to achieve the Sustainable Development Goals,* available at: https://www.sdgindex.org/reports/europe-sustainable-development-report-2021/.

Mazzola, A. (2018), *The role of Domestic Advisory Groups in monitoring the implementation of Free Trade Agreements,* available at: https://www.eesc.europa.eu/en/our-work/opinions-information-reports/opinions/role-domestic-advisory-groupsmonitoring-implementation-free-trade-agreements.

Moens, B., & Hanke Vela, J. (2022), "Brussels looks to evade EU capitals to get Mercosur deal done", *Politico,* 28 September 2022, available at: https://www.politico.eu/article/brussels-eu-commission-grab-trade-power-mercosur-deal/.

Nienaber, M. (2016), "Tens of thousands protest in Europe against Atlantic free trade deals", *Reuters,* 17 Setember, available at: https://www.reuters.com/article/us-eu-usa-ttip--idUSKCN11N0H6.

POLITICO Pro. (2022, 10 November 2022), Europe: Response to Single Entry Point complaint postponed, *Morning Trade Newsletter: Big Pharma threats — Foreign subsidies — Warning on China.*

Šajn, N. (2022), "Ecodesign for sustainable products", European Parliamentary Research Service, available at: https://epthinktank.eu/2022/06/09/ecodesign-for-sustainable-products-eu-legislation-in-progress/.

Shapiro, J. (2021), The Environmental Bias of Trade Policy. *Quarterly Journal of Economics, 136*(2), pp. 831-886, retrieved from: https://www.nber.org/papers/w26845.

Titie *vs.* kaia, J., Morgado Simoes, H., & Dobreva, A. (2022), "EU carbon border adjustment mechanism: Implications for climate and competitiveness", European Parliamentary Research Service, available at: https://epthinktank.eu/2022/01/24/eu-carbon-border-adjustment-mechanism-implications-for-climate-and-competitiveness-eulegislation-in-progress/.

Toni, A., & Tubiana, L. (2021), "Mercosur trade deal threatens to wreck EU's climate credibility", *Euractiv,* 2 April, available at: https://www.euractiv.com/section/energy-environment/opinion/eu-mercosur-trade-deal-threatens-to-wreck-the-blocs-climate-credibility/.

Transnational Institute (2022), "Six reasons NOT to ratify the EU-Mexico Global Agreement", *Tni,* available at: https://www.tni.org/en/article/six-reasons-not-to-ratify-theeu-mexico-global-agreement.

United Nations (2022), *The Sustainable Development Goals Report 2022,* New York: UN, available at: https://unstats.un.org/sdgs/report/2022/.

Van Beers, M. (2022), *On non-compliance by the Colombian and Peruvian Governments of Chapter IX, on Sustainable Development, of the Trade Agreement with the European Union* [pdf], available at: https://www.cnvinternationaal.nl/_Resources/Persistent/7/e/a/d/7eaded188057bc7dd0e1b6fbf1569d3a5883b119/CNVI-0334%20Complaint%20Colombia%20Peru%20SEP%20EU%20Trade%20Agreement.pdf.

Voituriez, T., Cremers, K., Guimarães, A., Moutinho, P., & Zerbini Benin, O. (2022), *Lula's election: A blessing for a green EU-Mercosur Association Agreement?* [pdf], available at: https://www.iddri.org/en/publications-and-events/policy-brief/lulas-election-blessing-green-eu-mercosur-association.

Wittkopp, K., Ghislain, S., Fournier, P., & Ulmer, K. (2018), "Planting the forest at the root of the EU-Indonesia trade relationship", *Fern*, available at: https://www.fern.org/publications-insight/planting-the-forest-at-the-root-of-the-eu-indonesia-trade relationship-joint-paper-15/.

CHAPTER 10
GLOBAL VALUE CHAINS AND THE SLOWING DOWN OF GLOBALISATION[152]

Pompeo Della Posta

Abstract: Global value chains (GVCs) have been a major feature of the phase of economic globalisation that began after the 1980s. After the global financial crisis of 2007-08, however, this phase has come to an end, being replaced by one characterized by a significant slowdown in the degree of international economic openness, due to not only economic but also geopolitical reasons. GVCs have also shown a slowing growth trend after then. The future scenarios for GVCs, however, suggest the possibility that they may be more resilient than expected. A first theoretical explanation provided in the literature argues that the *reshoring* of foreign intermediate production would be prevented by the high sunk costs that would have to be incurred. However, an additional possible reason for GVCs resilience — this is the main theoretical contribution of this chapter — is due to the option of *friendshoring* or *nearshoring*, rather than *reshoring*. Moving the production to more suitable foreign destinations, characterized by a political or geographical proximity with the domestic one, would avoid the newly perceived strategic and geopolitical costs, while retaining the economic benefits of *offshoring*, thereby making GVCs resilient.

Keywords: Global Value Chains, Extensive and intensive margins, offshoring, *friendshoring*, *nearshoring*, *reshoring*.

[152] I would like to thank an anonymous referee for the extremely significant help in improving the structure and readability of my paper. I am also grateful to the guest editors of the Special Issue and to the editor of the Journal for the encouragement and suggestions provided during the process of revision of the chapter. Needless to say, I am the sole responsible for any remaining mistakes or inaccuracy.

1. Introduction

Global value chains (GVCs) have been a major feature of the phase of economic globalisation that began after the 1980s. After the global financial crisis of 2007–2008, however, economic globalisation has started to slow down, as it is clearly shown by Figures 10.1–10.6, reporting the relevant indicators of international trade in the goods and services markets and in the markets of the factors of production, namely labour and capital (both financial flows and foreign direct investment) (see also Ikenson, 2022). Such a *slowbalisation* (as it has been dubbed recently by the Economist, 2019) is due to both economic and geopolitical reasons (Olson, 2022). Although GVCs across the world markets have exhibited a similar tendency to slowdown, it has been observed that GVCs shocks may be affecting the intensive rather than extensive margins of trade (Antràs, 2020). In other words, while the percentage of intermediate production abroad may be reduced temporarily, the number of firms involved in such a production may remain relatively more stable. This suggests, then, that future GVCs may be more resilient than expected. A first theoretical explanation for such a phenomenon, given by Antràs (2020), has to do with the fact that *reshoring* home the intermediate production processes previously *offshored*, would imply paying a new (this time domestic) sunk cost, thereby making *reshoring* too costly. Hence the GVCs resilience.

In this paper, however, I am arguing that the conclusion of an expected future resilience of GVCs should not be based exclusively on the argument that *reshoring* is too costly, but also on the fact that previously *offshored* companies may be moved to friendlier countries rather than *reshored*, what has been defined *friendshoring* (The White House, 2021, Olson, 2022). Examples of *friendshoring* are the relocation of the Apple production plants from China to Vietnam (Connors, 2022), or Japan's plan to move the production of chips and semiconductors from China to some other South East Asian nations (Harput, 2022). Although *friendshoring* has been subject to some criticisms (Harput, 2022, Grossman, 2021), it can be argued that even without *reshoring* the production into the US or Japan (or the EU), the former would still allow for the proposed *decoupling* of the US or Japanese economies from the Chinese one, thereby avoiding any perceived risk of economic and geopolitical dependency from the latter (although at the cost of increasing a more general global stability risk).

In this chapter I propose a simplified model (extending Antràs, 2020) to show how, after a geopolitical shock hits the initial GVCs arrangement, *friendshoring* may provide a solution to *offshoring* which is more cost-effective than *reshoring*. Antràs (2020) shows that the high sunk costs to be incurred to *reshore* an *offshore* production are such as to discourage the *reshoring*, therefore concluding that GVCs will be resilient in the future. My point, still within the modelling framework of Antràs (2020) is that GVCs resilience can be obtained also through *friendshoring*, that may become more convenient than keeping the production *offshore* in the initial (now unfriendly) country. This conclusion is reached by considering both the incentives provided by subsidies that may be offered by domestic governments in order to encourage the move to friendlier countries (therefore reducing significantly the sunk costs implied by moving the production from one country to another) and the fact that *friendshoring* would still allow enjoying approximately the same low labour costs of the initial *offshore* country (as it would be the case, for example, when moving the production from China to Vietnam). The resilience of GVCs, then, would be obtained not only because *reshoring* would be too costly as opposed to keep producing intermediate goods *offshore*, but also because *friendshoring* (and *nearshoring*) may provide an additional viable alternative to *reshoring*, thereby changing the structure of GVCs, while preserving them. This chapter is structured as follows. Section 2 accounts for the current phase of deglobalisation. Section 3 discusses the evolution and current situation of GVCs in developing countries. Section 4 outlines the current and possible future scenarios for GVCs and Section 5 provides a simple model to account for phenomena like *friendshoring*, as opposed to outright *reshoring*, thereby providing an additional theoretical justification for the expected future resilience of GVCs described in Section 4. Some concluding remarks close the paper in Section 6.

2. Deglobalisation or *slowbalisation*

The first phase of economic globalisation covers the years of the *Belle Époque*, included between the end of the XIX century and the outbreak of World War I. The second phase started at end of World War II and the third phase is usually considered as starting at the beginning of the 1980s after the elections of Mrs. Margaret Thatcher as Prime Minister in the UK and Mr. Ronald Reagan as US President (this section draws on Della Posta, 2018, 2020a, 2020b).

Some criticisms emerged a few years after the beginning of the third phase, focusing mostly on the negative effects it was producing on the economies of least developed and developing countries (Stiglitz, 2002, Rodrik, 2001) and to a minor extent on those of developed countries.[153]

Those critiques, coming mostly from a world Southern and 'left wing' perspective (referring, for example, to the fact that the world trade system was biased in favour of developed countries or that the 'losers' of globalisation in developed countries were not receiving the appropriate attention), were discarded as unreasonable and unrealistic attempts to stop the unstoppable, in line with the conclusions synthesized by the well-known TINA paradigm[154] (Bhagwati 2002, 2004, European Commission, 2002, Fischer, 2003 and Krugman, 1987). While stressing the expected benefits of globalisation, however, such rebuttals underestimated its actual costs, therefore 'overselling' globalisation (see Stiglitz, 2005 and Rodrik, 2007).

It has been argued that those positions contributed to undermine the confidence in the élites advocating globalisation, producing the (this time) Northern and 'right wing' criticisms and populism as represented, for example, by the "America first" Trump's policies in the US starting in 2017 and Brexit, in the UK in 2016 (Stiglitz, 2017). After the 2007/08 global financial (and, as a result, economic) crisis, then, attention had started to be given again to the negative effects of economic globalisation by the press (Saval 2017), academia (Krugman 2016a, 2016b, Rodrik, 2017, 2018a, Stiglitz, 2017), and international institutions (European Commission, 2017, OECD, 2017, IMF/WB/WTO, 2017). Those analyses show clearly that some of the critical aspects that had been pointed out in the past were still there, for example as for the costs resented by large sectors of the population of the otherwise winning Northern part of the world (see Della Posta, 2020a and 2020b for further details). It seems possible to synthesize those problems with the observation that globalisation produces winners and losers who inevitably, at some point, react (Williamson, 2005; De la Dehesa 2006).

Political events like the 2016 Brexit referendum, and the November 2016 election of Mr. Donald Trump as President of the USA, can be interpreted precisely as such a reaction. They have been followed by the spreading of the Covid-19 pandemic crisis (which broke out in China in late 2019-early 2020)

[153] Della Posta (2018a) provides a detailed account of the many critical aspects accompanying the process of economic globalisation.

[154] TINA is the acronym of the phrase, attributed to Ms. Thatcher, "There Is No Alternative" (to globalisation).

and by the growing tensions between the USA and China, suggesting then that the process of globalisation that started at the beginning of the 1980s has now changed nature, to say the least.

As a matter of fact, world exports of goods and services as a ratio of world GDP (Figure 10.1) have been showing over the last 14 years a clear downward trend, going from a peak of 31.2% in 2008 to 26.5% in 2020 (the clear effect of the pandemic) and 29.1% in 2021.

Figure 10.1. World Exports of Goods and Services (% of World GDP)

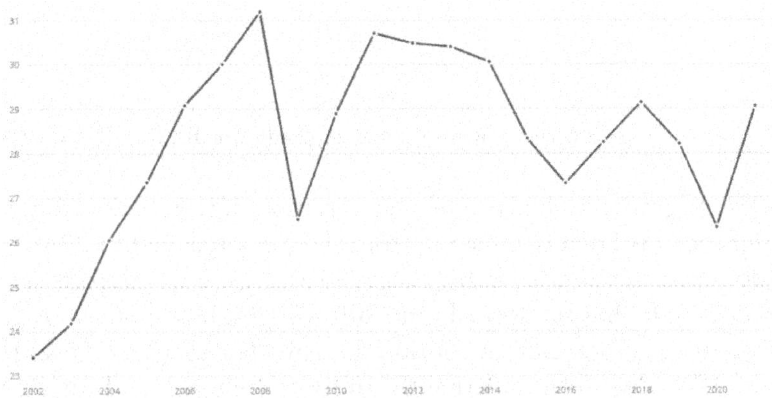

Source: https://data.worldbank.org/indicator/NE.EXP.GNFS.ZS.

The current degree of capital mobility is subject to tensions because of the negative consequences it is believed to produce in the countries of origin (for example because of the losses of domestic unskilled jobs that foreign direct investments [FDIs] imply). World FDIs net inflows for example, fell from a peak of 5.3% in 2007 to 1% in 2018 and 1.3% in 2020, again, with a clearly identifiable downward trend (Figure 10.2).

Figure 10.2. World Foreign Direct Investment Net Inflows (% of World GDP)

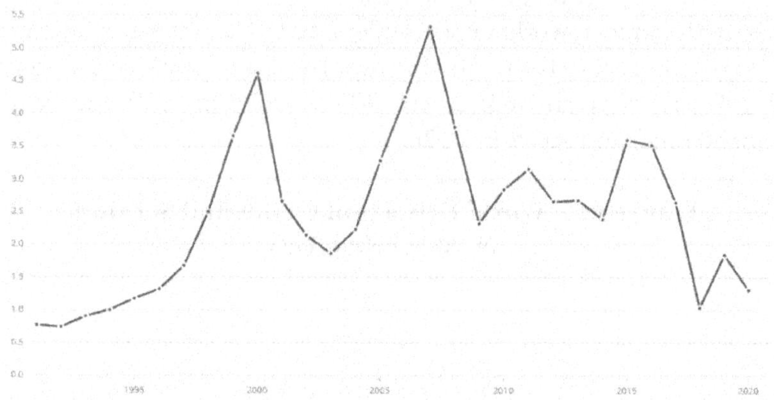

Source: https://data.worldbank.org/indicator/BX.KLT.DINV.WD.GD.ZS.

As for migrations, the year-to-year variation of the stock of international migrants has been decreasing from the peak reached in 2010 and has only recovered slowly after 2015 (Figure 10.3). Figure 10.4 depicts the trend in the ease of hiring foreign labour (2008–2020), based on the Executive Opinion Survey conducted by World Economic Forum (2020), over the last few years. What we observe is that the indicator relative to advanced economies has been worsening (in 2018 for the first time respondents from emerging and developing economies found it easier to hire foreign people than respondents of the advanced ones).

The overall picture, then, corroborates the idea of a *slowbalisation*. This phenomenon is also explicitly recognized by Catão and Obstfeld (2019), Frieden (2019) and Hoeckman (2015), among many others. Events have proved, then, that Mrs. Thatcher's TINA conclusion is far from granted and globalisation can be at least slowed down, if not halted, when people conclude or just believe that it is not in their interest anymore.[155]

[155] Rodrik (1999) had anticipated the risk that "economic integration" might be accompanied by "social disintegration" because of the social opposition and problems it raises.

Figure 10.3. Annual Rate of Change in the Migrant Stock in 5 years prior to 2020

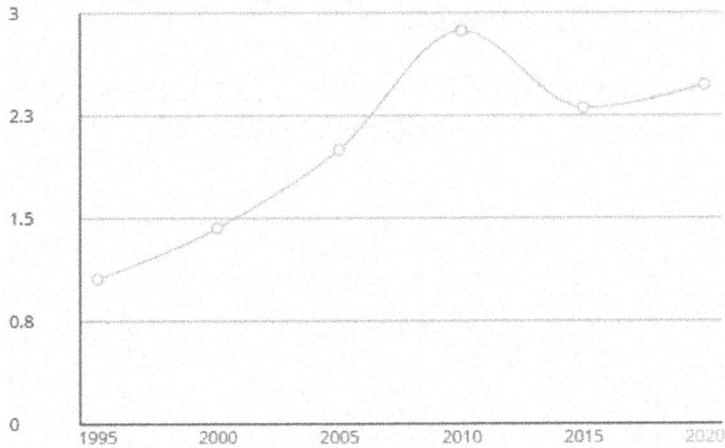

Source: UN DESA 2020 (https://www.un.org/development/desa/pd/content/international-migrant-stock).

Figure 10.4. Trends in ease of hiring foreign labour, emerging market and developing economies *vs.* advanced economies, 2008–2020

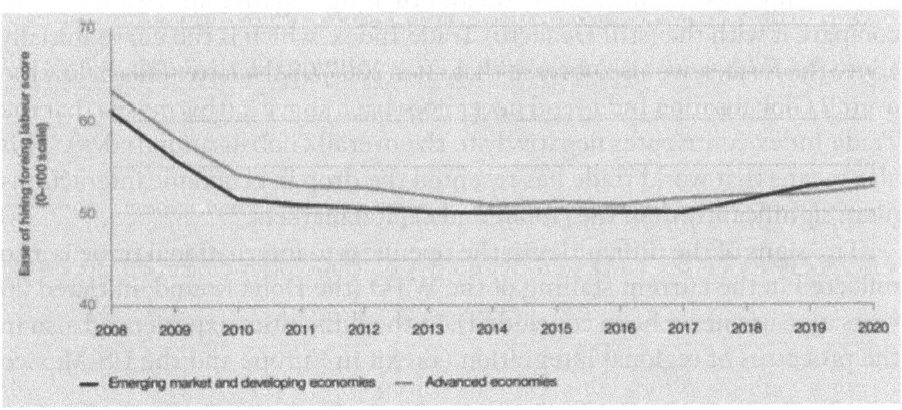

Source: World Economic Forum, Global Competitiveness Report 2020, Fig. 3.7 https://www3.weforum.org/docs/WEF_TheGlobalCompetitivenessReport2020.pdf.

A synthetic index of the evolution of globalisation is provided by Gygl *et al.* (2019), both 'De facto', namely as measured by the actual data reflecting the different aspects of globalisation, as 'De jure', namely by looking at the legal aspects affecting globalisation.[156]

Figure 10.5. De Facto Trade Index and De Facto FKO Globalisation Index

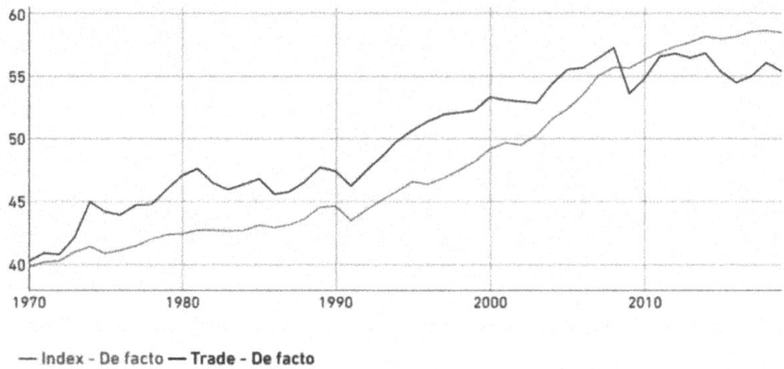

Source: Gygli *et al.*, 2019.

Focusing only on the De facto indexes, Figure 10.5 shows clearly how the overall Globalisation Index (represented by the initially lower curve) has been changing shape after the global financial crisis (with the second derivative being positive until 2007/08 and turning negative afterwards). If we compare it with the (still De facto) Trade Index, which is the curve initially above the former, we also observe that after 2007/08 the latter falls below the overall Globalisation Index and never goes back above it (this means that the Trade Index contributes negatively to the overall Globalisation Index). This also means that world trade has resented the drop in economic interactions more significantly than the labour and capital markets.[157]

The signs of the difficulties in the openness to international trade is also reflected in the current stalling of the WTO (the Doha Round, initiated 20 years ago, has never been concluded), in the difficulties experienced also in the processes of regional integration (Brexit in Europe and the US-Mexico

[156] The calculation of the KOF Globalisation Index was initiated by Dreher (2006).

[157] The data are available until 2019, which means that the effects of the Covid-19 pandemic and of the intensifying trade war between USA and China are not captured by the figure yet.

Agreement--USMCA-- revision, for example), in the failure of attempts to build transregional agreements (the Transatlantic Trade and Investment Partnership, TTIP, that should have integrated the United States with the European Union, and the Trans-Pacific Partnership, TPP, that should have integrated the Americas with Asia, and eventually went ahead without the USA under a modified designation), and maybe even more importantly, the recent USA-China trade war.

3. The evolution and the current situation of GVCs

An additional relevant feature of the wave of globalisation that started in the 1980s is the creation of complex global value chains (GVCs). ICT developments, a favourable international trade policy climate allowing for the reduction of trade barriers, and political developments that made it possible to increase the labour force available worldwide (Antràs 2020), have allowed for the fragmentation of the production process, scattered over different parts of the world (although with some significant exceptions, like most of the African continent, or some landlocked regions of central Asia, recently involved in the Belt and Road Initiative, for example).

The formation of complex GVCs has been accompanied (and made possible) by the capital inflows resulting from foreign direct investments. Figure 10.6 shows the clear correlation between respectively inward and outward FDIs and GVC participation for Low-, Middle- and High-income countries.

Figure 10.6. Foreign direct investment and GVC participation

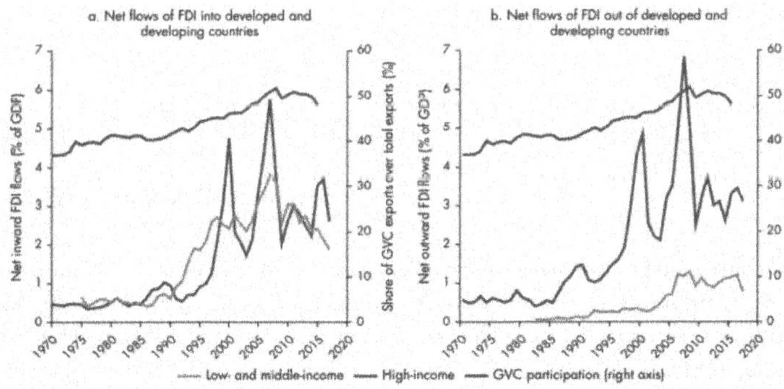

Source: WTO (2021) (Figure 1.15).

It is possible to measure GVCs by looking both at the *production* of the same good taking place in different countries as a ratio of the total production (Wang *et al.*, 2017), or by looking at the *exports* of finished and unfinished products occurring more than one time across borders as a ratio of total trade (Borin and Mancini 2019).

A further distinction refers to the different role played by a country in participating in a GVC. It is possible to distinguish, then, both *forward* GVC participation of a country (when the goods and services produced by that country are sold to foreign buyers), or *backward* GVC participation (when the country's production inputs are supplied by foreign countries). If the forward length is longer than the backward length, then that country is said to be relatively *upstream*, while it is said to be relatively *downstream* when the opposite applies (WTO, 2021).

Participation in GVCs differs significantly across countries in the world. Figure 10.7 provides a graphical representation of the situation in 2015.[158]

Figure 10.7. World distribution of GVCs participation by macro-sector of activity

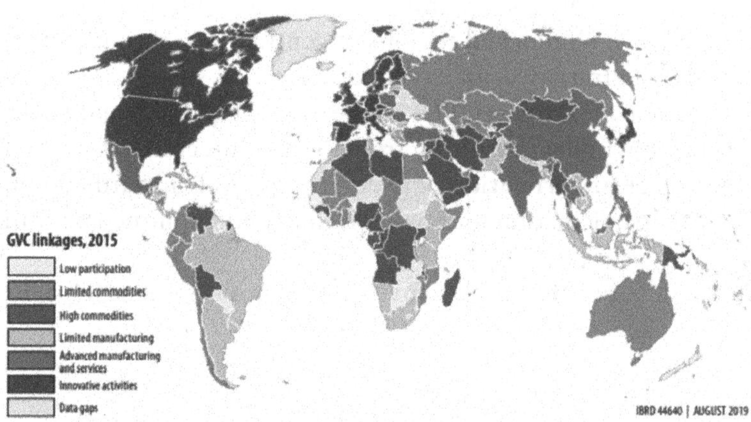

Source: WDR 2020 team, based on the GVC taxonomy for 2015 (see box 1.3 in chapter 1).

Note: The type of a country's GVC linkages is based on (1) the extent of its GVC participation, (2) its sectoral specialization in trade, and (3) its engagement in innovation. Details are provided in figure 1.6 in chapter 1.

Source: World Bank (2020) (Map 1.1).

[158] Clearly, the value added resulting from the participation in a GVC is not the same across all its different components. Specialization in some phases of the production process (advanced manufacturing and services, or innovative activities, for example), may result in value added that is much higher than others (on commodities, for example). This is why a crucial element to consider is the evolution in the GVC participation of countries, to verify whether they manage to upgrade their participation and secure an increasing value added. Rodrik (2018b) provides a very interesting, but skeptical, view on the potential for development of least developed and developing countries resulting from their participation in GVCs.

Figure 10.8 also shows the growing role of services with respect to goods in GVCs participation.

Figure 10.8. The growing role of services in GVCs

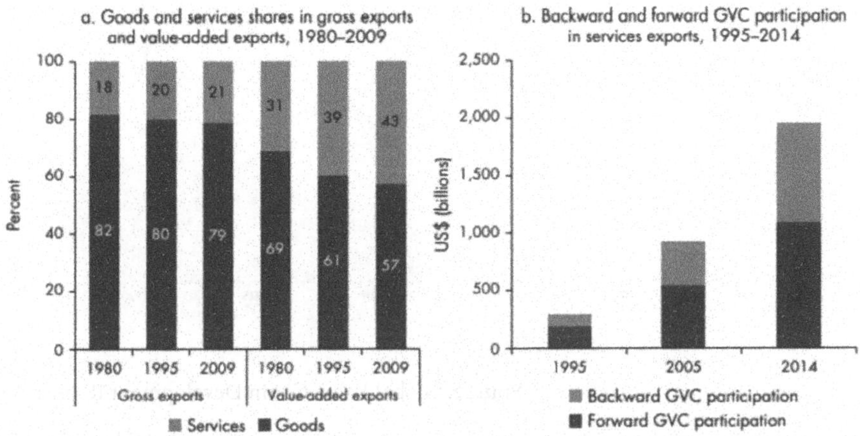

Sources: WDR 2020 team, using data from Johnson and Noguera (2017) for value-added exports measure in panel a and WIOD data from the 2013 release for 1995 and the 2016 release for 2005 and 2014 for panel b.

Note: Panel a reports the share of goods and services in gross exports and value-added exports, and panel b the GVC exports of services broken down into their backward and forward components. The GVC exports reflect exports that flow through at least two borders and indicate the extent to which sectors participate in GVCs. The GVC exports include transactions in which a country's exports embody value added that it previously imported from abroad (backward GVC participation), as well as transactions in which a country's exports are not fully absorbed in the importing country and instead are embodied in the importing country's exports to third countries (forward GVC participation).

Source: Source: World Bank (2020) (Figure 1.12).

When looking at the data, however, it is not surprising to observe that the current slowdown of globalisation is also reflected in the measures of GVCs intensity, in spite of the nominal growth (although at lower rates) of global indirect exports (the numerator of the trade-based GVC participation rate), Figure 10.9 shows that after the global financial crisis, participation rates (as resulting from both the *production-based* and the *trade-based* GVCs indexes) have stalled to say the least, with a dramatic drop in 2020 as a result of the pandemic crisis.

Figure 10.9. Global Value Chain Participation Rates, World 1995–2020

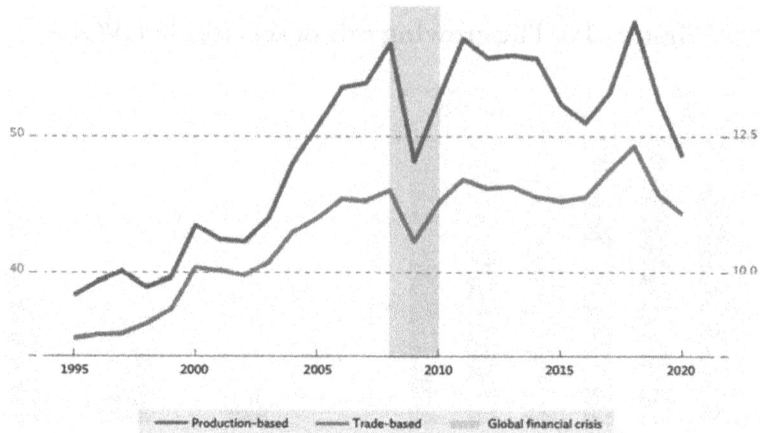

Source: Global Value Chain Development Report 2021.

New phenomena like the so-called *reshoring* (bringing most of the production back to the home country), *friendshoring* (moving the production abroad to countries that are more politically aligned with the home country), or *nearshoring* (moving the production abroad geographically closer to the home country) explain such a slowdown of GVCs (Olson 2022; Connors 2022) and may be playing an even larger role in the future (The White House 2021, Harput 2022), given the objective of *decoupling* the domestic economy (removing any dependency from abroad or at least from countries that are not perceived as "friends")[159]

In Figure 10.10, the WTO (2021) identifies the most relevant economies driving indirect trade both by magnitude and growth in three benchmark years: 2000, 2010, and 2019. *Slowbalisation* is apparent from the GVCs data by observing how in France, China, Germany and Netherlands (4 of the 5 top indirect exporting countries), the (still positive) rate of growth of the indirect exports of 2019 has decreased dramatically compared to 2010. The change is particularly significant for China, whose indirect exports dropped from a growth rate of 20.0% a year in 2010 to a mere 4.6% in 2019. This may be due to the rising cost of labour in China, to the efforts of the Chinese government

[159] Harput (2022) doubts that moving the production from one country to another abroad would really allow the desired *decoupling*.

to reduce the dependency on external channels for the country's economic growth, but also to some *friendshoring* or *nearshoring* process undertaken by foreign companies and penalising the Chinese production of intermediate goods. Such phenomena are clearly apparent in countries like Cambodia, Lao PDR and Nepal when comparing their 2010 rates of growth of intermediate trade with those of 2019. Figure 10.10 shows that Cambodia's rate of growth of intermediate trade has moved from 11.9% in 2010 to 17.1% in 2019, Lao PDR's from 12.4% in 2010 to 16.5% in 2019 and Nepal's from 1.8% in 2010 to 13.1% in 2019.

Figure 10.10. Economies with major indirect exports (million $)

	Gross Exports			Indirect Exports		
Economy	**2000**	**2010**	**2019**	**2000**	**2010**	**2019**
World	7,418,146	17,638,600	24,594,288	3,018,079	7,963,467	11,254,582
		(8.7%)	(3.7%)		(9.7%)	(3.8%)
Top 5 by Magnitude, 2019						
Germany	585,655	1,385,309	1,810,593	237,832	631,683	949,316
		(8.6%)	(3.0%)		(9.8%)	(4.5%)
United States	926,628	1,552,490	2,514,751	333,968	559,297	948,578
		(5.2%)	(5.4%)		(5.2%)	(5.9%)
PRC	262,018	1,697,752	2,664,103	80,676	595,559	903,902
		(18.7%)	(5.0%)		(20.0%)	(4.6%)
Netherlands	199,698	481,024	755,817	89,180	269,426	448,621
		(8.8%)	(5.0%)		(11.1%)	(5.7%)
France	356,767	649,302	862,767	144,159	295,172	424,097
		(6.0%)	(3.2%)		(7.2%)	(4.0%)
Top 5 by Growth, 2010–2019						
Cambodia	1,258	4,041	16,549	468	1,538	7,186
		(11.7%)	(15.7%)		(11.9%)	(17.1%)
Lao PDR	452	1,548	6,985	164	566	2,498
		(12.3%)	(16.7%)		(12.4%)	(16.5%)
Viet Nam	17,155	83,474	279,720	6,287	45,482	164,563
		(15.8%)	(13.4%)		(19.8%)	(14.3%)
Nepal	984	1,067	2,666	282	337	1,093
		(0.8%)	(10.2%)		(1.8%)	(13.1%)
Mongolia	441	2,955	8,413	196	1,315	3,433
		(19.0%)	(11.6%)		(19.0%)	(10.7%)

Lao PDR = Lao People's Democratic Republic, PRC = People's Republic of China.
Notes:
1. Magnitudes are in millions of current dollars.
2. Numbers in parentheses are compounded average growth rates for 2000–2010 and 2010–2019.
3. Estimates of indirect exports are based on the source-based decomposition methodology of A. Borin and M. Mancini. 2019. Measuring What Matters in Global Value Chains and Value-Added Trade. *Policy Research Working Paper*. No. 8804. Washington, DC: World Bank.
Sources: Asian Development Bank. Multiregional Input–Output Database. https://mrio.adbx.online (accessed 31 July 2021); Asian Development Bank estimates.

Source: WTO, 2021 (Figure 1.1).

The overall current difficulties of GVCs emerge clearly also by looking at their production lengths, namely the number of *backward* and *forward* passages of the production process. Figure 11 shows clearly that while the length increased in most sectors over the period 2000–2010, it decreased over the period 2010–2019.

Figure 10.11. Global Value Chain Production Lengths by Sector, World, 2010, 2019

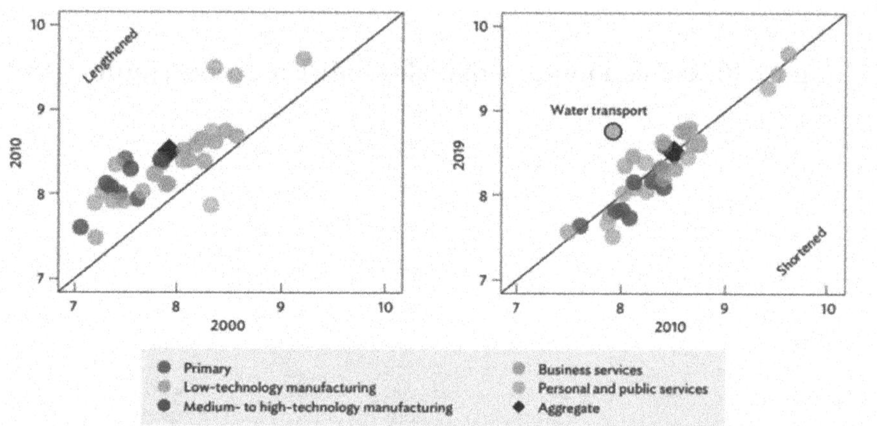

Notes: Global value chain production lengths are the sum of backward and forward lengths, computed following the methodology of Z. Wang, S. Wei, X. Yu, and K. Zhu. 2017. Characterizing Global Value Chains: Production Length and Upstreamness. *NBER Working Paper*. No. 23261. Cambridge, MA: National Bureau of Economic Research.
Sources: Asian Development Bank. Multiregional Input–Output Database. https://mrio.adbx.online (accessed 31 July 2021); Asian Development Bank estimates.

Source: WTO (2021) (Figure 1.3).

Evidence of the *slowbalisation* era emerges, then, both in the globally stagnant GVC participation rates and in the shortening of GVCs lengths, although some emerging countries are trying to take advantage of the retreat of China (this is the case, for example, also of Bangladesh in textiles and garments, the Philippines in business services, and Vietnam especially in electricals, see World Bank, 2020 and WTO, 2021).

4. Is the future scenario for GVCs really gloomy?

The current difficulties of the state of economic globalisation, as represented in the sections above) would suggest that the scenario that we should expect for the future of GVCs should be anything but gloomy. This is what Morgan Stanley (2022), for example, suggests.[160]

The current—increasingly significant—trade war between China and the United States, the Covid-19 pandemic crisis, and the Russian Federation's invasion of Ukraine, with the difficulties at different levels that all of these events have brought to the operation of GVCs (thus increasing the awareness on the part of individual countries and international institutions such as the European Union that the restoration of some form of industrial policy and the reduction of foreign dependence for some key inputs should be considered), are all suggestive of a future diminishing role for GVCs.

However, somewhat surprisingly at first sight, a recent survey on business leaders' opinions about the future of value chains' globalisation conveys a different picture (see Figure 10.12). The survey shows that for the large majority of the respondents from countries that play a rather significant role in the globalisation process (including China, the USA, Germany, Brazil, the Russian Federation, just to name a few) either globalisation is going to increase or it would remain like this (a neutral attitude).

Figure 10.12. Business leaders' opinion on the future of value chains' globalisation

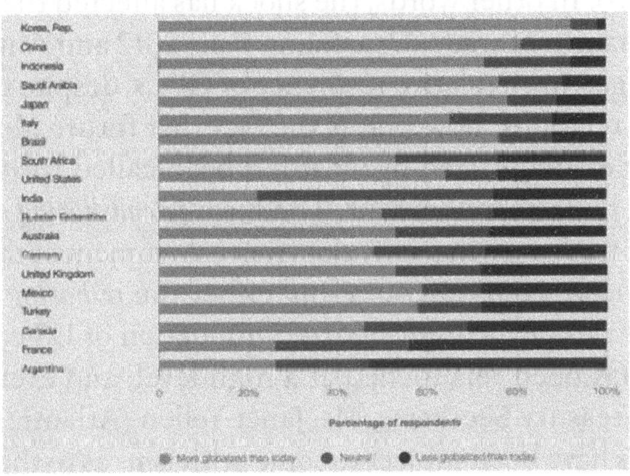

Source: World Economic Forum, Global Competitiveness Report 2020 (Figure 3.8). https://www3.weforum.org/docs/WEF_TheGlobalCompetitivenessReport2020.pdf.

160 Applying Rodrik's approach to GVCs (2018b) to this issue, we can argue that this might not be a serious problem if GVCs do not play a so significant role (at least in their current form) in favouring the development of the countries who are engaging in them.

So, a puzzle seems to emerge: the globalisation process has been scaled downwards, correspondingly GVCs have also stalled, but business leaders are still willing to assign a relevant role to GVCs. Moreover, some studies have also show that GVCs may be more resilient than expected (see for example, Antràs, 2000, Dadush, 2022 or Giglioli *et al.*, 2021). Antràs (2020), for example, argues that *sunk costs* must be borne by firms that want to take advantage of the low-cost production opportunities available abroad. *Reshoring*, then, would imply wasting the initial sunk costs and undertaking new ones (in addition to stop enjoying the lower labour costs available abroad). In other words, the past decisions to *offshore* part of the production process may be difficult to revert, being too costly. Needless to say, uncertainty in regard to the future perspectives may make this decision even more difficult. Only exogeneous shocks that are recognized as permanent would allow to calculate more accurately the expected benefit of a partial or complete relocation (Antràs 2020).

Still, Antràs (2020) presents a quite significant figure showing how, in spite of the 2007-08 global financial and economic shock (producing its negative effects also in 2009) that implied a dramatic drop of the three month moving average of exports, the three month moving average of the number of firms engaged in those export activities has been relatively more stable (see Figure 10.13). In other words, the shock has affected the *intensive* rather than *extensive* margin of trade (Bricongne *et al.*, 2012 and Antràs, 2020).

Further suggesting a relative resilience of GVCs, despite the bleak future of global trade relations, however, is the fact that future globalization may be increasingly characterized by what has been called *friendshoring*, which does not imply their abandonment. The term *friendshoring* originates from the USA-China trade war, in particular from a document of the White House (The White House, 2021) encouraging either the *reshoring* or the move to friendlier countries of the intermediate production of US companies. Such an indication has been relaunched at a high level, and even more explicitly, by the US Treasury Secretary, Ms. Janet Yellen (Atlantic Council 2022). These proposals have been subject to some criticisms as to their effectiveness and long-term sustainability (Grossman *et al.*, 2021, Harput, 2022), not to mention the more general negative effects on the perspectives of peaceful relationships at the global level.

Figure 10.13. The Extensive Margin of Trade during the Great Recession

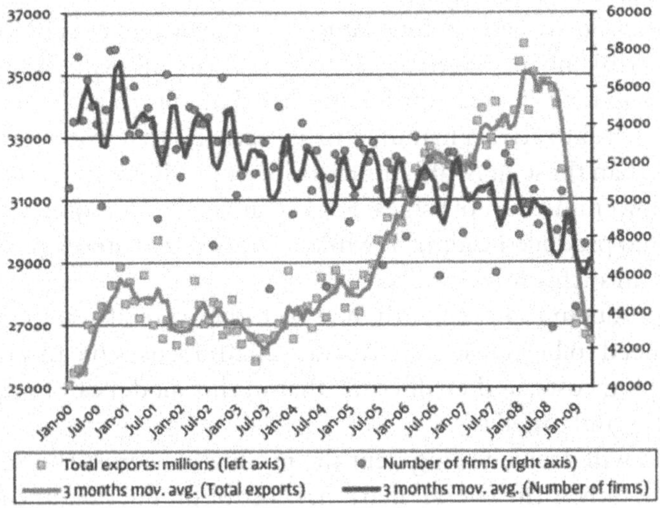

Source: Bricongne *et al.* (2012, Figure 1).

While keeping these criticisms in mind, in the next subsection I will extend the simple model of Antràs (2020) (in which he provides a theoretical explanation of the resilience that GVCs might show in the future, due to the high costs of *reshoring*), to provide a theoretical representation of the *friendshoring* tendency described above, a phenomenon that implies the absence of *reshoring* and thus may also contribute to determining the possible resilience of GVCs as described above.

5. *Reshoring* or *Friendshoring*? A simple theoretical formalisation supporting the conclusion in favour of GVCs resilience

Following Antràs (2020), let us consider a simplified two-country model (we can think of a developed Nord, *N* henceforth, and a developing South, *S* henceforth). Production is assumed to be made of two different phases, a managerial one, which needs mostly human capital (*K*) and a manufacturing one, requiring mostly unskilled labour (*L*). The two phases are assumed to be used in fixed proportions, and to produce 1 unit of product *Y* are needed both all of *K* (provided by *N* because of its comparative advantage resulting, for example from the historical evolution of the country) and all of L (provided by S, again because of the historical heritage). Y, however, could also be produced fully in N, although at a higher marginal cost than in the case it is produced in S. So, we can say, for example, that hiring an unskilled worker in N costs w^N, while hiring her in S costs $w^S < w^N$. Still following Antràs (2020), we can also assume (to account for the fact that, for example, not all lower wages are such as to attract manufacturing activity) that workers of S are less productive than those in N, although the lower productivity is not such as to nullify S's lower unit cost of wages. So we can say that N requires 1 worker at the cost w^N to produce 1 unit of Y, while S requires z^S workers (with $z^S > 1$) at the cost w^S, in such a way that $z^S w^S < w^N$.

When producing in the South, however, there are also some additional costs that need to be considered. Antràs (2020) focuses on ad-valorem ICT costs, shipping costs, and tariff costs, that in this model can be aggregated for simplicity and called $c^S > 1$.

The firm will decide to fragment the production across the South of the world, then, only if the overall marginal cost of production in the South is lower than the cost of producing in the North, as shown in Eq. (1) below:

$$z^S w^S c^S < w^N. \tag{1}$$

We have considered so far only the variable costs of manufacturing intermediate products abroad, but some fixed costs have also to be incurred. Let us define C_N the *sunk cost* incurred when producing in the North and C_S the *sunk cost* incurred when producing in the South. We should also assume, for reasons due to distance, differences in the legal and regulatory environment and so on, that $C_S > C_N$, and to economize the notation we can just consider the difference between the two, so that we have $C_{S-N} = C_S - C_N$. So, in the first period of production, in order to be optimal to produce in the South it must be that:

$$z^S w^S c^S + C_{S-N} < w^N \tag{1'}$$

Still following Antràs (2020), we can adopt the standard assumption of monopolistic competition in which consumers demand different varieties of the same product with preferences characterized by a constant elasticity of substitution (CES), so that a markup can be charged on the marginal costs depending on the value taken by the price elasticity of the demand faced by the firm, which is denoted with σ (so, when $\sigma < 1$ marginal cost differences do not matter fully and intra-marginal trade, characterized by trade in different varieties of the same products, takes place even in presence of cost differences, while when $\sigma \to \infty$ and products are therefore fully substitutable, the difference in the marginal costs when operating in *N* or in *S* matters fully). As mentioned above, the capital and labour services are used in fixed proportions, with a unit of output requiring a_K units of capital services and a_L units of manufacturing production. Let us consider, still to simplify the notation, a managerial zero marginal cost, and let us consider a price elasticity of the demand faced by the firm as constant and represented by σ. It turns out that the firm will want to engage in a fragmentation of the production process, moving the manufacturing phase abroad, if and only if:

$$B(a_L\, z^S\, w^S\, c^S)^{-(\sigma-1)} - C_{S-N} > B(a_L\, w^N)^{-(\sigma-1)}, \tag{2}$$

where *B* is the product demand that depends on the marginal costs of manufacturing ($a_L\, z^S\, w^S\, c^S$), on the net sunk cost of producing abroad (C_{S-N}) and on σ, the CES between the intermediate products produced in the two countries.

This inequality applies in the first period. If we consider, however, a second period, in which some negative shocks may be hitting the manufacturing costs abroad (for example because of the changed policy climate, like the one that we can see as occurring currently between the USA and China as discussed above), and in which the sunk costs undertaken in the first period do not matter anymore, the terms on the left hand side of Eq. (2) change and a new cost resulting from the production abroad, $g^S > 1$, may emerge. We can define g^S as the additional cost resulting from new international political friction or geopolitical costs. Geopolitical costs may result, for example, from the fact that some materials or some productive sectors are of strategic importance (after all, any standard international economics textbook has always acknowledged that national defence was an admissible reason for protectionism): when those geopolitical frictions and costs, that were absent when *offshoring* took place initially, emerge, they get added to the cost of *offshoring*. The term on the left-hand side, then, changes in the second period, so as to possibly reduce the final demand of the intermediate products produced in the initial *offshore* country, as represented in Eq. (3):

$$\frac{1}{B(a_L\, z^S\, w^S\, c^S\, g^S)^{(\sigma-1)}} < \frac{1}{B(a_L\, w^N)^{(\sigma-1)}} \tag{3}$$

So, the new source of international political cost g^S, may reduce the demand for the intermediate production abroad, and be sufficient to induce a reshoring of the foreign production.

The point that Antràs (2020) makes, however, is that an additional element has also to be considered when deciding to *reshore* the foreign production of intermediate goods: deciding to do so would imply undertaking some completely new sunk costs, that would increase the domestic production costs and decrease the overall demand for domestically produced intermediate products. So, in the second period, the changes are not only relative to g^S, but also (in the absence of any new foreign sunk costs, C_S) to the emergence of the *reshoring* sunk costs, C_N.

This means that the new equation, then, is as follows:

Eq. (3')
$$\frac{1}{B(a_L\, z^S\, w^S\, c^S\, g^S)^{(\sigma-1)}} > \frac{1}{B(a_L\, w^N)^{(\sigma-1)}} - C_N.$$

It is rather likely, then, that the necessary *reshoring* sunk cost, C_N, is such as to more than compensate the international policy friction costs g^S, and this would determine the absence of significant *reshoring* and would make GVCs resilient, at least in its extensive margins, as it has been observed above, as shown by Antràs (2020).

However — this is the novel contribution that I am adding to this literature — in the current phase we observe also the emergence of the different phenomena mentioned in the Section above, namely *friendshoring* and *nearshoring*. As already discussed, *friendshoring* occurs when the production of intermediate products abroad is moved to countries implying a lower international policy friction cost, while allowing to retain the same lower wage costs, ICT costs, and trade policy costs enjoyed when initially moving abroad the production of intermediate goods; *nearshoring* can be interpreted as being something similar, since it implies to move the intermediate production to a closer country, which is more likely to be a friend.

So, the point that I am making here is that while the higher costs of moving the production at home may well explain the relative resilience of GVCs (in their extensive margins) that we are observing, such a resilience may also be compatible with *friendshoring* and *nearshoring*.

In order to show this conclusion, let us consider a situation in which the comparison is between producing in the initial *offshore* country and *friendshoring* that production.

This would allow to benefit of the low labour costs of the previous country (z^S w^S), together with the other lower ICT costs and initial policy trade costs, c^S, while not incurring the international policy friction costs g^S. It might also well be that the new sunk cost to incur in order to move the production from the initial foreign country to a more friendly country, C^F_S, will be lower than the cost of *reshoring*, so that $C^F_S < C_N$. Even when that may not be the case, *friendshoring* may be encouraged by the provision of some government subsidies, S^F (Harput, 2022). The new "*friendshoring*" equation is then:

$$(3'') \qquad \frac{1}{B(a_L\, z^S\, w^S\, c^S\, g^S)^{(\sigma-1)}} < \frac{1}{B(a_L\, z^S\, w^S\, c^S)^{(\sigma-1)}} - C^F_S + S^F$$

In the left hand side of Eq. (3"), $\frac{1}{B(a_L\, z^S\, w^S\, c^S\, g^S)^{(\sigma-1)}}$ represents the product demand in the original *offshore* country (now not perceived as friendly anymore), while $\frac{1}{B(a_L\, z^S\, w^S\, c^S)^{(\sigma-1)}}$ is the demand obtained in the country in which the new *friendshoring* takes place. The benefits of such a larger demand (due to the fact that the geopolitical cost, g^S, is missing in the *friendshoring* country) is reduced by the sunk cost C^F_S, and increased by the subsidy S^F.

It is possible to conclude, then, that while not being convenient to do a *reshoring* of the foreign intermediate production, as shown by Antràs (2020), it may well be convenient, instead, to do a *friendshoring* of it. In other words, considering that switching from an *offshore* country to a (still *offshore*) *friendly* country may imply sunk costs that are lower than those incurred when moving back to the home country; that such a move may be encouraged by subsidies granted by the government of the country of origin; and, above all, that keeping the production in a friendly (Southern) country allows enjoying wage costs that are as low as those in the initial *offshore* country, the result of *friendshoring* emerges, thereby strengthening the conclusion of resilient GVCs, precisely as described in Section 4 above.

6. Concluding remarks

After the global financial crisis of 2007-08, economic globalisation in its different facets (goods and services, labour and capital, both real — foreign direct investment — and financial) began to slow down. The reasons are not only economic but also geopolitical.

GVCs have played a very important complementary role in economic globalisation and it is not surprising, then, to observe some slowdown also in their growth rates.

However, quite surprisingly, opinion surveys keep assigning an important role to GVCs, and past experiences suggest that the shocks that have been hitting intermediate trade have been affecting more the *intensive* than the *extensive* margins. In other words, GVCs may well be more resilient in the future than the current situation and data would suggest. The reasons for such a resilience have to be found in the fact that an outright *reshoring* of the foreign intermediate production would imply forsaking the sunk costs previously undertaken and incurring in new ones in the domestic country.

Such an explanation, however, assumes that *reshoring* is the only alternative to *offshoring*, whereas GVCs can be kept alive also by moving the production of intermediate goods to *friendlier offshore* countries.

The theoretical model presented in this chapter (extending Antràs, 2020) shows that while the relevant sunk costs for relocating home the *offshore* production discourages *reshoring* (as shown by Antràs, 2020), the subsidies that governments may provide to encourage *friendshoring*, the relatively lower sunk costs and the low labour costs that can still be enjoyed when doing so , would also allow the survival of GVCs (although differently composed).

Future research is needed to investigate, among other things, the consequences of such reshuffling processes on all countries involved, the effective *decoupling* that they would allow and, most importantly, their long-term sustainability and the risks they pose to peaceful relations worldwide.

REFERENCES

Antràs, P. (2020), "De-Globalisation? Global Value Chains in the Post-COVID-19 Age", November 16, Paper written for the ECB Forum on Central Banking, "Central Banking in a Shifting World".

Atlantic Council (2022), "Transcript: US Treasury Secretary Janet Yellen on the next steps for Russia sanctions and 'friend-shoring' supply chains", Atlantic Council, 23 April, available at: https://www.atlanticcouncil.org/news/transcripts/transcript-us-treasury-secretary-janet-yellen-on-the-next-steps-for-russia-sanctions-and-friend-shoring-supply-chains/.

Bhagwati, J. (2002), *Free Trade Today*, Princeton: Princeton University Press.

Bhagwati, J. (2004), *In Defence of Globalisation*, Oxford: Oxford University Press.

Borin, A. and Mancini, M. (2019), "Measuring What Matters in Global Value Chains and Value-Added Trade", World Bank Policy Research Working Paper, No. 8804, available at: SSRN: https://ssrn.com/abstract=3366657.

Bricongne, J.-C., Fontagne, L., Gaulier, G., Taglioni, D., and Vicard, V. (2012), "Firms and the global crisis: French exports in the turmoil", *Journal of international Economics* 87 (1), pp. 134-146.

Catão, L.A.V. and M. Obstfeld (2019), *Meeting Globalisation's Challenges, Policies to Make Trade Work for All*, New York and New Jersey: International Monetary Fund and Princeton University Press.

Connors, E. (2022), "Apple shift shows China's pain is Vietnam's gain", *Financial Review*, 2 June, available at: https://www.afr.com/world/asia/apple-shift-shows-china-s-pain-is-vietnam-s-gain-20220602-p5aqlm.

Dadush, U. (2022), "Deglobalisation and protectionism", *Bruegel*, available at: https://www.bruegel.org/sites/default/files/2022-11/WP%2018.pdf.

De la Dehesa, G. (2006), *Winners and Losers in Globalisation*, Malden (MA), Oxford and Victoria: Blackwell Publishing.

Della Posta, P. (2018), *The Economics of Globalisation: An Introduction*, Pisa: ETS.

Della Posta, P. (2020), "An analysis of the current backlash of economic globalisation in a model with heterogeneous agents", *Metroeconomica*, 02 September 2020, pp.1-20, 2020, doi: 10.1111/meca.12312.

Della Posta, P. (2020), "The economic and social costs of globalisation: a target zones analysis", *The World Economy*, 17 July, available at: https://doi.org/10.1111/twec.13008.

Dreher, A. (2006), "Does Globalisation Affect Growth? Evidence from a new Index of Globalisation", *Applied Economics* 38 (10), pp. 1091- 1110.

European Commission (2002), "Responses to the challenges of globalisation, a study on the international monetary and financial system and on financing for development", European Economy, Special Report Number 1.

European Commission (2017), *Reflection Paper on Harnessing Globalisation*, COM 2017 (240) final, 10.4.2017.

Fischer, S. (2003), "Globalisation and its challenges", *AEA Papers and Proceedings*, Richard T. Ely Lecture, Vol. 3, No. 2, pp. 1-30.

Frieden, J. (2019), "The backlash against globalisation and the future of the international economic order", in Diamond, Patrick (ed), *The Crisis of Globalisation: Democracy, Capitalism, and Inequality in the Twenty-First Century*, London: I.B. Tauris, pp. 43-52.

Giglioli, S., Giovannetti, G., Marvasi, E. and Vivoli, A. (2021), "The Resilience of Global Value Chains during the Covid-19 pandemic: the case of Italy", Working Paper n. 7/2021, Dipartimento di Scienze per l'Economia e l'Impresa, DISEI, Universita di Firenze, available at: https://www.disei.unifi.it/upload/sub/pubblicazioni/repec/pdf/wp07_2021.pdf.

Grossman, G., Helpman, E., and Lhuillier,H. (2021), "Supply Chain Resilience: Should Policy Promote Diversification or Reshoring?", mimeo, September 27, available at: https://economics.princeton.edu/working-papers/supply-chain-resilience-should-policy-promote-diversification-or-reshoring/ Princeton University.

Gygli, S., Haelg, F., Potrafke, N., and Sturm, J.- E. (2019), "The KOF Globalisation Index — Revisited", *Review of International Organizations*, 14 (3), pp. 543- 574, available at: https://doi.org/10.1007/s11558- 019-09344-2.

Harput, H., (2022), "The hidden costs of frienshoring", Hilrich Foundation, 15 November, available at: https://www.hinrichfoundation.com/research/article/us-china/the-hidden-costs-of-friend-shoring/.

Hoekman, B. (2015), "Trade and growth — end of an era?", in Hoekman, B. (ed) *The Global Trade Slowdown: A New Normal?* VoxEU.org eBook, pp. 3-19, available at: https://voxeu.org/content/global-trade-slowdown-new-normal.

IMF/WB/WTO (2017), *Making Trade an Engine of Growth for All: The Case for Trade and for Policies to Facilitate Adjustment*, Washington, DC: IMF, available at the web address: https://www.imf.org/en/Publications/Policy-Papers/Issues/2017/04/08/making-trade-an-engine-of-growth-for-all.

Krugman, P. (1987), "Is Free Trade Passé?", *The Journal of Economic Perspectives*, 1 (2), pp. 131-144.

Krugman, P. (2016), "Trade and tribulation", *The Conscience of a Liberal, The New York Times*, March 11.

Krugman, P. (2016a), "Globalisation and growth", *The Conscience of a Liberal, The New York Times*, March 14.

Morgan Stanley (2022), "Can Thinking Local Fix Global Supply Chains?", *Morgan Stanley*, available at: https://www.morganstanley.com/ideas/slowbalization-global-supply-chain

OECD (2017), *Fixing Globalisation: Time to Make it Work for All*, Better Policies Series, April, Paris: OECD.

Olson, S. (2022), "Yellen, Lagarde, and the death of the global trade system", *Hinrich Foundation*, available at: https://www.hinrichfoundation.com/research/article/sustainable/yellen-lagarde-global-trade-system/.

Rodrik, D. (1999), "Globalisation and labour, or: if globalisation is a bowl of cherries, why are there so many glum faces around the table?", in Baldwin, R., Cohen, D. *et al.*(1999), *Market integration, regionalism and the global economy*, Cambridge: Cambridge University Press.

Rodrik, D. (2001), "The global governance of trade: as if trade really mattered", *Background paper to the UNDP Project on Trade and Sustainable Human Development*, New York: United Nations Development Programme (UNDP).

Rodrik, D. (2007), "How to save globalisation from its cheerleaders", in *KSG Working Paper No. RWP07-038*, Harvard, MA: Kennedy School of Governance.

Rodrik, D. (2017), "Too Late to Compensate Free Trades Losers", *Project Syndicate*, 11 April, available at: https://www.project-syndicate.org/commentary/free-trade-losers-compensation-too-late-by-dani-rodrik-2017-04?barrier=accessreg.

Rodrik, D. (2018a), "Populism and the economics of globalisation", *Journal of International Business Policy* 1, pp. 12-33, available at: https://doi.org/10.1057/s42214-018-0001-4.

Rodrik, D. (2018), New Technologies, Global Value Chains, and the Developing Economies, Pathways for Prosperity Commission Background Paper Series; no. 1, Oxford, United Kingdom.

Saval, N. (2017), "Globalisation: the rise and fall of an idea that swept the world", *The Guardian*, 14 July.

Stiglitz, J. (2017), "The overselling of globalisation", *Business Economics*, 52 (3), pp. 129–137.

Stiglitz, J. (2005), "The overselling of globalisation", Chapter 10 in Epstein, M. (ed), *Globalisation: what's new*, New York: Columbia University Press, pp. 228-261.

Stiglitz, J. (2002), *Globalisation and its discontents*, London: Penguin Books.

The Economist (2019), "Slowbalisation: The future of global commerce", 24 Jan, available at: https://www.economist.com/weeklyedition/2019-01-26.

The White House (2021), "Building Resilient Supply Chain, Revitalizing American Manufacturing, and Fostering Broad-based Growth", *The White House*, available at: https://www.whitehouse.gov/wp-content/uploads/2021/06/100-day-supply-chain-review-report.pdf.

Wang, Z., Wei, S., Yu, X. and Zhu, K. (2017), "Measures of Participation in Global Value Chains and Global Business Cycles", *National Bureau of Economic Research Working Paper Series* 23222, March, doi: 10.3386/w23222, http://www.nber.org/papers/w23222.

Williamson J.G. (2005), "Winners and Losers over Two Centuries of Globalisation", in Atkinson, Anthony B., *et al., Wider Perspectives on Global Development, Studies in Development Economics and Policy*. London: Palgrave Macmillan, pp 136–174, doi https://doi.org/10.1057/9780230501850_6.

World Bank (2020), *World Development Report 2020: Trading for Development in the Age of Global Value Chains*, Washington, DC: World Bank, doi:10.1596/978-1-4648-1457-0. License: Creative Commons Attribution CC BY 3.0 IGO University Press.

WTO (2021), *Global Value Chain Development Report, Beyond Production*, Asian Development Bank, Research Institute for Global Value Chains at the University of International Business and Economics, the World Trade Organization, the Institute of Developing Economies — Japan External Trade Organization, and the China Development Research Foundation.

PART IV
CONCLUSIONS AND OUTLOOK

Summary

Part IV takes stock of what we have learned from the contributions in this book and summarizes how EU trade policy copes with new challenges. It brings together the different perspectives on global cooperation and trade, deep trade agreements, EU deep trade agreements and the lessons from CETA, the EU's Trade and Sustainability Chapters, and the European (economic, social, environmental) model.

CHAPTER 11
ON GOVERNANCE AND SUSTAINABILITY CHALLENGES FOR EU TRADE POLICY[161]

Annette Bongardt and Francisco Torres

Abstract: The EU is in a prime position in trade but faces an onslaught of challenges where a weakened open trading order, recent shocks with impacts on the international economic system (the Covid-19 pandemic, the Ukraine war, climate change), geopolitics and changing globalization patterns combine. This chapter (and special issue) takes stock of what we have learned and summarizes how EU trade policy copes with new challenges. It brings together the different perspectives on global cooperation and trade, deep trade agreements, EU deep trade agreements and the lessons from CETA, the EU's Trade and Sustainability Chapters, and the European (economic, social, environmental) model.

Keywords: Challenges to the international trade system, EU Deep Trade Agreements; CETA; geopolitics; sustainability.

1. Introduction

The European Union (EU), as the European Commission contends, is in a prime position in regard to trade.[162] Its assessment is based on the EU being the world's largest economy and trading bloc, ranking first in inbound and

[161] We would like to thank our fellow authors in this book as well as the reviewers for useful comments and discussions. The first author conducted this study at the Research Center in Political Science (UIDB/0758/2020), University of Minho / University of Évora, supported by the Portuguese Foundation for Science and Technology and the Portuguese Ministry of Education and Science through national funds.

[162] Source: https://policy.trade.ec.europa.eu/eu-trade-relationships-country-and-region/eu--position-world-trade_en

outbound international investments, being the top trading partner for 80 countries (the US for about 20) and the most open economy to developing countries. It is deeply integrated in global markets, a fact to which modern transport and communication facilities have contributed.[163] Being one of the most open economies in the world and a defender of free trade, it does recognize the importance of the development of trade. Doing so is important due to the impact that external trade has on EU economic growth and prosperity but is furthermore to serve wider EU's objectives by leveraging the EU's weight in global trade to shape an open and fair global trading system and by making sustainable development central to trade policy. In our view, those EU objectives are very much in tune with current challenges to global trade.

The increasing global economic integration that the world economy has become accustomed to over the last decades has brought about substantial benefits but is being challenged on various fronts. To start with, multilateralism's institutional framework has weakened in this millennium, as illustrated by the failure of the Doha round or the blocked World Trade Organization (WTO) arbitration panel. More acutely, in recent years successive crises have impacted world trade, most notably the Covid-19 pandemic, which erupted in early 2020, and Russia's invasion of Ukraine in early 2022. Highlighting weaknesses of existing globalization patterns such as the energy and food dependency and the fragility of global supply chains in the face of shocks, those prompted a reappreciation of cost advantages versus resilience in light of risks and pushed geopolitics to the fore as a factor on the trade agenda. In the process, issues that have arguably been lurking more in the background for long (benefits and costs of international trade and their distribution, labour and environmental issues, even climate change) have also surfaced.

As a result, a new global map of economic relationships started to take shape as of 2021, in which geopolitics increasingly influences the global economy (Lagarde (2022). The risk of trade wars and the return of confrontational politics is among the global risks that the EU faces, as is climate change that requires an immediate transition to a green economy (von der Leyen, 2023).

[163] Globalization here refers to the internationalization of markets that has taken place over the past three decades or so. Of course, globalization is not exactly a new phenomenon. Just recall the wide-ranging globalization that existed in Europe pre-WWI or the cultural globalization of Hellenism post Alexander the Great.

Aiyar *et al.* (2023) draw attention to the world now facing the risk of policy-driven geoeconomics fragmentation and to the costs of fragmentation costs through various channels. While fragmentation risks have multiple sources (the fact that not everybody benefited from global integration, declining public support for economic openness in various countries, a levelling-off of cross-border flows of goods and capital since the global financial crisis, trade tensions between blocs and the Russia's war on Ukraine), strengthening the international trade system and stepping up climate action should be among the (three) priorities to preserve the benefits from global integration and multilateralism in the face of multiple shocks (Georgieva, 2023).[164] As Lagarde (2023) argues, Europe should be leader and not a follower in writing the next chapter of globalization and has the capacity to do so.

2. What are the new challenges to today's globalized economy and how should the EU cope?

The contributions to this special issue can be grouped in three, if at times overlapping, categories. The first four chapters frame the discussion, looking at the need for cooperation in global governance in the light of crises, the political difficulties of doing so, seeking to better understand what the observed shift from multilateralism to preferential trade agreements, more specifically, the emergence and proliferation of deep trade agreements, means, and how the latter affect the European model.

In "Europe in the World circa 2030" Gaspar and Amaglobeli (2022) set out the challenges for cooperation in today's global governance setting. They remind us that international trade calls for a stable world economic system, which in present times however requires multilateral coordination that goes beyond trade rules and the traditional trade agenda. Successive shocks to the world economy (such as the coronavirus pandemic or Russia's full-scale invasion of Ukraine) have further underscored the importance of and need for multilateral cooperation in various domains. Among the challenges that the EU and the world need to address within the decade, Gaspar and Amaglobeli single out pandemic preparedness, progress on the United Nation's Sustainable Development Goals (SDG), and mitigation of and adaptation to climate change. A key takeaway is that important present challenges to

[164] The third priority is to help vulnerable countries deal with debt.

international trade and the international economic system that need to be addressed collectively with some urgency reside beyond the traditional trade area, with the need to factor in climate effects (carbon tax) being critical. In this regard, the EU, a staunch supporter of multilateralism (despite or rather because of its retreat, one may add), is well placed to play a role in multilateral coordination and has assumed a leadership role in combatting climate change.

The economic case for international economic integration to deliver public goods leads to the question as to the prospects for realization. It is where political economy factors come in.

In his chapter entitled "Global trade in the Age of Populism", Frieden (2022) discusses the future of international economic cooperation in the light of the politics of trade, calling attention for the domestic and international political factors to be reckoned with. The 2007-09 global financial crisis had ended a period of stability in globalization that many had come to take for granted.[165] Still, Frieden points out that this shock had less of a lasting effect on global trade (tellingly, discriminatory measures hardly rose) whereas it did cause perduring socio-economic impacts. The effects of globalization (notably an unequal distribution of benefits and costs along various dimensions) pushed the politics of trade to the forefront at a domestic level. The subsequent development of populist movements — anti-globalization, in Europe anti-EU — over the past 15 years, opposing economic and political integration, fed through into parties, governments and countries' trade policy. As a result, domestic politics has become an important factor for the feasibility of international economic cooperation.[166] At the same time, recent shocks to the international economic system — the global Covid-19 pandemic, Russia's full-scale invasion of Ukraine, the rise of China and the evolution of climate policy — nevertheless differed from the global financial crisis in that they have also had important impacts on trade openness (discriminatory measures went up sharply, global trade integration decreased for the first time). Thereby, those shocks cumulatively contribute to uncertainty about

[165] As Frieden reminds us, ours is the second period of globalization. The first period of globalization was prior to WWI, the second globalization period took off in the 1980s. Both achieved comparable trade openness. Democracy added additional challenges for the functioning of international institutions (for instance, in operating the gold standard austerity was not an issue). Rodrik (2011) has long argued that there exists a delicate balance between democracy and globalization.
[166] The article argues that populist movements tend to share a dislike of 'globalism' and the international collaboration and integration framework, which has been the norm since the 1940s.

the future of world trade and investment. Frieden argues that existing economic and political trends have called cooperation on trade among the principal economic centres, which would be critical to uphold and develop the open trade system, into question.[167] The chapter concludes that overcoming opposition to international economic integration within major Western powers presupposes addressing the domestic reasons for opposition.

The chapters by Gaspar and Amaglobeli and by Frieden cumulatively highlight the (economic) need for and the (political) difficulties to address challenges for the international economic system by means of international cooperation. Those challenges encounter a global governance system in trade where multilateralism and support for the global open trading order have become weaker. They are also in large part beyond the traditional trade domain. The rise of preferential trade agreements in general, and within those of deep trade agreements in particular, may hence be seen as an attempt to overcome perceived shortcomings of multilateral trade coordination. A better understanding of the nature and features (scope, depth) of deep trade agreements is however a precondition also for evaluating their consequences.

In their chapter "The Evolution of Deep Trade Agreements", Mattoo, Rocha and Ruta (2022) provide that important base, which is fundamental for shedding light on the nature and contents of deep trade agreements as compared to conventional preferential trade agreements and on their effects on trade. Its importance also for this special issue warrants a more detailed account.

The authors zoom in on international trade and globalization in a changed global governance system, in which regionalism has grown at the expense of multilateral governance, and where deep trade agreements emerged in the 2000s and have risen since within the preferential trade agreements notified to the WTO. Mattoo *et al.* clarify that while those preferential trade agreements are based on WTO rules, they drove the trade agenda beyond in terms of issue areas and towards regionalization. Two underlying causes are presented. First, because even traditional trade policy areas (tariff reduction, services liberalization) have become more frequently negotiated in a regional context than under the WTO umbrella and second, preferential trade

[167] As pointed out, in the US, the Biden administration's trade policies have not varied much from Trump's.

agreements have often gone further than countries' WTO commitments, augmenting their scope.

Mattoo *et al.* analyse deep trade agreements extensive and intensive margins (number of covered policy areas and specific commitments within a given policy area, respectively), drawing on new data on the content of preferential trade agreements up to the end 2017 that comprises 18 policy areas most covered in those preferential trade agreements. They shed light on two main issues — what are deep trade agreements and what are their main effects. As for the former, deep trade agreements are shown to aim at economic integration beyond trade. This deep integration sets them apart from traditional trade agreements that focus on market access.[168] Economic integration envisages establishing five types of integration rights, namely free (or freer) movement of goods, services, capital, people and ideas. deep trade agreements feature policy areas that can be classified according to three categories[169]: those that envisage establishing economic integration rights; those that aim at protecting economic integration rights (limiting government discretion to undo them), meaning enforcement provisions that limit the discretion of importing countries in these areas, as well as with provisions that regulate exporters' behaviour; and those that expand consumer rights and social welfare (obligations on exporters such as labour market regulations or environmental laws).

As for their effects, Mattoo *et al.* put forward five new stylized facts on preferential trade agreements that derive from their data. To start with, they lowered trade-weighted average tariff rates below WTO levels (to less than 5 percent for more than two-thirds of countries). The number of commitments in preferential trade agreements increased over time, particularly since the 2000s and in areas aiming at facilitating flows of services, goods and capital. Deepening commitments have been accompanied by an increase in regulatory requirements, namely on enforcement. As compared to developed countries, developing countries tend to have fewer commitments in preferential trade agreements, with larger gaps in areas such as labour and environment. Finally, preferential trade agreements are more similar within blocs although similarity can be significant even across blocs.

[168] By implication, the term trade agreement becomes somewhat misleading, given that coverage extends beyond trade into other policy areas (among which international flows of investment and labour, intellectual property right protection and the environment).

[169] With a possible overlap between the second and third categories in the case of some areas (competition policy, state-owned enterprises, subsidies).

Looking at the case of the European Union (EU), it, too, first reluctantly but then increasingly so, turned to bilateral and new generation trade agreements to advance its international trade agenda. EU deep trade agreements have become a major embodiment of EU trade policy. But what does that mean for the EU and its integration project?

In their contribution entitled "EU trade dynamics and the European model in the context of new globalization patterns and global governance", Bongardt and Torres (2022) stress that new generation EU trade agreements, going into non-trade policy areas, feed back into and influence the European model, which aims at making compatible economic efficiency and social and environmental objectives. That is so because deep trade agreements imply a qualitative change in EU trade, where external trade and EU regulation interact and impact on the European model (important for the EU's identity), potentially either strengthening or weakening it. Tellingly, EU deep trade agreements, unlike conventional trade agreements before, have been subject to contestation, with fears voiced that higher European standards could be undermined or pre-empted. Bongardt and Torres draw attention to the fact that the EU has to balance economic integration rights granted to third countries via deep trade agreements and ensuring the acceptability of domestic EU economic integration. In the EU, regulation recurs to harmonization provided that there is preference convergence, otherwise, by default, to mutual recognition (systems competition). However, and critically, the notion of similarity that makes mutual recognition possible and politically acceptable is already stretched within the EU (Bongardt and Torres, 2017).

A second group of chapters looks at the EU's new generation trade agreements with respect to the evolution of EU free trade agreements in terms of competences and the specific case of the EU-Canada Comprehensive Economic and Trade Agreement (CETA). CETA's importance derives not least from the fact that it has served as a blueprint for successive EU deep trade agreements and offers lessons. This bilateral new generation trade agreement, which had already been signed in 2016, is since 2017 in force but only provisionally as it is still awaiting ratification by all member states and some regions. The analysis of CETA — its nature, reach, enforcement and ratification — is hence of particular interest for getting a better understanding of issues surrounding EU deep trade agreements.

In her chapter "EU FTAs and divided sovereignty: Transformative shifts in trade authority", Guimarães (2022) points out that it is efficiency reasons that underlie the expansion in terms of policy areas of EU trade agreements.

Trade became an exclusive competence of the European Community in the founding Treaty of Rome (1957). Yet, it was only fifty years later, under the Lisbon treaty (2007), that additional areas were added to that EU-exclusive trade competence. The author puts forward that there had been competence creep on the part of the EU in trade pre-2007 and that there continued to be competence creep thereafter, only that it has come to face limits in terms of member state or sub-state competences.[170] Guimarães concludes that, as a result of the impact of the 2017 Singapore decision by the Court of Justice of the EU and of the engagement of subnational entities in trade policy (in federal systems), there have been transformative shifts in the locus of trade policymaking from centralized competences to divided sovereignty with national and subnational entities. Questioning or contestation in areas of the latter's competence has slowed down the Commission's activeness in trade-related regulatory provisions in second and third generation agreements, aimed at regulatory approximation.

Coutinho's (2022) chapter "On the Legal Nature of New Generation Trade Agreements: Lessons from the CETA Saga" looks into the reasons for and implications of EU trade agreements of a mixed nature (of EU and member state competences). He explains that a grey zone had existed in regard to EU trade competences, then clarified by the Court of Justice of the EU, in its 2017 Singapore decision[171], upon request by the European Commission. An essential implication is that portfolio investments and Investor State Dispute Settlement (ISDS) are member state competences. It follows that an EU trade agreement that is qualified as mixed, covering policy areas of member state competence, is void if it does not get unanimous approval by all parties involved. Coutinho points out that CETA's qualification as a mixed agreement hence determines that its application is limited and provisional (applicable to all other mixed agreements), and subject to a pending threat of termination until all member states and some regions have ratified the agreement. The separation of such a mixed agreement in two, in line with the competence distribution in the EU, offers a possible solution.

Leblond and Viju-Miljusevic's (2022) chapter is guided by the question of "CETA as the first EU third-generation trade agreement: does it act like one?". On the basis of their categorization of the three generations of trade

[170] She suggests that the creeping competence notion be widened.

[171] Available at: https://curia.europa.eu/jcms/upload/docs/application/pdf/2017-05/cp170052en.pdf

agreements (background, characteristics, examples and innovations) and having examined a 5-year period of CETA being applied, they conclude that CETA also behaves like one. They clarify that third-generation policy issues imply more extensive institutional mechanisms to facilitate cooperation between the parties (such as regulatory cooperation, government procurement or the mobility of persons), which is due to the anticipation that much work on the removal of existing or potential barriers to trade needs to take place and continue after the agreement has entered into force. While data suggests that CETA had a positive economic impact but is silent on the quantitative effect of provisions that pertain to third-generation trade issues when compared to tariff reductions (or elimination), Leblond and Viju-Miljusevic examine the qualitative progress on third-generation issue commitments, namely institutional and regulatory cooperation (in light of the difficulties associated with harmonization and mutual recognition). They conclude that economic benefits eventually materialize, but that beyond-the-border issues dealing with standards and regulations need time and efforts to make third-generation provisions work effectively since they require the cooperation of several actors.

A third group of (three) chapters centres on the reorientations of EU trade policy and on the issue of changing globalization patterns (the resilience of global value chains).

EU trade policy has undergone strategic reorientations over the years, most recently in 2021 with the Trade and Sustainable Development (TSD) Review. The question is whether the new approach to TSD chapters in EU trade agreements, will make trade more sustainable and bring it in line with the EU's sustainability objectives and the European Green Deal.

Couvreur, De Ville, Jacobs and Orbie's (2022) chapter "The good geopolitical trade actor? The European Union's discursive justification of the Anti-Coercion Instrument" looks at how the EU's justified a change in EU trade policy, examining the case of the anti-coercion instrument. They point out that the EU, normatively, has stood for free trade and multilateralism. While it is still a defender, it has been adjusting its trade policy since 2015. The discursive justification of why the EU has done so boils down to that its trade stance had been naïve. Emphasis is now placed on defensive aspects against others (the example given is China, which was not successfully domesticated by multilateral rules). Couvreur *et al.* conclude that neither argument is entirely correct. That is, neither was EU trade policy that naïve before (as illustrated among others by the Generalized System of Preferences plus (GSP+) or the Europe agreements), nor is it entirely defensive now (examples: sustainable development chapters, carbon border adjustment mechanism (CBAM)).

In Couvreur *et al.*'s view, EU trade policy has now switched to an active stance, at least in some areas. One of those are Trade and Sustainable Development chapters, which are the focus of Blot's chapter.

In her contribution entitled "Green horizons — Towards more sustainable trade after the TSD Review", Blot (2022) clarifies that TSD chapters are not new but date back to 2011, when they first made an appearance in EU free trade agreements (in the EU's first new generation agreement with South Korea). In her view, the TSD Review, reinforced by the 20-point TSD Action Plan in June 2022, represents an attempt to rebuild the climate credibility of EU trade policy. It moreover amounts to a recognition of the EU's contribution to the global environmental degradation embodied in trade and of EU trade patterns negatively feeding back into EU policy goals (which in turn motivated contestation at various levels). Reviewing the action points of the new TSD Chapter approach in terms of their effects (that is, in terms of their impact on leveraging free trade areas for sustainability, enhancing the environmental credentials of free trade areas, empowering broader civil society, targeted actions for the Domestic Advisory Groups, and strengthening enforceability of environmental and social commitments), she concludes that the new approach is ambitious and sets the EU on course to embed sustainability in free trade agreements, notably by committing to the Paris agreement and ILO conventions, by including concrete enforcement mechanisms in partner countries (for the first time), switching to a more tailored rather than the previous one-size-fits-all approach that is accompanied by building support through greater involvement of civil society and financial and technical assistance and dialogue. The effect of some non-committal phrases on implementation is as yet unclear. Overall, the Review fortified the EU's position as a global leader with respect to integrating sustainability in trade policy, although it missed out on some opportunities to further enhance the sustainability of EU free trade agreements.

Della Posta's (2022) chapter "Global Value Chains and the Retreat of Globalization" is interested in what lessons the global financial crisis holds for the evolution of global value chains (GVC). He shows that globalization already retreated after that crisis, with a significant slowdown in the degree of international economic openness, attributable not only to economic but also to geopolitical reasons. His argument draws on various indicators of the degree of openness of the global economy and its evolution (on international trade, foreign direct investment, labour mobility), and a slowing of GVC growth trend. Yet, as he argues, GVCs might be more resilient than expected. The reason is that firms may also opt to switch some production (say from China) to a location more near-by (with similar cost advantages but associated with a perceived lower geopolitical risk) rather than back home or to the same bloc.

3. Bringing different perspectives together

With the weakening of multilateralism, preferential trade agreements may have been seen as a second-best option and as one affording a more tailored response to globalization. Their proliferation in this millennium has resulted in more regional integration in the world economy centred around major trading blocs. The EU is a case in point. EU trade policy has ever more opted for preferential trade agreements, which are increasingly deep and comprehensive trade agreements. Recent crises appear to reinforce regionalisation, as countries have adopted measures to protect their economies and societies from their fallout or, more generally, from perceived geopolitical risk.

Against this background, the objective of this book has been, above all, to shed light on how EU trade policy has evolved within the wider global context and to discuss EU trade dynamics in light of old and new challenges. To do so, contributions have taken a closer look at the evolving global context and main challenges, at deep trade agreements in general and the EU's new generation deep free trade agreements in particular, at why the latter imply a qualitative change in EU trade, and discussed spillovers from external trade and the impact on the European social and economic model. As chapters also happened to speak to each other, let us consider some main points where things come together.

First, there is a necessity for economic cooperation in order to provide public goods, yet doing so hinges on overcoming an additional type of hurdles (public contestation). The international economic system faces challenges (pandemic preparedness, sustainable development, climate change) that call for collective action still in this decade, whose resolution requires cooperation beyond the narrow trade domain (Gaspar and Amaglobeli, 2022). However, creating and extending global governance has to reckon with political opposition from private and public actors (Frieden, 2022). As pointed out, the issue playing out in this second globalization is democracy (different from the first globalization prior to WWI, which was otherwise as deep). Globalization is also confronted with the rise of geopolitics in trade, which calls into question, among other things, the configuration of global value chains (Della Posta, 2022).

Second, the rise of preferential trade agreements may be seen as a response to a global trading order in retreat but it also affects global trade. There are two main reasons (Mattoo *et al.*, 2022). To start with, because deep trade agreements increasingly set trade rules. Those are about establishing economic integration rights (goods, services, labour, capital, ideas) and have been growing in terms of policy areas and complexity, in general terms but most among developed countries. Also, because there has been a regionalization of trade (preferential trade agreements being centred around the EU, the US and Japan), with trade agreements being most similar within those blocs (although there is similarity in regard to about half of the contents also across).

Third, the EU has been very successful on account of being able to conclude an ever-increasing number of deep and comprehensive free trade agreements, which however sits uncomfortably with the difficulties that it has been experiencing with respect to ratification. Explanatory factors include competence creep (if justified by efficiency reasons) in conjunction with the fact that some relevant competences are decentralized, resulting in divided sovereignty for trade issues (Guimarães, 2022). In legal terms, any agreement that is qualified as mixed (covering also specific areas of member state competence) rather than EU-only may still enter into force but only provisionally and in a limited way (like CETA); its fate is subject to uncertainty in the meantime. It becomes void if a single member state (or region, if applicable) does not ratify it (Coutinho, 2022). Splitting up a trade agreement allows for getting around the role of member states in ratifying the trade section part (Blot, Coutinho). It involves negotiating separate trade and investment and political and cooperation agreements. The Commission has adopted this approach already in the recently concluded EU-Chile agreement and proposed it for the politically contentious Mercosur and Mexico agreements (Blot, 2022). Moreover, judging by the case of CETA, the EU is undertaking some efforts to address (avoid) possible contestation a priori, notably by increasing transparency and making new generation free trade agreements more progressive in terms of objectives (Leblond and Viju-Miljusevic, 2022). As bilateral agreements receive greater scrutiny (Blot), the reaction to or contestation of other EU free trade agreements will be informative as to the EU's capacity to pursue a trade agenda that is supported by European society and member states and regions.

Fourth, the rules established in bilateral or regional deep trade agreements also feed back into the European economic and social model (Bongardt and Torres, 2022). As Mattoo *et al.* (2022) explain, deep trade agreements not only establish economic integration rights and enforcement rights but have recently also come to feature welfare-related areas such as the environment and labour. The impact on welfare occurs through an international spillover effect. With economic integration within the EU and its internal market being more profound than what the Union grants to third countries in deep free trade agreements, the risk is that the latter may still interact with and have a negative impact on European environmental and social standards. After all, the very logic of deep trade agreements is doing away with non-tariff barriers (once tariff barriers are already low). At the same time, establishing those economic integration rights necessarily reaches out into regulation and enforcement to ensure implementation beyond the border. For the EU, the challenge comes down to balancing the economic integration rights granted through (deep) trade agreements to third countries and ensuring an equilibrium internally. In the EU's internal market, the functioning and acceptance of regulation rest on preference convergence: harmonization if there is preference convergence, mutual recognition where there is not. However, the notion of similarity that makes mutual recognition (systems competition) possible is already stretched within the EU. In the end, the issue is to what extent systems competition via deep trade agreements could come to undercut those areas which are key components of the EU model and whether competence distribution in the EU (when involving member states and/or regions) provides a sufficient safeguard in the case of divergent preferences. What Rodrik (2011 and 2014) refers as the delicate balance in globalization poses an even larger challenge for the EU, as its own delicate internal balance could be potentially upset by new generation free trade agreements.[172]

[172] Rodrik has long pointed to the existence of a paradox in globalization, warning that if pushed too far globalization would undermine its own institutional foundations. As he puts it, there is hence a need to find a delicate balance. Bongardt and Torres (2022) argue that this is even more the case for the EU, where the resulting external balance impacts a delicate internal balance.

Fifth, with EU free trade agreements being a chief embodiment of EU trade policy, what can be said about the implementation of EU objectives in or through trade? On the one hand, EU trade policy has moved away from normative free trade and multilateralism, embracing (more openly) a more active trade policy and pushing for EU objectives. The EU discursive justification (of anti-coercion measures, for instance against China) centres on the assessment that the previous stance had been naïve (Couvreur *et al.*, 2022). On the other hand, the Commission's recent TSD review vows to bring trade policy in line with EU policy (SDGs, EGD) and external commitments (Paris agreement). Its stance has become more assertive in some respects (Couvreur *et al.*, Blot). TSD chapters had already been part of EU new generation trade agreements, but under the TSD review and action plan commitments will be strengthened in new agreements as is enforcement, with commitments binding and the possibility of sanctions in case of non-compliance (Blot).

Trade and the European model are intertwined. The above discussion allows us to conclude that the EU is well placed to push for cooperation on global public goods and/or to use bilateral or regional preferential trade agreements to further its objectives. There is also a strong economic case for dealing with negative environmental effects, at a global and multilateral level or else through modern free trade agreements. The EU brought its trade policy in line with its wider objectives and started to use new deep trade agreements as a vehicle to promote external trade that serves its objectives (sustainability, labour standards), domestically and in partner countries. The shift to welfare--related commitments in trade is also significant as it may also help address the issue of political contestation. However, as always, the devil will be in the details. Time will tell whether EU deep trade agreements manage to condition globalization in line with EU values and objectives or whether economic integration rights granted to third countries put pressure on the European model.

REFERENCES

Aiyar, Shekhar, Chen, J., Ebeke, C.H., Garcia-Saltos, R., Gudmundsson, T., Ilyina, A., Kangur, A., Kunaratstskul, T., Rodriguez, S. L., Ruta, M. Schulze, T., Soderberg, G., and Trevino, J.P. (2023), *Geo-Economic Fragmentation and the Future of Multilateralism, Staff Discussion Note,* New York: IMF.

Blot, E. (2022)."Green horizons – Towards more sustainable trade after the TSD Review". *Perspectivas - Journal of Political Science*, 27, pp. 93-107. ps://doi.org/10.21814/perspectivas.4566

Bongardt, Annette and Francisco Torres (2017), "Comprehensive Trade Agreements: Conditioning Globalization or Eroding the European Model?", *Review of European Economic Policy*, 52 (3), pp. 165-170.

Bongardt, Annette, and Torres, Francisco (2022), "EU trade dynamics and the European model in the context of new globalization patterns and global governance", *Perspectivas – Journal of Political Science*, 27, pp 13-21.

Coutinho, Francisco P. (2022), "On the Legal Nature of New Generation Trade Agreements: Lessons from the CETA Saga", *Perspectivas – Journal of Political Science*, 27, pp 77-92.

Couvreur, S., De Ville, F., Jacobs T., and Orbie, J. (2022), "The Good Geopolitical Trade Actor? The European Union's Discursive Justification of the Anti-Coercion Instrument", *Perspectivas – Journal of Political Science*, 27, pp 133-147.

Della Posta, Pompeo (2022), "Global Value Chains and the Retreat of Globalization", *Perspectivas – Journal of Political Science*, 27, pp 62-76.

Frieden, Jeffry (2022), "Global Trade in the Age of Populism", *Perspectivas – Journal of Political Science*, 27, pp 50-61.

Gaspar, Vitor and Amaglobeli, David (2022), "Europe in the World circa 2030", *Perspectivas – Journal of Political Science*, 27, pp 22-34.

Georgieva, Kristalina (2023), "Confronting fragmentation where it matters most: Trade, debt and climate action", IMF blog, 16 January.

Guimarães, Helena (2022), "EU FTAs and Divided Sovereignty: Transformative Shifts in Trade Authority", *Perspectivas – Journal of Political Science*, 27, pp 121-132.

Lagarde, Christine (2022), "A new global map: European resilience in a changing world", speech at Peterson Institute for International Economics, Washington, D.C., 22 April.

Lagarde, Christine (2023), "New challenges in a changing world", speech by Christine Lagarde, President of the ECB, at the Deutsche Börse Annual Reception in Eschborn, 23 January.

Leblond, Patrick and Viju Miljusevic, Crina. (2022), "CETA as the First EU Third-Generation Trade Agreement: Does It Act Like One?", *Perspectivas – Journal of Political Science*, 27, pp 106-120.

Mattoo, Aaditya, Rocha, Nadia , and Ruta, Michele (2022), "The Evolution of Deep Trade Agreements", *Perspectivas – Journal of Political Science*, 27, pp 35-49.

Rodrik, Dani (2011), *The Globalization Paradox. Democracy and the Future of the World Economy*, New York: W.W. Norton & Company

Rodrik, Dani (2014), "The paradox of globalization is that pushing it too far undermines its own institutional foundations", LSE-blog, 2 January.

Von der Leyen, Ursula (2023), "Special address by President von der Leyen at the World Economic Forum", 17 January.

NOTES ON CONTRIBUTORS

Annette Bongardt is an integrated member of the Research Center in Political Science (CICP), University of Évora, and Visiting Professor of European Political Economy at Católica Lisbon School of Business and Economics. She holds a Ph.D. in Economics (1990) from the European University Institute (EUI). In recent years, she was a Visiting Senior Fellow at the London School of Economics and Political Science, a Visiting Fellow at the Robert Schuman Centre for Advanced Studies of the EUI, and an Academic Visitor at St Antony's College, Oxford University, where she lectured in various modules of European Political Economy. She also taught at the Rotterdam School of Management, the University of Victoria, B.C., King's College London and the University of Pisa. She had also held positions as Robert Schuman Post-Doctoral Research Fellow of the European Commission at the Centre for European Policy Studies, Brussels, and as Research Fellow at the International Centre for Economic Research, Turin. In Portugal, she was, among others, a regular Visiting Professor (and National Coordinator) at the National Institute of Public Administration and UFP and Visiting Associate Professor at the University of Aveiro. She has extensively lectured and published on European political economy and European integration topics. Her latest publications include a book on Brexit (Edward Elgar, 2020) and her Lessons on the Political Economy of European Integration (UCE, 2022), co-authored with F. Torres. ORCID: https://orcid.org/0000-0003-3264-5519

Francisco Torres is Visiting Professor of European Political Economy at Católica Lisbon School of Business and Economics. He has been a Visiting Senior Fellow at the London School of Economics and Political Science (2014-19) and a PEFM Associate and Visiting Fellow at St Antony's College, Oxford University (2012-20), where he also lectured on European Political Economy (in various modules: PPE and MSc). He also taught at the U. Victoria, the U. Rome II (Tor Vergata) and King's College London. He holds a Ph.D. in European Political Economy (Católica, Lisbon), a Master in Economics (Nova, Lisbon) and a 5-year degree also in Economics (Católica, Lisbon). He also holds an MA in International Affairs from the Johns Hopkins University, SAIS, and held a one-year post-doctoral fellowship at the University of Oxford. Moreover, he was a researcher at the Economics Dept (Ph.D. programme) and a Visiting Fellow at the Robert Schuman Centre for Advanced Studies at the European University Institute in Florence and the 1st Robert Schuman Fellow of the European Commission at the Centre for European Policy Studies in Brussels. In Portugal, he taught mainly at Católica, both at the Economics Dept and at the Institute for European Studies (Executive Director and Head of the Studies Programme and Research), at the National Institute for Public Administration (Professor and Chair of Internationalization and European Integration) and at the University of Aveiro (Visiting Associate Professor). He has published numerous journal articles, (co-)authored and (co-) edited 15 books and various journal special issues and international reports on European integration and European political economy. ORCID: https://orcid.org/0000-0001-6396-7081

Aaditya Mattoo is Chief Economist of the East Asia and Pacific Region of the World Bank. He specializes in development, trade and international cooperation, and provides policy advice to governments. He is also Co-Director of the World Development Report 2020 on Global Value Chains. Prior to this he was the Research Manager, Trade and Integration, at the World Bank. Before he joined the Bank, Mr. Mattoo was Economic Counsellor at the World Trade Organization and taught economics at the University of Sussex and Churchill College, Cambridge University. He holds a Ph.D. in Economics from the University of Cambridge, and an M.Phil in Economics from the University of Oxford. He has published on development, trade, trade in services, and international trade agreements in academic and other journals and his work has been cited in the Economist, Financial Times, New York Times, and Time Magazine. ORCID: https://orcid.org/0000-0002-1584-8544

Crina Viju-Miljusevic (Canada) is Associate Professor and Director of the Institute of European, Russian and Eurasian Studies at Carleton University.

She is also the Associate Director of the Centre for European Studies at Carleton University, and she holds a Jean Monnet Chair in "EU External Relations: Competing Regionalism in Eurasia" funded by the Erasmus+ Programme of the European Union. Her research interests include the economic effects of different trade policies applied within the EU, US and Canada, European economic integration, and the EU as an external actor. Crina's current research focuses on the EU trade policy, Canada-EU Comprehensive Economic and Trade Agreement (CETA) as well as the EU, Russia and China as competing actors in Eurasia. She has an extensive publication record, including edited or co-edited volumes, and numerous journal articles, book chapters and conference presentations. ORCID: https://orcid.org/0000-0001-9705-5101

David Amaglobeli is a Deputy Division Chief in Fiscal Affairs Department. Previously he was an assistant to the director in Fiscal Affairs Department. Prior to that he has worked on intense surveillance country cases and on the design and review of IMF-supported programs in several crisis countries. Before joining the IMF in November 2009, he held several positions in his native Georgia, notably as acting governor of the National Bank of Georgia, and deputy minister of finance. ORCID: https://orcid.org/0000-0002-7258-9235

Eline Blot is a Policy Analyst at the Institute for European Environmental Policy (IEEP), a sustainability think tank. Her work focuses on the integration of environmental sustainability in the EU's trade policy and the coherence of the EU's internal and external policies related to climate, environment, trade and sustainable development. Her previous research on the EU's free trade agreements and accompanying Trade and Sustainable Development Chapters began in 2021 with a comparative analysis of the environmental credentials of the EU's trade policy (published on the IEEP website with co-author Marianne Kettunen) and continued in 2022 on ways forward to enhance the sustainability of the EU's free trade agreements (published on the IEEP website with co-authors Antoine Oger and James Harrison). ORCID: https://orcid.org/0000-0003-3117-1374

Ferdi De Ville is an Associate Professor in European Political Economy at Ghent University. His research and teaching focus on the political economy of European integration, and of EU trade policy in particular. He is the co-author (with Gabriel Siles-Brügge) of TTIP: The Truth about the

Transatlantic Trade and Investment Partnership (2016, Polity) and (with Mattias Vermeiren) of Rising Powers and Economic Crisis in the Euro Area (2016, Palgrave). He has published extensively in peer-reviewed journals, including Journal of Common Market Studies, Journal of European Public Policy, British Journal of Politics and International Relations and New Political Economy. Currently, he is doing research on the unilateralization of EU trade policy, with the introduction of new instruments like the International Procurement Instrument, the Foreign Subsidies Regulation and the Carbon Border Adjustment Mechanism. ORCID: https://orcid.org/0000-0003-4415-758X

Francisco Pereira Coutinho is Associate professor at Nova School of Law (Lisbon, Portugal). Bachelor (2002), PhD (2009), and Habilitation (agregação) (2021) in law from Nova School of Law. Vice Dean at Nova School of Law (2018-2021), President of Jurisnova (2015-2022) and Professor at the Institute for Political and Social Sciences of the University of Lisbon (2010-2015) and at Lisbon Autónoma University (2009-2012), as well as legal advisor at the Diplomatic Institute of the Portuguese Ministry for Foreign Affairs (2005-2011) and at the Secretary of State of the Presidency of the Council of Ministers of the Portuguese Republic (2003-2004). Member of CEDIS - R&D Centre for Law and Society, of the Portuguese Society of International Law, and of the Portuguese Association of European Law. Coordinator of SPARC, the Compliance Lab and the observatories for data protection and Portuguese Legislation. ORCID: https://orcid.org/0000-0001-9075-2537

Jan Orbie is Professor in European Union (EU) External Relations at the Department of Political Science at Ghent University (Belgium). He is a member of the Ghent Institute for International and European Studies (GIES), the Ghent Centre for Global Studies (GCGS) and the Human Rights Research Network (HRRN) at the same university. He researches and teaches about the European Union's global role with a particular focus on critical and normative approaches to EU external trade, social and development policies. He currently (co-)supervises doctoral research projects on the geopoliticization of EU trade policy, the GSP+ system of the EU, the EU's migration-development nexus, the human-nature divide in EU foreign policies, EU external deforestation policies, sustainable development in EU-Asia trade relations, financialization in EU development cooperation, and the post-Cotonou partnership agreement. He has recently published on EU trade policies from discursive, global justice, post-development and decolonial perspectives. ORCID: https://orcid.org/0000-0003-3080-3122

Jeffry Frieden is Professor of Government at Harvard University. He specializes in the politics of international economic relations. Frieden is the author of *Currency Politics: The Political Economy of Exchange Rate Policy* (2015) and the co-author (with Menzie Chinn) of *Lost Decades: The Making of America's Debt Crisis and the Long Recovery* (2012). Frieden is also the author of *Global Capitalism: Its Fall and Rise in the Twentieth Century* (2007; second edition 2020), of *Debt, Development, and Democracy: Modern Political Economy and Latin America, 1965-1985* (1992), of *Banking on the World: The Politics of American International Finance* (1987), and the co-author or co-editor of over a dozen other books on related topics. His articles on the politics of international economic issues have appeared in a wide variety of scholarly and general-interest publications. ORCID: https://orcid.org/0000-0003-0285-9284

Maria Helena Guimarães is tenured Associate Professor at University of Minho (Portugal) and holds a Jean Monnet Chair in European economic integration. Her areas of research are political economy of European integration, the Single Market, trade policy, trade and subnational markets, and political economy of non-tariff barriers. Currently she has been focusing on US subnational diplomacy *vis-à-vis* the EU and on Single Market (dis)integration. She teaches international political economy, European economic integration, political economy of international business, and the global economy. She was a Fulbright Visiting Scholar at American University (Washington DC) and Visiting Scholar at the University of Washington (Seattle). She has published in scholarly journals, including the Journal of Common Market Studies, Regional and Federal Studies, Business and Politics, The International Trade Journal, and Frontiers in Political Science. She has received various research grants, including from the Fulbright Program, European Commission, Luso--American Development Foundation, and Calouste Gulbenkian Foundation. ORCID: https://orcid.org/0000-0003-1432-4113

Michele Ruta is Deputy Chief in the Strategy and Policy Review Department of the International Monetary Fund, where he oversees the work on trade and trade policy. He had previous appointments at the World Bank, the World Trade Organization and the European University Institute, and holds a PhD in economics from Columbia University and an undergraduate degree from the University of Rome "La Sapienza". Michele's research focuses on international and regional integration and has been published, among others, in the *Journal of International Economics, the Journal of Development Economics* and the *Journal of the European Economic Association*. His books and edited volumes include *The Impact of the War in Ukraine on Global Trade*, the *Handbook of Deep Trade Agreements* and *Belt and Road Economics*. Personal website: https://sites.google.com/site/michelerutasite/. ORCID: https://orcid.org/0000-0003-1070-2279

Nadia Rocha is a Lead Economist in the Macroeconomics, Trade and Investment Global Practice at the World Bank. Prior to joining the Bank she worked at the WTO and she also served as a Senior Advisor on trade to the Colombian Ministry of Trade. She holds a PhD in International Economics from the Graduate Institute of Geneva, an MA in Economics from Pompeu Fabra University of Barcelona and a BA in Economics from Bocconi University in Milan. Nadia's work focuses on trade policy, regional integration, global value chains and trade and gender. ORCID: https://orcid.org/0000-0003-0045-7492

Patrick Leblond is CN — Paul M. Tellier Chair on Business and Public Policy and Associate Professor in the Graduate School of Public and International Affairs at the University of Ottawa. He is also Senior Fellow at the Centre for International Governance Innovation (CIGI), Research Fellow at CIRANO and Affiliated Professor of International Business at HEC Montréal. Dr. Leblond is an expert on economic governance and policy with a particular focus on Canada, North America, Europe and, increasingly, China. He has published extensively on financial and monetary integration, banking regulation, international trade and business-government relations. Before embarking on his academic career, he worked in accounting and auditing for Ernst & Young as well as in corporate finance and strategy consulting for Arthur Andersen & Co. and SECOR Consulting. ORCID: https://orcid.org/0000-0002-9889-7498

Pompeo Della Posta (PhD, EUI, Italy and MA, University of Warwick, UK) is Professor of Economics at the Belt and Road School of Beijing Normal University, Zhuhai Campus (Guangdong, China) and currently on leave from the University of Pisa. He is the director of *Scienza e Pace / Science and Peace* and member of the editorial board of the *Global Economy Journal*.

He has been President-elect for 2019 of the *International Trade and Finance Association*. He spent one academic year as Visiting Student at Princeton University (USA) and a Summer Term, still as Visiting Student, at Stanford University (USA). He has visited, among others: CIRANO Research Center (Montreal, Canada), George Washington University (Washington, USA), University of Victoria (BC, Canada), State University of Saint Petersburg (Russia), Yokohama University (Japan), Delhi School of Economics (India), University of Durham (UK), University of Krakow (Poland), University of Gdansk (Poland). ORCID: https://orcid.org/0000-0002-5379-7338

Sjorre Couvreur is a PhD Fellow at the Ghent Institute for International and European Studies, Department of Political Science, Ghent University (Belgium). His PhD research focuses on geoeconomics and EU trade and industrial policy. He holds a Master in EU International Relations and Diplomacy Studies from the College of Europe (magna cum laude) and a Master in International Politics from Ghent University (summa cum laude). Before starting his PhD, he worked at the European External Action Service (EEAS) in Brussels and the U.S. Foreign Service Institute in Washington D.C. ORCID: https://orcid.org/0000-0003-0037-913X

Thomas Jacobs is an Assistant Professor of Information and Communication at Engage, the Research Center for Publicness in Contemporary Communication, at Université Saint-Louis in Brussels. His research has been published in numerous international peer-reviewed journals including the Journal of Common Market Studies, the International Journal of Social Research Methodology, Contemporary Political Theory, Critical Review, Rethinking Marxism, and Critical Discourse Studies. It focuses on Post-Marxist Discourse Theory, which he deploys to analyse the strategic and discursive dimension of political communication within European politics. He is primarily interested in questions regarding hegemony, political strategy, and rhetoric. Thomas' first research monograph, entitled *Hegemony, Discourse, and Political Strategy: Towards a post-Marxist understanding of contestation and politicization*, was published with John Benjamins in 2022. ORCID: https://orcid.org/0000-0003-1723-325X

Vitor Gaspar, a Portuguese national, is Director of the Fiscal Affairs Department of the International Monetary Fund. Prior to joining the IMF, he held a variety of senior policy positions in Banco de Portugal, including

Head of Research and Statistics. He served as Minister of State and Finance of Portugal during 2011–13. He was head of the European Commission's Bureau of European Policy Advisers during 2007–10 and director-general of research at the European Central Bank during 1998–2004. Mr. Gaspar holds a Ph.D. and a post-doctoral agregado in Economics from Universidade Nova de Lisboa; he also studied at Universidade Católica Portuguesa. ORCID: https://orcid.org/0000-0002-9659-2914